Faith and War

Faith and War

How Christians Debated
the Cold and Vietnam Wars

David E. Settje

NEW YORK UNIVERSITY PRESS
New York and London

NEW YORK UNIVERSITY PRESS
New York and London
www.nyupress.org

References to Internet websites (URLs) were accurate at the time of writing.
Neither the author nor New York University Press is responsible for URLs
that may have expired or changed since the manuscript was prepared.

Library of Congress Cataloging-in-Publication Data

Settje, David E., 1970–
Faith and war : how Christians debated the Cold and Vietnam Wars / David E. Settje.
p. cm.
Includes bibliographical references (p.   ) and index.
ISBN 978–0–8147–4133–7 (cl : alk. paper) — ISBN 978–0–8147–4134–4 (e-book)
1. Christianity and international relations—United States—History—
20th century. 2. Vietnam War, 1961–1975—Religious aspects—Christianity.
3. Cold War—Religious aspects—Christianity. I. Title.
BR526.S48   2011
261.8'70973—dc22   2010053653

New York University Press books are printed on acid-free paper,
and their binding materials are chosen for strength and durability.
We strive to use environmentally responsible suppliers and materials
to the greatest extent possible in publishing our books.

Manufactured in the United States of America
c   10 9 8 7 6 5 4 3 2 1
p   10 9 8 7 6 5 4 3 2 1

In loving memory of my grandparents,
for wanting a better world for us:

Virginia "Toots" Serbu
Emil Settje
Earl Serbu
Hilda Settje

Contents

Acknowledgments

The stereotype of a historian toiling away by herself in archives and then writing in solitude is thankfully far from the truth. In the process of my writing this book, numerous people touched my life and factored into what you read here, in both tangible, measurable ways and more vague, subtle ways. I am grateful to each and every one of them. Since I inevitably will have forgotten someone, I beg forgiveness and simply want to say that there is no one in my life who did not somehow positively influence this study.

Numerous libraries and archives made the material for this book readily available. I am always honored by the many people at these institutions who go out of their way to help me. Though I cannot mention each of you individually, I thank you. So many of you went well above the call of duty to locate materials and get them to me quickly, all while doing your other work and fulfilling other requests. This effort on your part is humbling, to say the least, and indispensible for what I have accomplished on this project. These institutions include the African Methodist Episcopal Church Department of Research and Scholarship, the Billy Graham Center Archives, the Concordia University Library, the DePaul University Library, the Dominican University Library, the Harold Washington Library of Chicago, the North Central College Library, the Southern Baptist Historical Library and Archives (which also issued a much appreciated and needed travel grant), the United Church of Christ Archives, the Southern Illinois University Archives, the University of Chicago Library, and the Wheaton College Library.

A multitude of people at Concordia University Chicago both enabled and nurtured this project along the way. From the university I received summer research grants that made travel to the many archives possible. For a small liberal arts college with a heavy teaching load, this is a vital sign of the university's dedication to faculty research. My dean, Gary Wenzel, reminds me often that I need to balance my teaching and research when I lose myself in teaching too much or serving on too many university committees and phantom task forces. This rare push from an administrator to take me *away* from the university encouraged me to continue, and reminded me that sometimes it's okay to say no. My department is one of the most collegial environments that I could imagine. The friendships and cooperation there of Bob Hayes, Bill Pierros, and Kurt Stadtwald are invaluable to me. Other colleagues on the faculty and staff also inspire me to continue my scholarship. Conversations about it between meetings, in the halls, and at other functions consistently provide me with motivation and feedback. All of these colleagues make it a pleasure to work at Concordia.

I owe a special debt of gratitude to my students. I hope that the high standard to which I hold you will make you all better citizens of the world. Pushing you to do your best reminds me that I must do the same. Though I frequently fall short of that goal myself, I also pray that you see in this book the fruits of my placing that same standard upon myself. I also learn from you in class, from hearing your insights, opinions, and interpretations of the history that we study.

A number of colleagues read portions of this manuscript or talked through various aspects of it with me. Thanks to them, it is a richer text than I could have written alone. Thank you to my former students-turned-colleagues, John Hink, Elisabeth Unruh, and Jen Vaughn, and to fellow scholars Robin Bowden, Roger Fjeld, Kathryn Galchutt, Jill Gill, David Kyvig, Leslie Liedel, Earl Matson, Laura Pollom, Mary Todd, and Christine Worobec. My association with the Lutheran Historical Conference has been invaluable, too: thanks to all of you for our shared pursuit of religious, and especially Lutheran, history. One colleague spent more time than any other on this project, meticulously going over every chapter and offering invaluable feedback. Thanks to Michelle Gardner-Morkert, for encouraging me, for reminding me that every day we should be pursuing our academic interests, and for making Concordia a scholarly place to work.

New York University Press made this a far better manuscript than the one they originally received from me. Everyone at the press has been so kind, professional, and inspirational. Thank you to each and every one of you. The blind readers all pushed me for clarification and greater context. I know that I didn't answer every one of their concerns or questions, but I tried, and thanks to them this is a much stronger investigation. Most of all, my editor, Jennifer Hammer, deserves a great deal of credit for this book. She ripped it apart, nurtured the process of my putting it back together, and in the end collaborated to make this study a quality contribution to the literature.

Finally, I would like to thank my friends and family, for being so much a part of who I am. My thanks go to all of my friends, for occasionally listening to boring history stories and, more often, for taking me away from working on this book for drinks, dinner, good conversation, or movies and sports distractions. And as for my family, I love you all. You are incredibly important to me every day, in so many ways. I cherish our time together and love you more than you could ever imagine. Certain family members did more than anyone else, and on a regular basis. You know who you are, and hopefully how much you mean to me. Thank you to my dogs, Cindy, JR, Toto, and Dracula, for cherished memories, and Armand and Akasha, for reminding me that quite often a treat, walk, ball chase, pet, or snuggle is a lot more fun than working. Thank you to my parents, for once again believing in me and for their constant love. My parents also instilled in me the importance of family, in part by making sure that I was around both sides of my family as much as possible as I grew up.

This lesson from my parents especially brought me into contact with my grandparents, who shaped my life in countless ways. The faith life they instilled in their families guides not only my personal life but also my professional career as I follow their example in trying to make this a better world for everyone. My thanks go to Virginia "Toots" Serbu, so much more than a grandmother, whose presence is still with me every day; to Emil Settje, for the devoted love of a grandfather that nurtured me; to Earl Serbu, for doting on me as a young child and for the Cleveland Browns fandom in my family; and to Hilda Settje, who died before I was born but who had planted a legacy within her family that still influences us. It is to their memory that I lovingly dedicate this book.

Introduction: Christianity and Foreign Policy, 1964–1975

An Introductory Analysis

Introduction

Throughout U.S. history, Christianity has shaped public opinion, guided leaders in their decision making, and stood at the center of every contentious issue. One cannot study any period of time or major issue in American history without confronting Christianity's effect. Religious sensibilities have had positive and negative influences, but they have always *had* an influence. The founding of the nation incorporated intense discussion about church and state, including a constitutional amendment to separate the institutions. The Civil War stemmed from a battle over slavery, which emerged in part from the abolitionists' Christian calling to combat an immorality. Throughout two centuries, Catholic Americans struggled against Protestant hegemony and prejudice, discrimination that reached into political parties, immigration restrictions, and irrational fears of a papal conquest. Religious zeal led to the prohibition of alcohol and surrounded intense social debate about Darwinian theory. President after president has articulated a faith position and been sworn into office on a Bible. The list of important religious elements in the U.S. past continues infinitely. Historians must grasp the religious context of an era in order to gain complete knowledge about what transpired, why it happened, and how. Yet too little is known about the effect of American Christianity on foreign policy opinions during the Cold War and Vietnam War era. This book seeks to play a role in correcting this lacuna so that scholarship on the 1960s and 1970s more closely resembles the fullness of what we already know about other generations. Christianity influenced the culture war raging about foreign policy during this era, with many points of view adding a religious component to the debate.

This book traces the influence American Christians had on foreign relations opinions and analyzes what led Christian entities ranging from the Southern Baptist Convention to the periodical *Christianity Today* to take their particular position. It demonstrates that Christian institutions both reflected and shaped public opinion on the basis of their theology and history. Between 1964 and 1975, the United States found itself embroiled in the ongoing Cold War, which led to military engagement in Vietnam. There was a sharp divide in American society at the time about the validity of U.S. foreign policy, especially as it related to American fighting in Southeast Asia. Historians of the 1960s and 1970s have time and again explored this contentious period in order to better comprehend how Americans viewed diplomatic matters, and to discern their impact on overall opinions and the actions of American leaders. To aid us in better understanding the 1960s and 1970s, this book explores the foreign policy outlooks of a diverse sampling of Christian entities in order to offer a more complete picture of the United States during those decades. In so doing, it explores questions such as the following: Did the history of a particular religious institution factor into its position on war and diplomacy? How and to what extent did theology or spirituality guide this decision making? And what does this teach us about American Christianity specifically and the United States more generally during this pivotal decade?[1]

Scrutinizing the evangelical and conservative magazine *Christianity Today*, the mainline Protestant and liberal *Christian Century*, and a sampling of Catholic periodicals from a variety of political and theological perspectives, and also including an analysis of the right-leaning Southern Baptist Convention, the socially conscience African Methodist Episcopal Church, and the liberal United Church of Christ, this book explores the commingling of religion, politics, and foreign policy from 1964 to 1975.[2] It describes how the history and theology of each entity directly played into the way it viewed both the Cold and Vietnam wars. Christianity both reflected and sought to shape foreign policy opinions, though Christian outlooks included a wide range of theologies, political stances, and understandings of how church and state interact with one another. Fuller knowledge about the role that religious institutions played in these foreign policy debates offers us a better grasp of the factors influencing and mirroring public opinion at that time. This book details the way in which Christians participated in debating, formulating, and discussing foreign policy during a crucial period in U.S. history in which a contentious culture war consumed much of American society.

Time Period and Historical Context

This volume examines Christian reactions to U.S. foreign policy between 1964 and 1975. This decade occurred right in the middle of the Cold War, which had started after World War II and continued until the fall of the Union of Soviet Socialist Republics (USSR) in the early 1990s. Because of this standoff between the Western democracies and the Communist world, the United States found itself embroiled in a civil war in Southeast Asia, backing South Vietnam against an internal foe and North Vietnam. This war sets the specific time parameters for this book because U.S. military engagement in Vietnam escalated toward a full-blown war in August 1964, and North Vietnam defeated South Vietnam in April 1975.[3]

Because this book seeks to examine a large cross-section of Christianity in as concise a manner as possible, I have narrowed its primary focus to the following time frames: August 1964–December 1964, during the early buildup toward war in Vietnam; January 1968–December 1968, a presidential election year that sparked much commentary about foreign affairs; April 1970–July 1970, after Richard M. Nixon admitted the bombing of Cambodia and seeming escalation of the war; September 1972–February 1973, during another presidential election year and through the peace accord that withdrew U.S. military forces from Vietnam; and March 1975–June 1975, when the civil war came to an end with a North Vietnamese victory. These dates revolve primarily around the Vietnam War, though Cold War events occurred throughout them. It was easiest to conform to this scheme regarding the periodicals under consideration, but less so for the denominations. For example, if the denomination's national assembly met in an off year from this time sampling, this volume will nonetheless include those crucial records because they are fundamental to the church body's public articulation of its theology and opinions. Some of the periodicals and records have missing years and materials; whenever possible, this examination therefore supplements the data with dates that surrounded as closely as possible the parameters outlined here.

The Cold War context actually began following World War II and the development of an arms race between the United States and the Soviet Union. Dissimilar forms of government and opposing economic systems led leaders from both nations to mistrust and dislike each other, thus leading to a contentious and often dangerous standoff. Each nation ultimately manufactured nuclear arms and fought this "war" by threatening the other with total annihilation. For the United States, the Cold War created a firm belief in the domino and containment theories, which held that the United States had to contain communism where it already existed and therefore stem the tide of its alleged expansionist aims or risk nations falling one after another, like dominoes, to communism. By the 1960s, this diplomatic ideology had firmly entrenched itself in the minds of American leaders and civilians alike. Christian entities, too, took part in this discussion, as this book will demonstrate.

This foreign policy ideology stemmed from both irrational fears of the Soviet Union and proof that that country persecuted its citizens, especially religious believers. During the 1950s, Americans by and large condemned the USSR and feared its expansionism. The Soviet regime was oppressive, imprisoned many within its borders who dared question it, and especially harassed and fought against Christians because they contradicted and opposed the official Soviet policies of atheism. But by the 1960s, Americans had a difficult time articulating how they understood this Communist enemy. Some Americans, both civilians and government leaders alike, including Christians on both sides of the spectrum, continued to fear that communism intended to reach around the globe and conquer all non-Communist nations. Many people therefore persisted with harsh condemnations of any Communist government throughout the world. But others had developed a more complex understanding of the world situation, which assessed each nation and individual separately. Rather than seeing communism as a huge monolith, they saw separate nations with differing motivations. These divergent outlooks led to debate throughout American society, from high levels of the government to average citizens, about the true nature of the Cold War and communism.[4]

In other words, throughout the 1950s, a majority of Americans believed that communism represented one worldwide, monolithic force attacking capitalism and democracy with the hope of total conquest. But foreign policy realities and an influential contingent of intellectual liberals who had questioned Cold War policies from the beginning (including Christian leaders of the ecumenical movement) had softened this black and white approach by the 1960s. Some Americans continued to live in a world that denounced all communism and insisted that it was a unified force to combat. Others viewed the situation in more complex terms. The People's Republic of China (PRC) had grown strong enough to consider itself a Communist leader, much like the Soviet Union. This Chinese assertion led to tension between the two Communist giants over their leadership of world communism and shared border disputes. In addition, smaller Communist countries played the two giants off one another to gain economic and military aid from each. The monolith therefore proved illusory, and some Americans recognized this infighting. This recognition even came from the conservative Nixon administration under its pursuit of détente, which took advantage of the conflict to further split the USSR and the PRC by establishing relationships with both nations, including historic visits by Nixon to Moscow and Beijing.[5]

Yet if an alteration in the Cold War between the United States and Communist giants signaled reduced tension, Southeast Asia kept antagonisms high. There, the United States continued to rely on containment theory to determine its actions. Following the French pull-out from Vietnam in 1954, the United States took over protectorship of that nation in order to prevent it from becoming a Communist state. Nonetheless, Ho Chi Minh became the leader of North Vietnam and established a Communist nation that allied with the Soviet Union and People's Republic of China. In contrast, the United States, between 1954 and the fall of Saigon to North Vietnam in 1975, backed a series of corrupt regimes and dictators in South Vietnam simply because they opposed communism and because U.S. leaders did not think that a viable alternative outside of a Communist government presented itself. By 1964, South Vietnam and its war with southern insurgents and the North Vietnamese became unstable enough that Lyndon B. Johnson convinced Congress to pass the Gulf of Tonkin Resolution, which gave him war powers in Southeast Asia. U.S. involvement in the Vietnamese civil war escalated slowly thereafter, through Johnson's administration and into Richard M. Nixon's term in office. Both Johnson and Nixon argued, on the basis of the domino theory, that America had to protect the South Vietnamese from falling into Communist hands—an argument Nixon made even during his efforts toward détente with the USSR and PRC. Officials within the State and Defense Departments, however, were not of one mind regarding this war. Their previous Cold War harmony, which advocated containment and firmly believed in the domino theory, evolved into a vibrant debate during the conflict in Vietnam that focused on the legitimacy of these theories as applied to Southeast Asia. Where some officials, including the presidents, saw a dangerous Communist enemy, others depicted a civil war that had nothing to do with U.S. national security. Though this opposition group failed to win the governmental debate, their voice affected policy and had support from outside Washington, D.C. Throughout all of this dialogue, Christian Americans were vocal on both sides in the debate.[6]

From the very beginning, various Americans questioned U.S. involvement in Vietnam on the grounds that this "civil war" hardly endangered the United States. They also disagreed with America placing itself on the side of dictatorial regimes in South Vietnam. Continuing a long legacy of pacifist advocacy in American history, an intellectual movement from the 1940s and 1950s that had opposed the Cold War arms race began the Vietnam antiwar movement, including and often led by Christian leaders. They were followed quickly by college-age students who agreed with this earlier movement and had the added incentive of being subject to the draft. Throughout the Vietnam War, this antiwar advocacy grew steadily to the point that, by the early 1970s, more and more Americans outside of the vocal demonstrators agreed with their cause and sent politicians to Congress to vote on their behalf. Those who condemned the war had a variety of reasons for doing so. Some felt that the United States had no business fighting in this war, while others felt that a war the United States showed no sign of winning had simply gone on for too long. They therefore wanted to end the bloodshed and loss of life as soon as possible. Those Americans who opposed the Vietnam War agreed with the government officials who had come to question containment theory. Christianity played an enormous role in this antiwar crusade.[7]

The complexity of this period makes it impossible to place Americans into one ideological category, especially as related to the war. While many came to protest it either publicly or privately, the neoconservative movement that emerged after World War II—advocating a strong state and especially championing Cold War antagonisms—remained vibrant throughout the 1960s and supported the Vietnam War, again with a sizeable Christian participation. Their presence helps to explain the election of Richard M. Nixon in 1968 on a law-and-order platform in the midst of antiwar protests and, even more so, his landslide reelection in 1972 despite the continuance of a war he had promised to end. These Americans continued to fear communism, and persisted in their belief that this monolith still worked to encircle the globe and had to be stopped in Southeast Asia. The far right in Nixon's party went so far as to condemn him for détente with the USSR and PRC and for not prosecuting the Vietnam War vigorously enough. The common perception of a decade rife with rights movements, student unrest, and antiwar protests misses the full reality of America at that time. Scholarship has begun to amend this misperception with detailed analysis of conservatism's resurgence beginning in the 1960s. However, little is known about the Christians who contributed to this movement, including a foreign policy stance that maintained a faith in the government and trust in containment theory.[8]

The history of the United States from 1964 to 1975 was profoundly affected by foreign policy issues, especially regarding the Cold and Vietnam wars. A complete understanding of this time period must include knowledge about America outside of its powerful elite, government leaders, or even the vocal antiwar movement. These constituencies are important but did not exist in a vacuum. Christianity has influenced public reactions to and comprehension of every significant era of and issue within U.S. history. This book will shed light on Christian America and its effect on and reactions to the Cold and Vietnam wars, from the domestic debate about Vietnam to popular perceptions of foreign policy to nongovernmental actions overseas. It seeks to add a more complex understanding to what we know about Christianity's participation in this culture war.

Background Context

Christians during the Cold War era generally disdained the atheist mantra of the Soviet Union and People's Republic of China and felt duty bound to assist Christians oppressed inside the Communist nations.[9] Furthermore, a number of religious leaders intensified McCarthy-era paranoia, none more famously so than Billy Graham, who took advantage of Cold War fears during his crusades to warn of an imminent Communist victory that would signal the end times. Christians thus added a religious fervor to the Cold War during the first two decades of the standoff. Yet other Christians, especially those passionate about the ecumenical movement, countered this harsh anticommunism by questioning America's militarization and global antagonism, even as they agreed on the dangers posed by the USSR and PRC. As with the rest of the nation, Christianity was further factionalized along these lines by the 1960s debate about foreign policy. Two of the primary ways of viewing diplomatic concerns that emerged were, on the one hand, a persistent Cold War fear that backed the Vietnam War as necessary and, on the other, a belief that the war was unjust and the domino theory outdated. While this split specifically concerned Vietnam, it relates to significant theological arguments within American Christianity that had been brewing throughout the twentieth century. Quite often, the conservatives who supported the Vietnam War also espoused a fundamentalist view of the world, or at least a very conservative theology, that denounced modernism and interfaith dialogues between Christians who disagreed theologically, between Jews and Christians, between Christians and Muslims, and especially between religious believers and atheist Communists.[10] Other Christians, in contrast, advocated global cooperation. Discussions with people of diverse religious backgrounds gave them a very different view of the war. Instead of viewing politics or theology as black-and-white issues, they saw variances that separated people religiously and politically but that did not necessarily mandate contention. The Christians who advocated a modernist understanding of the world— one that allowed for engagement with other faiths and with scientific thinking—also felt that the United States could coexist with Communist nations peacefully. Those on this side of the debate had spent much of the 1940s and 1950s promoting dialogue among Christian denominations, espousing religious cooperation, and working through organizations such as the National Council of the Churches of Christ in the United States of America (NCC) to foster unity. They continued this approach into the 1960s. While the above examples represent but two of the Christian modes of analysis regarding foreign policy, they demonstrate the amount of attention that Christianity gave to diplomacy during this decade. They show that Christianity participated in the culture war over foreign policy.[11]

In addition, this Christian contemplation included musings on the justness of the Vietnam conflict. By this time seven "just war" criteria had emerged in Christianity, having begun with Augustine and then having been refined through the ages: (1) the cause of the war must be just; (2) the war must be waged by a legitimate authority; (3) the war must be formally declared; (4) it must be fought with the right intention of instituting a just peace; (5) there must be a reasonable chance for success; (6) war must be a last resort; and (7) the means of waging it must be proportional to the ends. The prowar side during the Vietnam conflict felt that the war met these criteria while antiwar advocates insisted that it did not. In other words, religious exegesis provided no more concrete answers to the debate over Vietnam than did the secular political/diplomatic debate. Yet we still must understand how this religious voice added to America's culture conflict over foreign policy during this era.[12]

Finally, beginning in 1973 and certainly by the time North Vietnam took control of the South in April 1975, this vibrant debate over foreign policy tapered off for many people, though this book will demonstrate that this was not true for all Christians. Many Americans had become weary of the constant fighting, breathed a sigh of relief when Nixon withdrew American troops from Southeast Asia in January 1973, and tried to ignore the collapse of South Vietnam in 1975. For some, the war had gone on for too long for a nation with a historically short attention span. Student unrest disappeared, questioning of U.S. foreign policy faded, and discussions about the Vietnam War ceased to exist in a public way. Even many religious institutions put behind them much of the tension that had characterized this decade. Others, especially within liberal Christianity, insisted that Americans could not ignore international events that easily and emphasized that the United States had to learn from losing the Vietnam War how to behave differently in the future in the international arena. They championed efforts to learn from mistakes made in Vietnam and thereby to alter the nation's foreign policy regarding the Cold War.

Despite evidence that American Christians addressed the Vietnam War from both pro- and antiwar perspectives, we have given more attention to Christian involvement in the antiwar movement, thus providing a strong portrait of what motivated Christians toward this stance. Antiwar Christians disparaged the United States' reliance on containment theory, as did a number of Americans, and many had done so since the early 1950s. Numerous Christians therefore belonged to the Vietnam antiwar movement, in which they picketed, protested, wrote letters to the government, and generally fought against the war from the very beginning because they thought it unjust and immoral. They also created interdenominational organizations to lobby their fellow Americans, Congress, and the presidency to their point of view. The most extreme of these individuals became famous for their vocal opposition, none more so than the Catholic priests and brothers, Daniel and Philip Berrigan, who even broke into draft board offices and poured blood over files. Christian organizations attempted to change American opinion about the war as well: Clergy and Laity Concerned about Vietnam, an organization obviously created specifically to protest the Vietnam War, and the National Council of Churches of Christ, an interdenominational cooperative body, represent the most prominent of ecumenical efforts to embolden the antiwar movement with a moral, Christian message. Christians who protested the Vietnam War asserted that they represented prophetic voices who realized that the war injured innocent people and did nothing to fortify U.S. interests. My study will build further upon this scholarship when I examine the liberal voices that I have included here.[13]

Much of the Christian antiwar argument stemmed from Christians' knowledge about Vietnam and its history; they saw a complexity to the civil war taking place in that country. Where prowar advocates saw all Communists as one entity, antiwar Americans pointed out the many factions involved in the war. The National Liberation Front in South Vietnam was organized in the early 1960s as a cooperative venture between a number of South Vietnamese factions to fight against the dictatorial regimes in that country and included Communists and North Vietnamese spies but also middle-class South Vietnamese, religious protesters, such as the Buddhists, and assorted other groups that simply despised South Vietnam. These groups had plenty of reason to complain because the series of regimes backed by the United States, despite frequent changes in leadership, stole U.S. aid and put it on the black market for profit, arrested those who dared question the government, and forced people into the army, all of which outraged the Vietnamese. In addition, Vietnam had a long history of opposing foreign domination and not giving up, even when militarily overpowered. Antiwar Christians in America examined all of these realities and denounced the opinion that America fought for freedom against monolithic communism. They used churches and other organizations to make their point and brought many moderate Americans into their sway as more and more people came to question U.S. policy in Southeast Asia.[14]

Yet, as noted, not all Christians opposed the war. Statistical evidence, though scant and subjective, lends credence to the notion that Christian Americans disagreed about American policy in Vietnam. If anything, early opinion polls counter an emphasis on the antiwar movement within Christianity by suggesting that most American Christians supported the war. In 1965, 49 percent of Protestants and 59 percent of Catholics believed that the United States should be involved in Vietnam, versus just 27 percent and 23 percent, respectively, who said it should not be involved. Yet by 1970, this relative support had shifted when a poll asked whether or not the United States had erred in sending troops to fight in Vietnam. Fifty-six percent of Protestant and 58 percent of Catholic respondents answered yes, versus no votes of 32 percent and 35 percent. Yet this response did not necessarily signal a total loss of support for U.S. interests in South Vietnam, as many Americans maintained hope that an anti-Communist ally could be kept in power in South Vietnam. Still, in August 1972, 49 percent of Protestants and 57 percent of Catholics stated that the United States should continue to send economic and military aid to South Vietnam even after a withdrawal of U.S. troops. Other questions and polls reveal a similar trend: Protestants and Catholics held a variety of opinions about the Cold and Vietnam wars.[15]

American Christianity obviously voiced its will regarding the Cold and Vietnam wars between 1964 and 1975. But it hardly created a unified point of view. A spectrum of opinions about both wars reveals the complexity of studying the convergence of foreign policy, religion, and American citizens. The scholarship that contributed knowledge about Christian reactions to our understanding of America during this decade began the important process of teasing apart all that occurred within Christianity and its response to foreign policy at that time. This book further complicates the picture.

Methodology

This book examines six Christian entities: the Southern Baptist Convention, the African Methodist Episcopal Church, and the United Church of Christ, as well as *Christianity Today*, the *Christian Century*, and periodicals from American Catholicism. It provides a variety of viewpoints, including conservative evangelicals, liberal mainline Protestants, Christian moderates, and Catholics of various religious and political perspectives. As a whole, these Christians provide a sense of the many religious responses to the Cold and Vietnam wars, and also offer specific examples of how and why pastors and lay people arrived at their opinions about global issues in the context of their faith lives. This group offers a spectrum of diplomatic, political, racial, and theological outlooks that illuminate the complexity of Christian reactions to foreign relations and begins the process of developing a more complete understanding of this era.

I came to this project in the wake of my previous book, *Lutherans and the Longest War.* A number of colleagues recommended that I continue on the path laid out by this book with a broader study of Christianity, comparing other institutions to the Lutherans. I resisted for some time, frankly because I wanted to move in a new direction. However, once I had a firm grasp on the political, diplomatic, religious, and social circumstances swirling around the topic, I found that it made sense to expand my coverage of Christian reactions beyond Lutheranism. In part, some of the same questions plagued me even after I had completed the Lutheran study. I knew that Lutherans had offered a glimpse into middle America, or the silent majority, but I wanted to know if other Christians did the same. Was there more to discover and learn by doing a similar study with a broader range? Would they tell a similar or different story? This book answers those questions. But first, a word about why I chose each individual denomination or periodical and a brief overview of its history offer some needed context.[16]

I included *Christianity Today* because it provides a nationally respected voice for evangelical Americans with a broad readership and its reach extends beyond any one particular denomination. Though affiliated with a number of Southern Baptist Convention members, the periodical's link to the Reverend Billy Graham and other evangelical leaders who transcended particular denominational affiliations gave it an even greater impact. For a Christian periodical, too, it had a large circulation of 253,579 in 1968. This means that a number of Americans and institutions looked to it as a news source covering political, international, and social affairs from a conservative Christian theological viewpoint. Following in the path of the many historians who have used it to gauge conservative religious responses to a variety of matters, I considered it logical to scrutinize this periodical's 1960s and 1970s foreign policy perspectives.[17]

Christianity Today is a nationally distributed evangelical magazine with a heavy Baptist influence and a view enmeshed in traditional Cold War anticommunism. This foreign policy position stemmed from communism's hostility toward religion. Because the periodical's theology emphasized missionary work and Christian outreach, Communist nations came under fire because they forbade evangelical programs inside their borders and thereby thwarted a fundamental theological tenet of those who wrote in and read *Christianity Today*. In other words, more played into the periodical's anti-Communist stance and support of containment theory than mere politics or desires for global freedom. Regarding the Vietnam War, the periodical remained supportive of both Johnson and Nixon administrative policies and worried throughout the conflict about the "danger" of a Communist takeover of that nation. However, it seldom did so in a reactionary manner; it is clear from the material published that editors, writers, and even readers studied the war and formulated opinions based on their perception of factual information, not visceral feelings.[18]

This response makes sense given the periodical's history. Created in 1956 as a journal for evangelical outreach and opinion making in the United States to counter the more liberal mainline Protestant journals, *Christianity Today* grew rapidly, in part because of its affiliation with founding member Billy Graham, who maintained an active role with the periodical and helped to shape its outlook. Throughout its history, the journal proclaimed a conservative theology that warned of God's impending judgment and emphasized the need for evangelical outreach, and it was the first news magazine dedicated to fostering the evangelical message to a wide U.S. audience. As historian D. G. Hart states, the periodical "by the 1960s had emerged as the magazine of record for evangelical Protestantism."[19]

One of the theologically and politically liberal periodicals that *Christianity Today* was meant to counter with its founding was the *Christian Century*. I have included the *Christian Century* in this analysis to shed light on the elite intellectual perspective of mainline Protestantism. While hardly indicative of the entire population, it represents the foreign policy analysis of an influential group of thinkers who often had the ears of political leaders and could sway their readership with carefully argued and well-documented analysis. Again, the use of this periodical by numerous historians attempting to ascertain public opinion about various issues throughout the twentieth century testifies to its importance. Admittedly, it had a smaller circulation than *Christianity Today*, with only forty-five thousand subscribers in 1968. But it also had more competition from other liberally and intellectually minded Christian periodicals, such as *Christianity and Crisis*, whereas *Christianity Today* stood virtually alone. Though historians strive to get at popular opinion, not just that of a highbrow minority, it is still crucial to understand the elite point of view. Adding a liberal intellectual perspective to this study through the *Christian Century* balances the lay opinions that appear elsewhere and that often paralleled the point of view found in its pages.[20]

By the 1960s, the *Christian Century* had become the leading voice of liberal intellectual thought within American Protestantism. It persistently campaigned on behalf of the civil and women's rights movements, welfare programs, and interreligious dialogue. The *Christian Century* strove to assess academically various issues with the goal of uniting people in an effort to live together peacefully, whether within the United States or in the larger global community. Interdenominational in nature, it championed human rights issues and, having weaned itself off a 1950s Cold Warrior mentality, instead backed arms reduction and peaceful coexistence with communism.[21]

The writings of this periodical demonstrates that, while still disdaining Communist oppression and lamenting the treatment of religious believers inside Communist borders, some American Christians learned a different lesson from the Vietnam War: according to liberal, intellectual Protestantism, the United States could not force its will on people simply because it believed its ideology was superior. Except for a few very subtle nuances to the contrary, the articles and editorials about Vietnam within this periodical presented a unified antiwar voice, without disagreement or rancor. This conclusion contrasts with Mark Hulsether's findings for *Christianity and Crisis*, its sister publication. The *Christian Century* provides a crucial counterpoint to *Christianity Today* with its antiwar point of view in the context of an anti-Communist doctrine that nonetheless questioned containment theory and called U.S. actions imperialistic.

Yet Protestant America hardly had a corner on the market when it came to debating foreign policy during the 1960s and 1970s, as revealed in an examination of Catholic periodicals. With a roster of approximately 46,865,000 and thus by far the largest Christian denomination in the United States, the Catholic Church exercises an influence that is pivotal to consider. Gaining a sense of Catholic opinion, however, proves a formidable task; I selected a sampling of periodicals to reflect the diversity of opinions that existed in Catholic America. This selection includes periodicals edited by both lay and clergy members and reflects the variety of perspectives that I found after initially reviewing over thirty possible choices. I have incorporated the five periodicals that best reflect the diversity of foreign policy viewpoints that I saw without including any that seemed to represent a small minority opinion. The size of the Roman Catholic population in America alone explains why its leadership and membership published so many periodicals, and why it had an array of opinions about diplomacy.[22]

Dating to the colonial era, American Catholicism manifested a diversity of opinions, some agreeing with Vatican doctrine and others defying Rome with an independent American Catholicism. Additionally, each new wave of Catholic immigrants brought changed perceptions and ideologies, such as the contrast between Irish Catholics of the mid-1800s and Italian Catholics at the turn of the twentieth century. By the mid-twentieth century, it was impossible to paint Catholicism in America with one brush stroke. As historian Jay P. Dolan wrote, "By the 1960s, Catholics in the United States were becoming more like the rest of the American population." Catholic America included conservatives who began to side with the evangelical right in America, liberals among the working class who leaned toward far left politics and advocated social welfare programs, and a myriad of people somewhere between these extremes. Since this study begins shortly after the liberalizing of Catholic worship brought about by Vatican II, the research in this book demonstrates how new trends further splintered this denomination.[23]

In representing a moderate to liberal political outlook that emphasized Catholic charitable outreach and compassion, this study utilizes the lay-written *Commonweal* (43,000 circulation as of 1968); *Catholic World,* published by the Paulist fathers (20,500 circulation in 1968); and the Claretian Fathers' *U.S. Catholic* (54,562 circulation in 1968), which later merged with the liberal *Jubilee* and therefore took on a more leftist political bent. These periodicals provided a Catholic antiwar voice by the 1970s, though during the 1960s they struggled to shed the harsh anticommunism that had also characterized Vatican attitudes toward the Cold War throughout the 1950s. Indeed, the Holy See moved toward advocating peace and global tranquility throughout the 1960s and 1970s, a shift reflected in these American journals. This attitude continued the social Catholicism that evolved throughout the twentieth century and engaged the American church body more and more with secular, political issues.[24]

In contrast, other Catholic opinion makers insisted that communism still posed a threat to global religion and maintained 1950s Catholic conservatism regarding foreign affairs. While the Vatican inched toward a pacifist platform, it hardly became a bastion of liberal ideology and therefore allowed for these varying American perceptions between the periodicals. The Jesuit-published *America* (103,222 circulation in 1968) and the Catholic Publishing Center of the College of St. Thomas's *Catholic Digest* (600,000 circulation in 1968) provide a conservative counterpoint that clung to traditional Cold

War hostilities against communism because of its attack on Christianity, and especially on the Catholic Church inside Communist borders. These journals upheld the legacy of such luminary Catholic figures as Cardinal Francis J. Spellman, who championed hard-core anticommunism and backed the U.S. insistence on containment theory and confrontations with Communist doctrine. They also indicate that historians' focus on popular antiwar figures in the Catholic Church mischaracterizes a denomination that supported conservative periodicals with much higher subscription rates than those of its liberal counterparts.[25]

Edward T. Brett's *U.S. Catholic Press on Central America* also utilized periodicals to study American Catholic reactions to international events, finding the same disagreements and evolution of thought relating to foreign policy regarding Central America that this book will outline regarding the Vietnam War. He argued that the Catholic press began the Cold War by supporting U.S. policy but that experiences and knowledge about what it wrought in Central America moved many to change their minds, resulting in the first time in history that Catholics so vociferously challenged the government. Brett's argument about Central America's influence on changing Catholic opinions mirrors the findings in this book about Vietnam. As a whole, these Catholic periodicals echo the debate taking place in the Protestant press between *Christianity Today* and the *Christian Century*, as well as the varying viewpoints manifested in Protestant denominations.[26]

Protestant denominations also engaged in foreign policy discussions, as the Southern Baptist Convention (SBC) demonstrates. To further explore a Baptist, evangelical point of view, I included this, the largest Protestant denomination in America, with 11,140,000 members in 1967. This denomination offers an interesting comparison to *Christianity Today*, especially because I could get a better grasp of Baptist lay opinions in the SBC than was available through that periodical. I also wanted a church body with a decentralized polity. No denomination more fiercely protected local congregational rights than did the SBC. It also mixed patriotic/conservative backing of the government with a staunch stand in support of the separation of church and state. Finally, the SBC reflects an interesting regional perspective in that it predominantly represents the southern United States, a nice contrast to my earlier study of the more midwestern-focused Lutherans.[27]

Southern Baptist Convention history indicates that this predominantly white church body, headquartered in and with a vast majority of its members hailing from the South, aligned with a conservative political and diplomatic agenda by the 1960s in all aspects of its church life, not simply foreign policy.

Born in 1845, it began this conservative journey by defending slavery and breaking away from northern antislavery Baptists. It instituted a polity that fiercely defended local congregational control, allowed a secondary reliance on state conventions, and reserved the auspices of a national church office only for crucial national endeavors—a demeanor that held true for the 1960s and 1970s. The twentieth century brought with it a retrenchment of Baptist conservatism, particularly in relationship to the fundamentalist/modernist controversy. This eventually led to the ouster of even moderate Southern Baptists from power in the 1980s, a tension often reflected in the foreign policy disputes this book examines. For example, Foy Valentine, as leader of the Christian Life Commission, offered a moderate political point of view with an antiwar stance, and Valentine became one of the purged moderates in the 1980s. Furthermore, the denomination lived with an interesting dichotomy regarding its view of the nation. On the one hand, it maintained the strong Baptist legacy of championing the separation of church and state because of historic persecutions of Baptists by governments. On the other hand, it often sounded patriotic in its portrayal of American democracy and values, even becoming defensive when people questioned U.S. aims in Southeast Asia. SBC convention resolutions, periodicals, official papers, and lay sources contribute an important denominational voice to this study with a southern, white, and evangelical mantra that paralleled that of fellow evangelicals at *Christianity Today*.[28]

Examining denominations with a predominantly white membership, alone, hardly seemed to achieve an accurate portrayal of American Christianity. I therefore also included the African Methodist Episcopal Church (AME), which had a membership of 1,166,000 in 1951. Though generally without the publicity of its black Baptist counterparts, it contributes a Methodist voice to the study while at the same time paralleling the black Baptists' willingness to engage in political, social issues in a public way. But those in this denomination were generally more theologically conservative than many black Baptists, another factor that influenced its foreign policy points of view. The AME also offered the opportunity to scrutinize the oldest black denomination in the United States. Furthermore, as religious historians know, the black churches have scant accessible archival materials, except that the AME has a Division of Research and Scholarship that made available a great many sources not easily housed in one central location for the other black denominations.[29]

Founded in 1816, the African Methodist Episcopal Church came about because of racism within the Methodist Church that segregated congregations and gave black leaders such as Richard Allen a secondary status to that of white clergy. Theologically, therefore, the AME church paralleled that of all Methodism, emphasizing living a strict life, advocating temperance, and spreading the Gospel through mission work and revivals. But it diverged from white Methodism and the white churches and periodicals studied here due to race. Because its inception came about because of a social issue rather than a theological dispute, the AME matched the history of other black churches with regular commentary on race relations and social activism on behalf of the antislavery movement, education and literacy for black people, desegregation, and civil rights. The ability to congregate and thereby discuss race issues had prompted African Americans in all denominations to utilize the church as a bully pulpit and to fight for equality from the early 1800s to the present. This differed sharply from many white Protestant denominations that often avoided such activism for fear of alienating members or creating dissension. The very safety and livelihoods of black church members demanded social-justice participation from their congregations. AME leaders and members alike therefore had few qualms about bringing social issues into the church because doing so had been central to its function from the very beginning.[30]

Regarding the Vietnam War, this comfort with engaging contemporary issues clashed with the AME heritage of black church activism: members disagreed about how far the church should go in opposing the Vietnam War. Some believed that the AME had to criticize the war on moral grounds, especially because of the disproportionate number of blacks who were called to fight it. But others shied away from demanding such activism because antiwar statements could alienate Lyndon B. Johnson and his Democratic Party, which had done so much to champion civil rights, most notably by getting the Civil Rights Act of 1964 and the Voting Rights Act of 1965 passed into law. This conundrum included disagreement about Martin Luther King Jr.'s denunciation of the Vietnam War. Some within the AME applauded the civil rights leader's prophetic voice, while others agreed with black Americans who said it would undermine the civil rights gains that African Americans had made by mixing war with domestic concerns. This contention within black America and the AME Church tapered off during Richard M. Nixon's administration, partially because more and more within the AME joined the rest of America in weariness about the Vietnam War and partially because Nixon did little to assist the civil rights movement, thus removing the fear that antiwar advocacy would alter the government's view of civil rights matters. Black Americans understood Nixon's courting of white southern racists into his constituency and responded accordingly.

The AME elected leaders to local and national offices, thus further intensifying dialogue within the denomination about a range of societal issues.
When a bishop, especially at that national level, spoke contrary to the will
of an individual, congregation, or district, she or he found it necessary to
defend himself or herself from attack and struggled for reelection. The division into districts that held annual meetings also fostered debate about current issues, including foreign policy, because each could pass its own resolutions. The African Methodist Episcopal Church contributes a Protestant
perspective that both parallels and contradicts the voices found elsewhere in
this study: it parallels the debate about foreign policy and the way the church
should respond but differs in that race was central to all of its reactions.

Finally, I included the 2,053,000-member (1967) United Church of Christ
in this book. The United Church of Christ (UCC) contributes a unique voice
because of its unflinching liberal activism. Because the SBC embodied a
conservative theological and political example and the AME a conservative
theological but moderate to liberal political perspective, I wanted to examine a theologically and politically liberal counterpart. Furthermore, the UCC
provides the viewpoint of a more eastern Christian element and often paralleled the thinking found in the *Christian Century*. This UCC similarity to the
Christian Century gives weight to using a Christian liberal intellectual voice
because of the lay opinions that it included. It therefore contributes further
to our already strong understanding of Christian participation in the antiwar
movement with a new denominational voice.[31]

Most people affiliated with the United Church of Christ strongly opposed
all American military action in Southeast Asia.[32] Such a strong position
makes sense, coming from a denomination committed to social justice
since its founding in 1957 with the merger of the Congregational Christian
Churches and Evangelical and German Reformed Church. Because polity
had so dominated merger discussions, especially the issue of local congregational control, and because ecumenism and unity were foremost in the minds
of leaders, UCC theologian and historian Louis H. Gunnemann argues that
the founders spent little time articulating a firm theological direction for the
UCC. Furthermore, the new constitution specifically called the denomination to "Christian action in society." This fact left it to the new leaders, and
especially the denomination's periodical, *United Church Herald*, to create
the United Church of Christ's approach to national and global issues. They
focused on human improvement. From its inception, therefore, these leaders took up the cause of civil rights, the women's rights movement, poverty,
and other social justice issues and made them the business of the church.

Members soon followed, so that already by the mid-1960s, the UCC became known for its activism on behalf of a liberal Christianity that wanted equality and justice for all peoples. The Vietnam War began in the context of this denominational outlook, therefore bringing the wrath of the denomination down upon U.S. actions in Southeast Asia.[33]

This volume also attempts to transcend examinations that strictly consider intellectuals or denominational leaders by including as much lay and reader opinion as possible.[34] In addition to denominational and print data, it includes analyses of letters to the editor and to denominational leaders and committees, voting results at national conventions, and any lay correspondence or materials available in the archival sources. While not as complete and whole a picture as I would have liked because so much of lay opinion is lost to history, this work at least incorporates as much lay perception as possible into the study. Adding these items into the opinions of leaders and intellectuals broadens the perspective to offer a more complete sense of American reactions from a variety of levels. This analysis transcends the perspective of theologians, writers, and denominational leaders to include the viewpoints of denominational members and periodical readers wherever possible.

Nonetheless, a certain amount of "elite" church history remains in this work, as it does for many who attempt to research American religious history. My sources are predominantly, though obviously not exclusively, from white middle- to upper-class citizens with a higher education. The conservative members of this group clearly belonged to the "silent majority" as labeled by Nixon. It behooves us to research more about them, so long as they do not become the sole focus of our examinations. As historian Michael S. Foley argued in his study of the silent majority based on letters written to Dr. Benjamin Spock, we can learn about voices otherwise lost to us from the limited sources that survive. The denominational sources and periodicals that I examined offer another means for us to view the American home front during the Vietnam War. I am not arguing that they are a perfect source or entirely comprehensive; but they *are* a vital component to American life and give us a unique perspective on that era. Furthermore, much—but again not all—of the material included here centers on intellectual elites because they led the churches. Whether Protestant or Catholic, laity or clergy, highly educated individuals shaped the course of Christianity during this decade in profound ways. That their voices are heard more than many lay voices is only natural, because they recorded their thoughts, housed information in archives, and served through elections as the voice of Christianity. To avoid the "gap-theory," in which denominational leaders swing more to the left than their lay constituents, I researched as many lay sources as possible and added them to this book. Additionally, the use of convention minutes and resolutions assisted with this problem, because delegates were elected by congregations for all of the denominations studied herein. The popular vote at national assemblies, especially for the Southern Baptist Convention, indicates that at least this population of elected lay and clergy people agreed with their leadership. While I strive to weave lay and atypical voices into the conversation wherever possible, a certain amount of "higher leadership," even among evangelicals that resisted such hierarchy, becomes natural for this study. Surviving sources almost make it inevitable that a survey of this many institutions over such a long period of time will still suffer to some extent from the laity/clergy-gap concern. Yet if we take seriously the lay voices that we do find, and trust in the democratic process that the three denominations in this study employed for sending members to national and regional conventions, then we avoid this becoming a study that *solely* examines elite church leadership. I strove to be as precise as possible about what sources I engaged, so that readers will know if a given viewpoint came from a resolution, letter to the editor, or other kind of source. While this approach may not be as satisfying as polling numbers (which do not exist) or a deeper and more extensive collection of lay documents (again, which do not exist), it at least gives more lay opinion than a more traditional top-down approach would offer.[35]

Furthermore, for each time period examined, I combed through the periodicals page by page, examining every reference to foreign policy. I saw all editorials, guest columns, featured articles, book reviews, and letters to the editor for each issue. All of the periodicals included in this study commented frequently on foreign policy issues, at least a couple of times per issue; I chose a representative sampling from these editorials and articles to quote and cite because they encapsulated the vast amount of foreign policy commentary for each journal. This approach offered a solid overview of the publication and its general approach to diplomatic matters. I also researched in archives for unpublished letters to the editor when available, as well as editorial correspondence and private memos, to gain a broader perspective about the journals. Again, the letters I cite herein are a representative sampling unless I indicate otherwise. Similarly, I spent weeks in the denominational archives for the SBC, UCC, and AME. I uncovered as much material as they had preserved to include in this study. From private letters written by lay people to denomination leaders to churchwide resolutions, I gathered as much information as possible to gain a holistic view of that particular denomination's take on foreign policy matters. I then used a representative sampling to give readers a sense of what I learned. When I quote someone, whether denominationally or from a periodical, either that person/entity was a good sample of something that I saw in multiple locations or I note in the text that it was from a unique voice. For example, I used lay letters to the editor that voiced an opinion heard from several lay sources, while I allowed a denomination leader to speak on her or his own, knowing that readers would recognize the particular nature of that opinion. Sadly, a lot of denominational materials have been lost over time, because individuals take their correspondence home when they retire, because of natural disasters, and simply because other stuff is never processed and is accidentally thrown away. Researching American Christianity can be a haphazard enterprise, but I strove to overcome this challenge with a breadth of material to give as complete a sense as possible of each of the entities I examined.[36]

As noted above, the sampling outlined here furthers the process of understanding Christian reactions to the Cold and Vietnam wars. It provides a spectrum of belief systems and histories, all of which played into the way a particular periodical or denomination shaped its positions on foreign policy. Not only will this information better illustrate how Christian America reacted to war, participated in it, and contributed to American attitudes about it; it also provides historians with a more accurate sense of U.S. opinions in general during that decade. Liberal, moderate, and conservative Americans all voiced their opinions and shaped the way the United States acted in the world. Each of the Christian entities studied here had a history of global action and viewpoints that also influenced how they responded to the conflicts of that time. In other words, they came to understand these wars in the context of their historic stances on world issues, American politics, and theology. While no smoking gun unequivocally proves that the Christian debate about foreign affairs had a decisive influence on American policymakers, the material in this study demonstrates that the Christian debates were a key element to American responses to war and that these Christians at least thought that they could alter the course of diplomatic affairs. Taken together, they illustrate the myriad ways that Christians and Americans in general approached foreign policy between 1964 and 1975. Christianity engaged in the culture war over foreign policy during this era, and we must better understand how it did so.

Few would argue today against a depiction of the contemporary world that highlights the profound influences of diplomatic policy, war, and religion on America. One cannot study the wars in Iraq or Afghanistan, the War on Terrorism, or domestic militarism without also examining the influence of ideology and faith. Similarly, Christian America and the nation as a whole benefited and suffered from theological reflections on the Cold and Vietnam wars as presented in this book. Grasping more fully the dynamics of these debates enables us to comprehend more completely that volatile time in U.S. history, and the one swirling around us today.

1

Christianity and the
Cold War, 1964–1968

Introduction

In September 1964, Billy Graham held the Greater Omaha–Council Bluffs Crusade. Graham told the 16,100 participants that teenage rebellion, sexuality, and a collapse of law and order endangered the United States, and he emphasized that this situation paved the way for Communists, who were "just waiting until we get soft enough" with moral standards and anti-Communist vigilance to swoop in and conquer America. The Cold War continued to threaten America and demanded action from Christians to help defeat communism. A conservative Christianity during the 1960s undergirded U.S. public opinion about Cold War policy and thereby assisted the government in its continued faith in containment theory. Yet fellow Christians in the United Church of Christ disagreed. *United Church Herald* editors cautioned that "political zealots" in the United States who warned that the government and society did too little to protect against communism were the real domestic threat because they rejected the democratic system with "a fervid willingness to take the law" into their own hands. They argued that curtailing open debate and constantly promoting fear of communism harmed innocent citizens with false hysteria. Despite scholarship showing that the Vietnam War prompted some Americans to begin to question Cold War hostilities, such liberal Christian editorials demonstrate that a push against this worldview had been initiated even earlier. Religious standpoints played a role in shaping and reflecting public opinion, but they also teased out some of the tension and disagreement inherent in this culture war dialogue.[1]

By focusing our examination primarily on the periods August 1964–December 1964 and January 1968–December 1968, periods of time during presidential election years in which Christian Americans frequently voiced political opinions as they readied to vote with the rest of the nation, we can see how Christians addressed the Cold War in relation to their particular theological positions and historical legacies. Because most Christians felt that communism's doctrine of atheism needed to be combated, religious institutions added important reflections to the national conversation. Government officials, anti-Communist organizations, and even popular culture sources were rife with language about fighting the "evil empire," warnings against Communist atheism, and declarations that the "Democratic Christian world" had to combat this sinister force. Scholars have clearly demonstrated that this religiously charged language was used to mobilize U.S. society throughout the Cold War. For example, historian and former director for Strategic Planning on the National Security Council, William Inboden, has shown that Harry S. Truman spoke publicly at the beginning of the Cold War and throughout his presidency about using America's spiritual strength to help defeat atheist Communists. Richard Nixon, too, added a religious component to his foreign policy when he utilized the evangelist Billy Graham's anti-Communist messages to justify the United States' actions around the globe. Moreover, while histories of American Christianity have made clear that churches and religious leaders employed the language of a holy war when describing the Cold War, they have tended to focus on the 1950s and early 1960s, without pulling this important thread through the Vietnam War.[2] Most studies have failed to look at Christian Americans' viewpoints into the 1960s to see why and how they employed this language of a holy war and crafted a theology to fit this ideology well into the 1970s. In addition to shedding light on the religious component of this conservative message, this study's examination of the religious rhetoric of the 1960s and 1970s adds to our growing understanding of the conservative political resurgence that started in the 1960s by contributing a religious voice to the conversation.[3]

During the 1950s, many American religious institutions had supported U.S. antagonism toward all things Communist because of communism's atheist ideology, though a minority (especially among Protestant leaders of the ecumenical movement) had resisted the arms race as antithetical to Christian ideals and dangerous for the world. This small group of committed opponents grew by the 1960s and generated a fuller Christian debate about the Cold War. Some conservative Christians continued to view communism as a monolithic Other wedded to expansionism and bent on oppressing its citizens and especially religious freedom, in line with the traditional Cold War viewpoint that called upon containment theory and a bold foreign policy to stop Communist aims, both political and religious. Other Christians questioned this worldview, and in increasing numbers. They argued that communism was not a global monolith and instead sought cooperation with Communist nations in order to reduce tension and especially the danger of a nuclear war, often drawing on particular biblical mandates of peace as God's will. Additionally, they insisted that the United States must first address problems within its own foreign policy before it could continue as a free example to the rest of the world. Morality and Christian obligation played into both points of view, despite their differing opinions. Conservatives believed that Christians had a moral responsibility to combat the evil force of communism, while their liberal counterparts argued that morality dictated reduced global tension and more cooperation with Communist nations. For most Christians, the Cold War was a moral issue, though they hardly agreed on what that meant.[4]

While the Cold War had burned hot through at least the Kennedy administration, it had cooled a bit by the mid-1960s. The near nuclear catastrophe of the 1962 Cuban Missile Crisis and subsequent improved communication between Moscow and Washington in part explained the reduced tension. The United States and the Soviets also had internal and external problems to address, which led them to focus attention away from the standoff that so dominated the 1950s. Under Nikita Khrushchev, the Soviet Union also reduced persecutions within Russia, especially those previously aimed at Christian institutions and believers. This, too, served to soften the American point of view. Yet, at the same time, the two nations remained wary of each other, continued to carve the world into spheres of influence, and maintained the arms buildup. Debates within the churches were thus mirroring those in which American policy makers were engaged: hard-line traditionalists backed containment theory as still necessary while moderates argued for a new approach due to changed circumstances.

This national debate over Cold War foreign policy, including American Christian attitudes, intensified during the 1960s because of global events. The 1968 Soviet invasion of Czechoslovakia clouded perceptions of the true nature of communism and of what U.S. foreign policy should do to combat the Cold War. The Soviet Union had seized control of Czechoslovakia in 1948 and thereafter supported a Communist puppet regime. This rigid system began to crumble in late 1967 because of an internal student movement that combined with political dissidents' demands for reform. In January 1968, the Central Committee took heed of this uprising and replaced Antonin Novotny, a dictatorial Soviet-style Communist, with the more moderate Alexander Dubcek. The new government attempted to balance its traditional Communist control with liberalized reforms, efforts that found global approval simply because they signaled change and challenged Soviet control.

Christians especially found heartening a trend toward more tolerance of religious belief. This attempt at self-rule came crashing down on 21 August 1968, when the Soviet Union, backed by its supporters in Prague, invaded the nation. Though it took almost two years for the Soviets to regain their previous hard-line control, by the end of 1968 few questioned the fact that they would succeed or could ignore the oppressive tactics used against Czech resistance. For Americans discussing the Cold War, this proved a setback for those seeking dialogue with Communists and proof positive for conservatives of Communist expansionism.

Yet, at the same time, Communist rifts contributed to a more liberal thinking. Almost from the rise of Mao Zedong as the People's Republic of China's (PRC) leader following World War II, friction erupted between the PRC and the Soviet Union over leadership of the Communist world. China followed a harder line than did the Soviet Union when it came to rhetoric and support for revolutions. The Soviets, leery of confrontation with the United States, often tempered their enthusiasm, while the PRC held fast to its advocacy of all wars for national liberation. This situation was further compounded by the USSR's presence in the United Nations and the PRC's exclusion from it until 1971. Though often outvoted and ostracized at the UN because of U.S. leadership, the USSR took the organization seriously and worked with it when possible. In contrast, the United States managed to keep the PRC out of the UN by propping up the exiled Chinese government then located in Taiwan, which Mao had defeated, as the UN China representative. The PRC's exclusion from world dialogue further intensified its renegade philosophy when it came to supporting a "global Communist effort." In addition, the Sino-Soviet relationship was strained because of disputes along their shared border, a region that both sides had armed and occasionally skirmished over. U.S. officials and many "average" Americans recognized this tension within the Communist camp, which led some to cast aside faith in a philosophy that framed a Communist monolith as an enemy because this characterization did not ring true anymore.

The ambition of negotiating disarmament agreements between the United States and the Soviet Union further clouded Cold War philosophies by the 1960s. Under Dwight D. Eisenhower and John F. Kennedy, the notion emerged but never made headway because of American distrust of the Soviets and contentious relations over several international issues. The Eisenhower administration had come close to a treaty in 1955 but decided that the Soviets would not abide by it and so abandoned negotiations. Under the Kennedy administration, hot spots such as Berlin, a contentious city because

West Germany controlled West Berlin in the heart of East Germany, took precedence and underscored this mistrust. Tension about Berlin, for example, overshadowed a Kennedy-Khrushchev meeting in 1961 that was supposed to consider disarmament. By the middle to late 1960s, little had been accomplished, a reality that played into both conservative and liberal points of view. While conservatives saw this failure to reach an agreement as proof that a strong stance against communism was needed and that Communists could not be trusted, others viewed the mere possibility of a disarmament agreement as evidence that Communists did not represent the total evil previously portrayed and wanted to soften anti-Communist rhetoric in order to promote an arms limitation that might make the world safer. Conservative Christians helped support a right-leaning anticommunism within the government, while liberal Christians questioned this very same policy on moral grounds, long before the harsh lessons of the Vietnam War.

Opinion on the Cold War thus ran the gamut within Christian America, though most stances were informed by specific Christian worldviews. Historian David F. Schmitz, in his examinations of U.S. alignments with right-wing dictatorships and the resulting conflict between American ideology and practical security concerns during the Cold War, argues that by the 1960s and 1970s American foreign policy experts no longer agreed about this strategy or the idea of combating communism at any cost. Many American Christians struggled with the same dilemma, though couching their positions in the context of their religious tradition, beliefs, and ideologies.[5]

Conservative Christians and the Evils of Monolithic Communism

As we have seen, the traditional Cold War view of communism insisted that the Soviets and Chinese led this international movement and that it endangered all freedoms. Many Americans, including conservative Christians, who maintained a fear of monolithic communism fought to keep the United States hostile to all things Communist. While the mere worry about monolithic communism on the part of conservative Christians adds little new information to our understanding of conservative opinion on this issue, it lays important groundwork for enabling us to see how this dread of a worldwide Communist force was intensified by conservative religious principles. In other words, this secular/political view of the world provided a foundation upon which conservative Christians could link their religious convictions to events in the secular, international arena. Indeed, conservative Christians' depiction of a monolithic Communist Other that threatened the United

States was not couched simply in secular terms but added strong religious language to the conversation as well. As we seek to discern the motivations of the American Right and learn more and more about its resurgence beginning in the 1960s, we would do well to remember that religious institutions framed much of this dialogue in religious terminology. In turn, this religious language undergirded a national trust in America's traditional Cold War foreign policy. Conservative Christians characterized communism not only as evil but even as an agent of Satan. This kind of language became part of the American dialogue about communism: secular politicians, columnists, and everyday Americans routinely employed it without feeling any need to prove its validity because the churches had done so for them. Amidst the liberalism and revolutionary activity of the 1960s, conservative Christians offered a counterpoint that intensified people's fears about fighting communism as not only a political battle but a religious crusade against the devil.

Christianity Today, for example, embodied a conservative agenda regarding foreign policy during the 1960s with a 1950s posture against communism that continued to view it as a monolithic threat to the globe that targeted Christianity in particular. Though the periodical claimed to serve the evangelical conservative movement and not focus on political concerns, it commented on politics and global affairs as they pertained to the spreading of the Christian message. To its editors and writers, the Cold War was both an American diplomatic and military effort and a Christian crusade against evil. They backed the government's firm stance against all things Communist because of these beliefs.

Maintaining a fear of monolithic communism was crucial to the way *Christianity Today* ultimately added its brand of faith to the conversation. In 1964, excerpts from a pamphlet written by John C. Bennett, president of left-leaning Union Theological Seminary, prompted *Christianity Today* to criticize him and to explain why they believed their fear of a monolithic foe was justified in the midst of the new realities presented during the 1960s. A few satellite nations in Europe, Asia, and Latin America had begun to resist Soviet and Chinese leadership despite their continued communism. Bennett explained that "the changes under Communism make the old 'red or dead' contrast quite meaningless today. Polish 'red' is different from Chinese 'red.'" Without a giant monolith to threaten the United States, Bennett and others felt that the U.S. could cooperate with some Communist countries who did not like the USSR or PRC, either, thereby reducing global tension. Bennett had argued such a position since the 1950s, demonstrating that even then a rift brewed within Christianity regarding Cold War policies. *Christian-*

ity Today chided that Bennett's assertion "may not be so true as he thinks." Poland had recently convicted a Polish-American author, Melchior Wankiwucz, of "slandering the People's Republic of Poland," which *Christianity Today*'s editors saw as evidence that "there is no true freedom under Communism wherever it prevails." Wankiwucz had been arrested because the elderly novelist, correspondent, and journalist had a large following and had spoken out against the Communist government. Wankiwucz had fled Poland during the Nazi invasion and settled in the United States, but returned to his homeland in the 1950s because he missed it. The Communist regime initially lionized him for returning, but he grew increasingly vocal about condemning the oppression of intellectuals and free speech, which led to his 1964 arrest, a sure sign according to *Christianity Today* that nothing had changed within the Communist bloc. Referring to the fact that Bennett lived in New York, the editors concluded that "red may not be red in some sectors of New York, but evidence persists that it remains red in Poland no less than in Russia." Where Bennett saw tension between Poland and the Communist superpower as evidence against a Communist monolith, Wankiwucz's plight told *Christianity Today* that, regardless of inter-Communist squabbling, Communist nations were united in oppressing dissent within their countries. They added to the culture war over foreign policy an insistence that all Communists everywhere endangered human freedom.[6]

Christianity Today's reporting of the *Pueblo* affair in 1968 continued to propagate this fear of monolithic communism. On 23 January 1968, North Korea seized the *U.S.S. Pueblo*, an intelligence ship that they claimed ventured into their territory but that the United States insisted had never left international waters. One American died attempting to defend the ship, the crew was held by North Korea for nearly a year before being released, and North Korea possesses the ship to this day. A *Christianity Today* editorial reflected the periodical's traditionalist Cold War point of view, which suspected all Communists of being in league, and asserted that, rather than an action by North Korea, this event personified a global Communist action merely played out by the North Koreans. A 1968 book review in *Christianity Today* well summarizes its opinion about the threat of communism: "True, the Communist thrust in the world is broken into nationalistic expressions and is less politically monolithic than it used to be. Yet whether monolithic or fragmented, the communism emanating from both China and Russia clearly represents imperialistic perils as dangerous to a democratic society, as any that have appeared in recent history." This writer's statement, reactions to the *Pueblo* affair, and the Bennett rebuttal exemplify how *Christianity Today* framed its views throughout the 1960s about communism as a dangerous monolith.[7]

The 1968 Soviet invasion of Czechoslovakia added fuel to this anti-Communist fire. Editorials throughout the year leading up to the invasion hardly indicate a blind reactionary impulse from the evangelical periodical. At first, writers applauded the Czech reforms and hoped for at least an easing of anti-Christian persecution. In August, when it still appeared that a new, freer Czechoslovakia might emerge, an editorial rejoiced at the fact that these reforms had come "not through revolution, in the usual sense, but through evolution. This might give pause to those who think that only the exercise of military force will reverse the tide of Communism." This hope for a peaceful end to Communist oppression evaporated when Soviet tanks invaded Prague. To an American religious community already leery of Soviet aims, this confirmed that "the Soviets cannot understand or tolerate any brand of socialism other than their own. To them, moderate socialism is a dangerous dilution." Though *Christianity Today* was staunchly anti-Communist and persistently condemnatory of the Soviet Union, Communist actions in Czechoslovakia—not a blind reactionary impulse—solidified this perception even when the periodical had softened its stance. Editors called the USSR a "big bully" that picked on smaller nations and had to be stopped, thus prompting their backing of a vigorously anti-Communist U.S. foreign policy. But they asserted that that policy standpoint alone would not solve the problem: it was not the United States that had to fight Communist Russia but "let Christians and all free men raise their voices in protest before and not merely after another act of aggression takes place." This stance demonstrates how the periodical attempted to sway its readership toward a conservative foreign policy, as well as how it reflected the perception that conservative Americans had of the Soviet Union. These secular/political concerns also laid a foundation for fearing communism that only became exacerbated when the periodical added its religious beliefs and concerns to the conversation.[8]

Christianity Today regularly made condemnatory remarks regarding the threat that communism posed to religion, and in particular Christianity. In almost every discussion during the 1960s that pertained to foreign policy, the editors and writers reminded readers that the Cold War was a religious battle against evil and not simply a political confrontation between the superpowers. None better demonstrated this Cold War religious mentality than *Christianity Today*'s editor, L. Nelson Bell. In an editorial in which he warned readers of the fact that "Satan is *real*," Bell stated that evidence of Satan's presence included the existence of Communist nations that promoted atheism.

Indeed, this link between communism and the devil built upon the dualistic theology regularly discussed within the periodical's pages, where God and Satan dueled for control of humanity. Academic experts, using logic and research, added weight to this religious need for combating communism. This combination of professional expertise with a sacred topic solidified the message being sent to readers. In 1964, Bela Udvarnoki, professor emeritus of social science at Chowan College in North Carolina, warned readers about the danger Christians faced inside Communist countries because "there are secret informers in every religious organization" who report illegal activities to state officials in a "diabolical" effort to isolate church leaders from their followers and each other so as to eliminate the church's role in society. Such religious reasons for combating communism played into conservative America's backing of traditional Cold War diplomacy well into the 1960s.[9]

Other authorities added their voices to this depiction of a religious war. *Christianity Today* often used charged religious language when referring to communism, Marxism, or any countries, organizations, or individuals it deemed to be in league with this ideology. J. Edgar Hoover wrote articles for *Christianity Today* that illustrate this portrayal of a religious war against a demonic foe. Hoover, the Federal Bureau of Investigation chief since 1924, gave the periodical a respected government official to offer expert testimony to its readership. Hoover had staked much of his career on a crusade against alleged Communist infiltrations in the United States, dating back to World War I. As he established the FBI as a major force in American life, he consistently pushed it to attack not only alleged Communists but also liberal groups that disagreed with his own politics. By the dawn of the Cold War and the eventual onslaught of McCarthyism, the FBI and Hoover had investigated, slandered, and often arrested numerous people and groups for Communist activities, frequently without merit. Nevertheless, many Americans within and without the government heralded him as a protector of the United States and valued his opinion. Fitting this pattern of zealous anticommunism into a religious framework came easily for the FBI director. In a September 1964 article, Hoover asserted that "no man can deny the demonic power of Communism." To confront such a nemesis, Hoover told readers that Americans needed to place "our hope in the only faith that can move men to the most noble purposes in life, the faith of our fathers." In short, Hoover told readers that only God could combat communism.[10]

Conservative Catholics often articulated the same message within this cultural war, as reflected in the Jesuit-run periodical *America*. The Roman Catholic Church had a historic opposition to Marxism that had engendered

a hard-line stance against Communist countries since the 1920s. It therefore allied with the Christian West but tempered this antagonism in order to
protect churches and adherents that remained inside Communist borders.
The Second Vatican Council from 1962 to 1965 muddied the waters in terms
of the church's Cold War mentality. Its prior alliance with the United States
against communism came into tension with a new policy of becoming a
neutral force that sought peace while still denouncing communism. American Catholics therefore received mixed signals from the papacy regarding
the Cold War, which helped to promulgate disparate opinions, which were
expressed in various Catholic periodicals. Some of the journals deliberately
reflected on diplomatic issues from a theological standpoint, while others
simply commented on foreign policy concerns. *America* during the 1960s
did not change its stance from a hard-line Cold Warriorism, thus buttressing
support for those who wanted the Johnson administration to maintain its
conservative approach.[11]

America saw nothing positive in world communism, reported on its
nations with disdain, and persisted into the 1960s with a 1950s-style American Catholic hostility to all things Communist. *America* did take note of the
split between Moscow and Peking described above by asserting that while
this split signaled "that the Cold War is changing its character," Communist
ideology still mandated that "the Soviet Union remain fundamentally hostile
to the West. We must expect the Soviet regime to foster and support revolutionary movements wherever they serve its purposes. This will be the case
especially in Asia, Africa, and Latin America." In other words, the editors
and writers of *America* believed that Communist expansionism would continue. A later editorial explained that the Sino-Soviet feud, rather than easing global tension, forced both countries into bellicose rhetoric in an effort
to appear in control of world communism. Red China's development of a
nuclear arsenal not only increased Cold War hostilities but had also "succeeded in pressuring Moscow into its 'hard-line' statement" of support for
revolutions around the world. *America* saw no reason to change its perception of communism on the basis of its understanding of the Sino-Soviet rift.
As with *Christianity Today*, a secular understanding of the Cold War became
an important underpinning onto which conservative Catholics layered religious sentiments to form their argument.[12]

The *Pueblo* affair with North Korea seemed to validate *America*'s concern.
Editors asserted that North Korea had committed "piracy" as part of the
monolithic global conspiracy; rather than viewing the event as an isolated
act by North Korea, *America* theorized that Kim Il Sung seized the U.S. ves-

sel as a way to put pressure on the United States and thereby assist North Korea's "ally" in North Vietnam. An editorial explained that the affair had everything to do with the Vietnam conflict, but never even discussed the North Korean–American animosity that had existed since the end of World War II. Associate editor Benjamin Masse stated that "there is plenty of additional evidence . . . to suggest that nothing much in the Communist drive for world power has been abandoned—or been radically changed."[13]

The Soviet invasion of Czechoslovakia solidified this hard-line posture. The journal merely added this incident to its list of reasons to distrust all Communist states. In fact, editors prophetically predicted in May 1968, three months before the Soviet invasion, that "the Kremlin might send the Red Army clattering across the border" to halt Czech liberalization. When Soviet troops invaded, *America* stated that "a shocked world was suddenly brought back to realities from which, in recent years, it had sought to escape. As Russian, Polish, East German, and Hungarian troops poured over the Czech frontiers, it learned that the Stalinist mentality that had crushed a similar revolt in Hungary in 1956 was not dead." For Catholics who had adhered to the Vatican's hostility toward communism and had supported U.S. Cold War policy since the 1950s, the invasion of Czechoslovakia indicated that any discussion of an altered world communism was based on illusion. It certainly solidified *America*'s Cold War hostility and the value it placed on the United States persisting with a traditional Cold War policy toward communism, thus contributing a Catholic voice to American conservatism as it organized to reassert itself during the 1960s.[14]

The Southern Baptist Convention (SBC) joined these conservative periodicals to add another religious voice to the concern that a Communist monolith still threatened the United States. The Southern Baptist Convention proclaimed a conservative point of view that both reflected the typical anti-Communist rhetoric of American society and also emerged from actual Baptist experiences within Communist nations. Often articulating a generic fear of communism as evil and atheist, Southern Baptist Convention leaders and members buttressed this anxiety with proof of Communist oppression obtained from missionaries and fellow believers inside Communist countries. A moderate minority did question the blanket anticommunism of most SBC adherents, but overall this denomination embraced a solid fear of communism and therefore belonged to the host of Americans wanting their nation to stand strong against communism even in the face of liberal criticism.

Private correspondence among Baptist officials often paralleled the anti-communism of *Christianity Today* and *America*. Roy W. Gustafson from the

Billy Graham Evangelistic Association Team Office wrote Fred B. Rhodes Jr., an active leader within the SBC and high-ranking Republican operative, after a trip to various African countries about his backing of containment theory. He revealed a strong bias against the Democratic Party by stating that "had the Hump [Hubert H. Humphrey, 1968 Democratic presidential candidate] made it, we felt that the judging Hand of God was upon us as a nation." He trusted that Richard Nixon would reverse Johnson administration initiatives, including foreign policy attempts to cooperate with Communist nations, because he worried that "if we lose these countries [Rhodesia and South Africa], as the present State Department policy is endeavoring to do, they will tumble into the Communist bloc."[15]

SBC colleagues echoed this fear that Communists posed an immediate danger to the United States. This kind of commentary usually appeared in the context of a Baptist theology that warned of God's judgment if society failed to heed an evangelical message. Southern Baptists maintained that God might punish the United States by allowing communism to infiltrate and influence American life, if not take over the country. Some of this rhetoric was manifest in generic discussions about the types of political leaders SBC members should support. Jack U. Harwell, editor of the Georgia Baptist Convention's *Christian Index*, explained that "deep, pervasive Christian commitment is essential to the man who leads the world's largest free nation" because this person faced dangers such as communism and global struggles for freedom. Without this Christian commitment, the president might flounder or fail to see the proper way to conduct foreign affairs. A writer for the *Alabama Baptist* more directly asserted that failure to keep the Ten Commandments would lead God to punish the United States because "the godless hordes of communism stand ready to enslave us if we let our national moral fiber weaken." As we have seen, Billy Graham echoed this concern during the 1964 crusade in Omaha, Nebraska. Bemoaning a trend he saw toward "moral decadence," Graham cautioned that this downward slide would lead to generational rebellion and the loss of government control over society, finally ending when "the Communists will move into the vacuum." This spirit of anticommunism also manifested itself when a contingent of college-aged students picketed the SBC 1968 convention in Houston, Texas, to ask messengers to condemn racism, the Vietnam War, and poverty. As Baptist Press reported, "messengers challenged them as being 'Communist inspired' while others questioned the genuineness of their faith." The available sources make it impossible to determine if this theology of fear of God's retribution led to anticommunism, or if a fear of communism induced or played into this theology. Regardless, most Southern Baptists connected the two intimately when looking at domestic issues and seeking to shape American perceptions of the Cold War.[16]

The perceived Communist threat even affected the way many in the SBC viewed the civil rights movement. Many critics accused civil rights leaders of communism or claimed that the movement would lead to a Communist revolution in order to discredit it without using overtly racist language. Yet historians have demonstrated that the civil rights movement and communism created only an uneasy alliance. Especially during the 1920s and the 1930s, the Communist Party U.S.A. promoted racial equality and gained support from African Americans, who knew all too well the United States' deplorable history of racial discrimination and proved susceptible to Communist assertions that democracy failed to protect black rights. Recent scholarship illustrates that this cooperation was tenuous because African Americans forged a unique political activism that used some ideals from the Communist Party without actually promoting communism. Furthermore, the civil rights movement never took direction from Moscow or relied upon Communist initiatives to propel its activism. No proof exists for claims that Communists inspired the civil rights movement in order to foment a revolution in the United States. Studies of anticommunism, however, indicate that American conservatives, from average citizens to J. Edgar Hoover and other leaders, persistently linked communism to the civil rights movement to discredit it and protect white supremacy, even though communism remained on the periphery and never controlled the fight for black equality.[17]

Regardless of historical reality, some within the Southern Baptist Convention believed that there was a connection between the civil rights movement and communism. Editors of convention papers often made public comments about this alleged link. In the midst of the violent year of 1968, with assassinations, student protests, and urban rioting, the editor of the *Baptist and Reflector* cautioned that Communists took advantage of the situation. Telling the people of the Tennessee Baptist Convention that "Communists are profiting from the violence," Richard N. Owen maintained that "whether or not civil riots are directly inspired by Communists, they are exploited by them." Later in this editorial, he claimed that "communism expects to make advances in the Negro freedom movement." Owen's colleague at the *Alabama Baptist* had the same message for his readers: "We have pointed out the evidence of Communism in these disturbances and the FBI has made a report that Communism is in the racial troubles." Ample historical documentation has revealed that the FBI did indeed attempt on numerous occasions to associate the civil rights movement with communism and throughout the 1950s and 1960s maintained illegal surveillance on its leaders and participants. Although even the FBI has admitted that no connection existed, this reality only came out years later and did nothing to stop conservatives in the 1960s, such as those within the Southern Baptist Convention, from believing in the Communist ties and using this connection to justify their opposition to racial-equality movements. The SBC's documents provide evidence that some religious institutions agreed with the FBI's fear of communism within the civil rights movement. Even before Richard Nixon became president, the politics of race was leading white southerners toward a new brand of conservatism, including some within American Christianity. Importantly, though race dominated the reason for this change, foreign policy/communism also drove this movement. The monolith had crept into the United States, and these conservative Christians wanted a vigilant anti-Communist government to stop it.[18]

The Southern Baptist Convention often added more overtly theological language to the conversation. Though a theological feud between moderates and conservatives was already brewing in the 1960s within Southern Baptist ranks, none of this tension manifested itself on this issue, where a hard-line conservatism held sway. *Baptist Message* from the Louisiana Baptist Convention explained this reality in describing how communism claimed to want to help people, just like Christianity, but then "wants to keep those whom it helps. And it really does. It enslaves them. And it kills them too. So here we see keepers of men who become killers of men—like Cain." The editor of *Baptist and Reflector*, the newspaper of the Tennessee Baptist Convention, explained that Christianity historically had remained too silent when confronted with dangerous political realities. Richard N. Owen compared the silence of church leaders about communism to the fact that "the pulpit was told to be silent in Nazi Germany. Hitlerism had its day." In short, Christians acquiesced to evil political forces such as communism by failing to speak against them.[19]

Baptist convention newspapers followed such blanket concerns about communism with comments about the unique danger that this ideology posed because of its subversive nature. Discussion of subversion was often couched in theological language about fighting evil. Erwin L. McDonald, editor of the *Arkansas Baptist*, explained how communism first pulled people into its realm by providing basic needs, such as food, and making promises about future freedoms. But after captivating people with this goodwill, communism turned on them by implementing its oppressive governments and stripping them of their religious liberty. Only a Cold Warrior's mentality could stop this spread of an evil force, a stance that supported the Johnson administration's traditional foreign policy approach.[20]

The Southern Baptist Convention paid close attention to the Soviet invasion of Czechoslovakia as one such example. The SBC news media first viewed the evolution of events with applause, then with despair, and finally with cautious hope. The liberalization of the country at first brought praise from the Baptist Press, the SBC news imprint that sent stories to convention papers and the national media, especially after a Czech delegate to the Seventh Baptist Youth World Conference announced that "he and his fellow countrymen have a new freedom for Christian witnessing." *Christian Index* editor Jack U. Harwell brought Cold War hostility back into the conversation after the Soviet invasion, asking if people "with sense enough to read a daily newspaper or watch a television news program have any doubt in their mind now about the true nature of communism." In response to Czechoslovakia seeking freedom but not wanting to leave the Soviet sphere, they "got in reply—tanks and guns." Yet the spirit of Christian belief persisted within the Southern Baptist community despite displeasure with this sign that Soviet communism continued to threaten the world. Even after the Soviet crackdown, news came to the Baptist World Alliance that Baptist worship services in Czechoslovakia continued. Stanislav Svec, the secretary of the Baptist Union in Czechoslovakia and pastor of First Baptist Church in Prague, later confirmed that "the 26 Baptist churches and 100 mission stations" continued to worship without government intervention or restraints. This reaction reveals a thoughtful Baptist response. Despite a tendency at other times toward knee-jerk Cold War anticommunism, the SBC condemned the Soviet actions but never gave up on Christian evangelism within Communist countries.[21]

The African Methodist Episcopal Church in many respects fell in line with conservative support for the Cold War but presented a unique voice due to its heritage of fighting for racial equality. The AME's ties to a Methodist evangelism at times led to a conservative Christian outlook, especially in regard to the Cold War, because of communism's attempt to thwart missionary outreach and religious practices. Yet the AME had, since its founding, involved itself in combating racism. Of the periodicals and denominations we are considering, the AME alone came into creation because of a social issue, not a theological debate. This social justice advocacy continued to affect the denomination into the 1960s. At times a conservative, Cold War stalwart, the AME also linked this global struggle to the African American plight in the United States in ways that transformed its right-leaning foreign policy outlook into a left-of-center domestic argument about race. And this entire approach played into supporting Lyndon B. Johnson's presidency.

From its very founding due to segregation in the Methodist Church, the AME had mixed religion and social issues. While this activism traditionally focused on race relations in America, it also established a pattern of the church voicing its opinion on a myriad of issues without concern for placing that opinion in a specifically theological context. African Americans often discussed the Cold War in relation to race relations within the United States, and the AME voiced an opinion along similar lines. Black leaders throughout the twentieth century articulated two general principles regarding race and foreign policy. First, they linked racial discrimination in the United States to global racial problems, thus unifying with those facing discrimination around the world. Second, they argued within the United States that fixing the racial problem at home was necessary for rehabilitating the United States' international reputation. In this they bought into the U.S. Cold War effort to thwart Communist movements worldwide by insisting that American democracy allowed for a successful fight against discrimination. Civil rights would help protect America from Communist expansionism. Bishop H. T. Primm presented a motion to the Thirty-seventh Session of the AME General Conference in May 1964 to display both the flag of the church and the U.S. flag on the conference platform because "the A.M.E. Church loved and respected our Christian faith and our nation." The conference passed this motion. It resolved, too, to applaud and assist the Peace Corps as a way "to gain friends for America in the present cold war with the Soviet Union." The resolution especially noted the importance of the medical assistance this program offered people around the world and stated that such assistance would support the United States' efforts to thwart future Communist uprisings. In this regard, the AME sought to shape a conservative foreign policy for its membership by stoking a persistent fear of expanding communism and calling for members to therefore support U.S. foreign policy against it.[22]

Indeed, this fear prompted the AME to use militant language to describe a Christian's responsibility toward the Cold War. *Christian Recorder* reported on a 1964 conference entitled "Christianity Confronts Communism" that implored Christians of all denominations to stand against the forces of communism. Not only did it request such action; it declared it mandatory for committed individuals to support those oppressed the world over. Another article described communism as a "'missionary movement' dedicated to winning the world to atheism and tyranny and materialism." However, it continued that "a massed force of Christians everywhere is the one thing that Communism fears. That is why it seeks to throttle the Church first, everywhere it goes." With the image of combat against Christians generated by this perception, the editorial therefore asked those in the AME to give their total effort toward defending the global Christian community. A pastor at St. Stephen AME Church in Jacksonville, Florida, provided one of the most forthright statements in this regard, asserting the AME's Cold War position in the context of this Christian militarism: "The present-day struggle for world supremacy and to build a fifth World Empire is between the free and slave worlds (Democracy and Communism). Communism cannot win because it has left God out of the equation. Communism does not recognize the sovereignty of God, therefore it cannot win." AME religious belief of this sort helped to solidify traditional Cold War mentalities within this denomination well into the 1960s.[23]

The 1968 Soviet invasion of Czechoslovakia strengthened the AME's anti-Communist resolve. Members reacted with horror when Soviet tanks invaded Czechoslovakia to crack down on its liberalization. A report about the reaction of the Eighty-eighth Session of the West Kentucky Annual Conference of the Thirteenth District summarized much of the AME response. Not only did delegates deplore this use of force upon another country; they related the events to the Vietnam War. Thinking that the Soviet Union wanted to control North Vietnam in the same way, a committee report explained the difficulty in believing anything that the Soviet Union promised about freedom given its behavior in Czechoslovakia. Reverend Dr. Sam M. Davis also criticized this Soviet action in the *Christian Recorder*, the official newspaper of the AME:

To the Communist freedom means deliverance from what he considers to be the exploitation of Capitalists [sic] society. To him it signifies the power to re-make the whole world, even though he may have to suppress Freedom of Speech, and freedom of the press to accomplish his aims, turn elections into a farce and deny the right of a people to choose their own rules, or send dissenters off to prison, Exile, and Death.[24]

Despite this similarity to the way other conservative Christian institutions and denominations regarded the Cold War, the AME also contributed a unique point of view because of its particular history relating to race and social justice. Founded as a social protest against segregated congregations, the denomination had always balanced a relatively conservative theology with an activist social agenda regarding race relations. Given that the Cold War and the civil rights movement happened at the same time, this balance was particularly well illustrated in the denomination's positions on these issues. Throughout the 1960s, the AME General Conferences sent repeated resolutions and calls to the White House to support Lyndon B. Johnson's civil rights agenda and to try to push the president and Democratic Party to do even more. Their simultaneous Cold War advocacy in part therefore parallels that of other civil rights leaders who backed the president's foreign policy agenda because they trusted his judgment and did not want to lose his civil rights support. For example, civil rights leaders Stanley Levison, Whitney Young of the Urban League, Bayard Rustin, and officials at the Southern Christian Leadership Conference all tried to dissuade Martin Luther King Jr. from marching against the Vietnam War for fear that this action would alienate President Johnson.[25] Also noteworthy, civil rights advocates increasingly tried to disassociate from violence and separatist rhetoric throughout the 1960s, as more militant black youth questioned nonviolence and paved the way for the black power movement. AME resolutions attempted to distance the civil rights movement from "the violence and tragic events which have occasionally resulted from these demonstrations," such as the Los Angeles Watts rioting, because it in part led to charges of Communist backing of the civil rights agenda. AME delegates decried the fact that the rioting "has led many to believe that extreme radicals were in control of all efforts for civil rights in these days and that Communists and/or Black Nationalists were actually in leadership." In many respects, this attitude answered the criticism seen above in the Southern Baptist Convention. The AME wanted its anti-Communist record to debunk such myths and further propel the nation toward civil rights. Interestingly, the SBC and AME stances, though emerging from disparate views about civil rights, both led to the maintenance of a conservative Cold War mentality that feared a Communist monolith, a link few historians have made because too few studies of religion and foreign policy exist.[26]

Cold War rhetoric often sought to frighten Americans into backing U.S. foreign policy. Whether it was the president, other politicians, or organizations such as the John Birch Society, conservatives warned against communism. Well into the 1960s, religious entities contributed to this discussion by intensifying this culture war with charged religious language. Conservative Christians argued that communism not only represented a dangerous political ideology but an evil, devil-inspired one at that. All the way into the 1980 presidential election, Ronald W. Reagan referred to the Soviet Union as the "Evil Empire." This should hardly surprise us, as politicians had employed such religious language to describe communism throughout the Cold War.

When Reagan and others mobilized conservative Christians in this way, they relied upon a foundation of conservative Christian anticommunism that had a long history, dating back to the 1950s. Studying conservative religious reactions to foreign policy contributes to what we are uncovering about the rightist resurgence in America during the 1960s.

Communism, U.S. Missionaries, and Conservative Christian Voices

Not all Christian depictions of communism as evil were based on mere rhetoric or general news stories. First-hand accounts from U.S. missionaries from within Communist countries provided proof that Communists oppressed religious believers. These accounts lay at the heart of conservative Christian anticommunism well into the 1960s. Such reports went beyond theory or secular politics to hit directly at the core conservative fear that communism wanted to purge the world of religion.

Christianity Today's reporting on the Congo in 1964 demonstrated all of the categories of analysis regarding conservatives and the Cold War we have been discussing: fear of a monolithic force, the charge of Communists as evil, and a worry about the well-being of missionaries in Africa. Congo fell into disarray shortly after Belgium granted independence to this former colony in 1960. The first elected prime minister, Patrice Lumumba, lost favor with Western powers, and his grip on the nation dissolved quickly as it degenerated into civil war. Various players thereafter included the United Nations, primarily acting with U.S. financial support and leadership, rebel movements, and ultimately Soviet and Chinese assistance for Lumumba, which during the Cold War automatically pitted him against the United States and Western interests. Civil war persisted after Lumumba's assassination in 1961 and threatened to allow a Communist victory in Africa. This failed to occur because the dictator Sese Seko Mobutu took control of the nation in November 1965 with U.S. backing, particularly from the CIA. But *Christianity Today* hardly knew this outcome in 1964 when it reported on events taking place in Congo.[27]

Again a mixture of faith and foreign policy informed *Christianity Today's* point of view. After rebel forces in the Congo killed two Protestant missionaries, editors worried about remaining missionaries and their children trapped in rebel-controlled territory. These ostensibly innocent bystanders had gotten caught in the midst of a civil war while spreading the word of God. *Christianity Today* connected this African rebel movement, American missionaries, and their anticommunism by asserting that "the rebel movement is reportedly assisted by Chinese Communist embassies in nearby countries." By the end of 1964, with more missionaries dead and the Congo in an uproar, editors claimed that "Mao's Chinese Reds poured in money, men, and material to gain a foothold in Africa and to foment trouble. They succeeded so well that the Congo became a Communist wilderness of hatred, strife, rapine, and murder." The lines between church and state were quite blurred for this evangelical magazine. It demanded that the U.S.-led Cold War coalition protect Christian missionary efforts throughout an often volatile world from Communist dangers. In the case of the Congo, *Christianity Today* lamented that America had lost because the Chinese had outmaneuvered it. Another domino had fallen to Satan, as proven by the martyrdom of missionaries in this region.[28]

Catholic periodicals added their voice to this concern for Christians inside Communist-controlled areas. Instead of evangelical-style missions, though, Catholics relied on the church's long-time presence in many Communist nations for the same type of news. The Catholic Church's significant presence in Latin America amidst growing Communist insurgencies differentiated the way *U.S. Catholic* reported on religion within Communist countries, but the periodical still expressed concern for the safety of fellow Christians. Tracing back to the Spanish conquest of the region, the Catholic Church had a storied and multifaceted history there. By the twentieth century, much of the Catholic Church in Latin America had splintered along the lines of the political and economic factions of the region. Despite the Catholic Church's official opposition to communism, some Latin American Catholics sided with Communist sympathizers against the moneyed gentry and/or oppressive dictators. Historian Edward T. Brett has demonstrated how the U.S. Catholic press evolved regarding Latin America from a staunch anticommunism in the 1950s to social justice advocacy in the 1970s.[29]

The Catholic press we are examining here reveals that the 1960s were indeed a transitional period, as Brett described. Georgie Anne Geyer wrote about the Catholic Church in Latin America for *U.S. Catholic* and highlighted the tension between communism and the church in this volatile region. She insisted that Latin American church representatives and Marxists were "cooperating in the very forming of a new society" because both understood the historic oppression of people in Latin America who needed liberation. She applauded the fact that the local church took a pragmatic position that neither supported communism nor alienated the people attracted to it because it offered empowerment to people kept down by repressive regimes and corporate interests. By the late 1960s, moderate Catholic journals *U.S. Catholic* and *Jubilee* thus portrayed a clouded reality when they discussed Christians inside Communist areas. On the one hand, they recognized communism's atheistic and totalitarian nature; on the other hand, they accepted its continued presence and hoped that the church could survive within Communist borders and even cooperate with Marxists if it assisted the underprivileged.[30]

Yet other Catholic periodicals agreed more with *Christianity Today's* staunch position, as evidenced in *America*. This conservative Jesuit periodical warned about the negative treatment of Christians in Communist lands. Where the moderate Catholic journals had seen Marxist-Christian cooperation in Latin America as a sign of hope, *America* viewed it as evil. The Communist opposition to the Catholic Church as manifested in Cuba served the periodical as evidence. Imitating Soviet and Chinese hostility toward religious institutions, Fidel Castro and his government suppressed religious belief after his takeover and persecuted Christians in Cuba, especially the Catholic Church. This included the imprisonment in 1965 of the Catholic bishop in Havana. *America* framed its opinion about Cuba on the basis of this context: it began a report on the Catholic Church in Cuba by stating that "the state's hostility toward all religions, but especially toward the Catholic Faith, has not abated despite the government's proclaimed neutrality." While it applauded church officials there for "striving imaginatively to adapt their apostolate to these conditions," it concluded that "all in all, the Church in Cuba lives under persecution." For *America*, this threat to Christians provided a sound basis for its opposition to communism.[31]

America had the company of *Catholic Digest* in taking this conservative Catholic stance toward communism. While not positioned as a news magazine, *Catholic Digest* did offer various opinions about foreign policy. *Catholic Digest* lamented the plight of Polish Catholics under the regime of Wladyslaw Gomulka because "their stubbornly held faith makes them a bone in the throat" of the Communist leader. Though the article outlined how Poland harassed seminarians and followed the lead of the USSR in outlawing religious education for young people, the writer did applaud the continuing faith of the people and saw it as a sign of God's action on behalf of those oppressed in that country. *Catholic Digest* took numerous such stances, allying with conservative Catholics, including *America*, in its staunch Cold War anticommunism and seeming disregard for the Vatican's softening of its stance after Vatican II. The periodical sought to shape Catholic opinion toward this conservative foreign policy and utilized the plight of Christians inside Communist nations to that end.[32]

The Southern Baptist Convention was also alarmed by reports from its missionaries about Communist atheism and its known attack on religion. Reports in *Commission*, published by the Southern Baptist Foreign Mission Board, emphasized the danger Christian missions faced in Communist nations. In 1968, claims by Albania that it had become the first completely atheist state in the world startled Baptists: Communist leaders there heralded "the closing of 2,169 churches, mosques, monasteries, and other religious institutions during the past six months." *Commission*'s reporting about this reality served to demonstrate to the SBC why it had to fight communism and support the United States: not only did Communists repress their citizens; they attempted to strip the world of God's word. *Commission* later reported something equally concerning when the Russian newspaper *Pravda* hailed a Russian ship, which it dubbed "an atheist missionary" vessel, that cruised up and down rivers north of Moscow, promoting state atheism and denouncing Christianity. This tactic, reported by the SBC division responsible for foreign missions, served for Baptists as concrete evidence of the godless campaign communism waged.[33]

Indeed, Baptist foreign missions often reported on the realities of atheism within Communist-controlled areas. American Baptists in general and Southern Baptists in particular had a long and vibrant history of missionary outreach around the globe that by the 1960s included a presence within many Communist nations, which led to both real reasons to fear communism and a simultaneous terror of all things Communist. Strong belief in the need for individual conversion and adult baptism led to an evangelical fervor to spread this Christian witness in order to save people the world over. Despite its emphasis on local congregational control and regional affiliations, this fervor within the SBC led to national organizations that proselytized both within the United States and around the globe. Wherever Baptist missionaries existed within Communist nations, they faced hostility, state harassment, and even arrest for their beliefs. As *Commission* explained in June 1968, "within the last four decades, this adversary has gained control of roughly one-third of the world's population and one-fourth of its land surface." Baptists explained that within Communist borders the state outlawed religion and closed churches, thus directly threatening the salvation of its citizens. These true circumstances forced Baptists to see the Cold War fight in religious as well as political terms. Once again the periodical for the SBC Foreign Mission Board articulated this stance when it mandated that "the philosophy of atheistic materialism constitutes a life-and-death challenge for Christianity. We must not let ourselves be deceived by this point."[34]

Specific experiences by Southern Baptist missionaries in Asia often underscored this Communist danger but also kept the evangelical spirit alive with stories of successful conversions accomplished despite the Communist threat. The corrupt and repressive presidential regime of Achmed Sukarno in Indonesia suffered not only from its oppressive tactics but also Sukarno's advanced kidney failure by 1965, which paved the way for an attempted Communist coup facilitated in part by Communist spies in Sukarno's government. Led by Dipa Nusantara Aidit, the large Indonesian Communist party collapsed in disgrace after it attempted to orchestrate this coup but failed, leading the government to arrest and execute many party members. This failed coup alarmed Southern Baptists the most when the missionaries discovered a death list drawn up by the Communists that cataloged all religious leaders, including Southern Baptist missionaries, and had them "marked for extermination." One SBC mission concluded that "it was only God's intervention that saved this country." The article then rejoiced at the number of conversions experienced since that moment but emphasized, too, that "a hard core of the Communist Party is still intact underground and . . . its original goal of conquest by 1970 still stands." This mixture of fear and hope characterized most Southern Baptist missionaries and their view of communism. Indeed, the first-hand knowledge that missionaries reported represents one of the more forceful ways in which Southern Baptists articulated their opinions regarding the Cold War.[35]

U.S. missionaries abroad gave American Christians first-hand accounts about what happened to faith inside Communist borders. This news intensified conservative anticommunism because of the risk to Christianity posed by Communist states. While it is impossible to determine the exact effect these conservative attitudes had on public opinion, the thousands of people who read these periodicals or belonged to these denominations could not avoid this mantra about the need to protect fellow Christians. Historians have shown that the U.S. government's conversation about fighting the Cold War regularly utilized the language of defending innocent people around the world and advancing the cause of democratic governments. When historians seek to understand the entirety of American public opinion and why people agreed with their leaders in this regard, understanding Christian America plays a vital role. The danger faced by missionaries and believers in Communist nations inspired conservative Christians to champion the foreign policy goals of their anti-Communist government.

Monolithic Myths and Liberal and Moderate Voices

Yet the American Christian landscape hardly presented a unified front entrenched in traditional Cold Warriorism. McCarthyism and the Vietnam War brought many Americans, including leaders in Congress and the State Department, to question containment theory and hard-line diplomacy.

Such rethinking of foreign affairs occurred within Christian forums as well, in addition to the fact that a large and vocal contingent of Protestant leaders had been questioning it since the late 1940s. Liberal Christians, as with conservative Christians, did not always place their foreign policy convictions in a specifically religious context, especially when considering the notion of Communist expansionism. Still, another critical voice in public opinion came from religious elements that denounced the fear of a Communist monolith as outdated and dangerous. While a number of studies, such as Charles DeBenedetti's and Charles Chatfield's *An American Ordeal* and Lawrence Wittner's *Rebels against War*, claim that most Americans began questioning traditional Cold War diplomacy because of the Vietnam War, these Christian voices reveal that such opposition was developing much sooner: they had entrenched themselves with this liberal outlook before the war intensified, many dating back to the very beginning of the Cold War. In their case, the Vietnam War merely served to sharpen their angst over the course of American diplomacy.[36]

The *Christian Century* stood as a liberal counterpart to *Christianity Today*. Already by the mid-1960s, it had shunned traditional Cold War views of monolithic communism as its editors and writers displayed a nuanced understanding of global affairs that allowed them to simultaneously condemn Communist tyranny, question U.S. foreign policy, and hope for disarmament and peaceful resolutions to world problems. The periodical took more overtly political positions in its writings than did its evangelical brethren, often with only cursory references to the way their stances related to religion. This approach stemmed from *Christian Century*'s editors and writers embracing of a humanistic theology that concentrated on people and their needs more than on ideology. In other words, while advocates of humanistic theology maintained their strong Christian faith, they felt it inappropriate simply to spread a Christian message around the world without reacting to local circumstances and situations. Rather, their Christian calling led them to focus on alleviating human need, regardless of the faith of the people being helped. Indeed, this theology lay at the heart of why the periodical had come to denounce hard-line anticommunism *prior* to the Vietnam War.

As with conservative publications, the *Christian Century* followed the 1960s Sino-Soviet rift over their shared border and leadership of world communism. Its editors saw the feud as proof that no Communist monolith existed and concluded that this fact might ultimately reduce friction in the global struggle between democracy and communism. When Soviet and Chinese military forces fired upon one another at the nations' border, these editors and writers found it impossible to persist with a Cold War dogmatism that lumped all Communists into one group. U.S. officials in both the Johnson and Nixon administrations used this tension within communism to the advantage of American foreign policy, though they mostly kept this fact from the public to protect their images as staunch anti-Communists. Yet some Americans paralleled the thinking of these officials with the belief that this schism could only assist the United States. When *Christian Century* editors and writers took this stance, it hardly signaled a sympathy for the Communists or disregard for the threat they posed. Rather, it acknowledged the multifaceted nature of global diplomacy and pondered the possibility that the United States could use this reality to foster world peace, the Christian principle that this periodical emphasized time and again when discussing both religious and secular issues.[37]

Also unlike its conservative counterparts, editors at the *Christian Century* viewed the 1968 Soviet invasion of Czechoslovakia with introspection and refusal to revert to Cold War jingoism. The periodical applauded early Czech reforms and viewed them as a sign of Communist reform. It especially saw "reason to hope for a genuine church-state rapprochement" because the country's reformed leadership allowed churches to choose their own leaders, thereby stripping Communist-backed church officials of their power. Editors resisted, however, seeing this as a U.S. triumph, and instead explained that the Czech liberalization "was not brought to pass by our power. It is an evolutionary movement coming out of communism itself. It is something democratic and good emerging from the communism we were so certain was totally evil. The impulse of the satellites to be free is beyond our political power or our alleged relative moral superiority." Even after the USSR revealed its continued oppressive aims by invading Czechoslovakia and thereafter reversing these freer trends, the *Christian Century* portrayed the situation in all its complexity. After stating that the Soviet Union was certainly guilty of perpetrating "a superbly self-defeating, stupid, treacherous" act upon Czechoslovakia, editors wrote that it had the unfortunate effect in the United States of making it a "good year for Red baiting" because "Russia has allowed us to bask in sanctimonious outrage." In other words, the Soviet invasion buttressed the fear of expansionism and permitted conservatives to question any appeasement with Communist nations that might ease global tension. Alan Geyer made this point in his first editorial after taking over as editor. He lamented Soviet treachery but applauded the Czech "spirited repudiation of Soviet intervention." He wrote that such Communist infighting debunked the myth of a Communist monolith but the Soviet invasion unfortunately allowed American Cold War traditionalists to "proclaim themselves vindicated by events." Yet the events did not change the negative view of traditional Cold Warriorism that had been held by this periodical for some time.[38]

Some Catholic periodicals agreed with this more liberal foreign policy outlook. *Catholic World* consistently aligned itself closely with the liberal *Christian Century* in foreign affairs. The periodical carried to print a position vocally supported by a Catholic pacifist contingency that had fought together with like-minded Protestants since the 1950s against nuclear armaments. Historian and Catholic priest William A. Au has revealed the Catholic peace movement's influence on anti–nuclear proliferation and antiwar advocacy after 1960, while other historians have examined the Catholic peace movement's influence on American society since the turn of the century. *Catholic World* belonged to this history of U.S. Catholic social justice advocates who campaigned against a militarist foreign policy. By 1968, *Catholic World* discredited the domino theory and declared that "there is good reason to believe that this concept of absolute evil incarnated in a monolithic Communist monster is fast becoming a myth." *Catholic World* represented a liberal Catholic voice when it aligned with left-leaning Christians to denounce nuclear arms and demand a new U.S. foreign policy void of containment theory. In this it articulated a much different viewpoint on foreign policy than its conservative counterparts, such as *America*.[39]

The complexity of Christian views on communism is illuminated even further by the challenge of a Southern Baptist Convention editor to his conservative colleagues' stances. Often suffering from criticism and isolation from fellow SBC leaders, *Arkansas Baptist* editor Erwin L. McDonald braved the anger of his constituents and peers to decry the unproven accusation that the civil rights movement supported communism and to disagree with the idea that a Communist monolith threatened the domestic United States. McDonald especially deplored that such statements continued after Martin Luther King Jr. was assassinated: "the length to which some who despised Dr. King and his cause and his methods are going to try to discredit him is deplorable. We refer particularly to those who are branding him a traitor and a Communist." This debate over communism and the civil rights movement highlights the growing tension between conservative and moderate Baptists as it brewed throughout the 1960s. McDonald attempted to push SBC members in a different direction than the majority of his counterparts. In the end, conservatives already carried a stronger voice within the SBC than did their moderate colleagues, as evidenced by a widespread belief that civil rights did indeed cater to communism. But McDonald and others like him waged a valiant fight against the notion of Communist infiltration into the United States.[40]

Liberal Christians decried traditional Cold War norms, and had done so long before the Vietnam War solidified this position. They no longer saw a Communist monolith encircling the globe (some never had), as evidenced by events around the world and at home. Though often secular in their framing, these Christian attitudes toward the Cold War added another liberal voice to the national deliberation. The fight by these Christian leaders against staunch anticommunism no doubt brought some of their followers with them, especially when couched in the Christian language of peace.

At the heart of this liberal Christian outlook on foreign policy lay the hope for a more peaceful world. Almost twenty years of an arms race that threatened global annihilation gave these Christians pause. Bellicose language and brinkmanship had not reduced Cold War tension or averted war. With the notion of a Communist monolith reduced to myth, these Christians used moral suasion during the 1960s to fight to reduce tension between the United States and its adversaries.

The arms race prompted the *Christian Century* to delve into the 1964 U.S. presidential election and back President Lyndon B. Johnson's reelection. Of the periodicals we are examining, the *Christian Century* most frequently made itself an actor on the larger national stage by speaking about political and social justice issues. It attempted to use its editorial voice to influence the nation's course regarding a myriad of issues, including civil rights, women's rights, poverty, and also foreign affairs. Editors viewed nuclear armaments as the biggest danger to the world, not the ideologies behind them. Cooperation on treaties with the Communist superpower to ease this concern therefore appealed to the *Christian Century*, which often warned of God's judgment against those who relied too much on military might. When Barry Goldwater, the conservative Republican candidate who had taken a hard line against communism throughout his presidential bid, stated that disarmament was "a dangerous exercise in complete and total futility," the periodical attacked him. Goldwater included in his platform a Cold War view that clung to containment theory and despised all things Communist. This line of thinking frequently crept into his speeches and was used by the Johnson campaign against him, especially in its allusions to the fact that Goldwater was willing to use nuclear arms more readily than Johnson. Goldwater's position stood in stark contrast to the *Christian Century*'s desire for cooperation with Communist nations with the hope of avoiding nuclear war. Favoring Johnson, *Christian Century* editors mirrored the Democratic strategy. Earlier, the periodical had stated that "if we wish civilization to survive" there was no alternative but "to keep trying" to work toward disarmament. It therefore blasted the Republican candidate because his uncompromising posture made it "unlikely that much progress can be made toward disarmament until after the election." The *Christian Century* hardly backed communism. However, neither did it display reactionary Cold War stances that uniformly supported all U.S. policy and condemned all Communist nations or diplomatic efforts out of hand. A Christian longing for peace drove editors to take this stance that opposed the nation's traditional reliance on containment theory and hostility to all things Communist.[41]

Even when it condemned Communist countries for persecuting innocent people, the *Christian Century* hoped for peace between those nations and the United States. The periodical routinely reported on the arrest of people within the USSR who dared question the government and castigated Communist officials for it. Such arrests proved to *Christian Century* editors the cruel nature of communism. For example, after the Soviets jailed a group of writers for questioning state policies in January 1968, an editorial called this action "deplorable" and censured anyone who thought the Soviet Union might liberalize. Yet after outlining such Soviet tyranny, the article pointed out that under the Stalinist regime "the dissidents would have been shunted off to prison or perhaps executed." In other words, editors noticed a slight change in Soviet behavior that gave them hope. The same posture held true for the *Christian Century*'s approach to Red China. It criticized the PRC for following a "hard, imperialist line which demands the subjugation of all opposition" and for adopting Maoism as a religion that "tolerates no heresy." However, it simultaneously prayed that the next generation of Chinese rulers would take a softer stance on global relations than Mao Zedong: "the present, aging clique of intransient, Stalinist-type rulers will not last forever." Editors then explained their opinion that history demonstrated a tradition of less hostility in second-generation leaders of governments and thus pleaded for the world to admit the PRC into the United Nations. *Christian Century* editors in the 1960s disdained the PRC and its praetorian tactics but advocated its admittance into the UN in order to pave the way for reduced tension in the future. In short, regarding the USSR and PRC, the journal displayed a Christian version of *realpolitik*.[42]

Christian Century editors and writers took the same approach to other Communist nations, including Cuba. The periodical denounced Castro and Cuban Communists for "the postponement of elections, the establishment of a Castro dictatorship, the drift of the Cuban government toward the Soviet Union and Red China, the government's seizing of church properties, the adoption of police state techniques in controlling the people," and so on. Numerous examples from Cuban refugees about the suffering of people who questioned the government infuriated the *Christian Century*. But editors pointed out that

> Cuba is a reality. No exorcism can make it disappear. It represents a new form of society which, for all its internal and external problems, could be destroyed only through a massive invasion launched by the United States. Socialist Cuba is a fact in the Caribbean as socialist China is a fact in Asia. To ignore the fact, to continue to blockade this island [in 1968], only makes it more determined to resist.

Again the threat of war caused the *Christian Century* community to hope for coexistence with a Communist regime long before U.S. involvement in Southeast Asia had escalated. Furthermore, editors here and throughout liberal Christianity felt that isolating Communist nations only pushed their citizens farther away from Christianity. They hoped that peaceful coexistence might one day allow the return of missionaries to nations such as Cuba and China.[43]

In many respects, *Commonweal's* lay leadership mirrored the *Christian Century's* stance. The moderate Catholic journal never condoned the Communist governments' acts of oppression and always maintained a hostility toward communism in line with Catholicism's Cold War mentality. The fact that the PRC tried to control the Catholic Church in China, to the point of wanting to appoint bishops, added to American Catholicism's fear in this regard. Yet the threat of global war moderated this temperament with a hope for peaceful coexistence that also allowed editors to question U.S. policy when appropriate. Thus, when a U.S./Soviet conference on disarmament was recessed without an agreement in late 1964, *Commonweal* pointed out that "Russia did offer certain modifications on this formula [disarmament proposals from 1962] two years ago. The United States has yet to match this gesture through certain changes in its own more reasonable and responsible disarmament proposal." Editors sided with the United States in applauding its more "reasonable and responsible" point of view but felt that negotiators had to work harder with Soviet representatives for a solution. The periodical aimed the same reflective attitude at the PRC, specifically concerning its admittance into the United Nations: "our refusal to recognize a stable regime that has governed the world's largest nation for fifteen years, and which now has entered the nuclear club, makes no sense at all." *Commonweal* often condemned Communist nations but wanted its readers to also see hope for a more peaceful world.[44]

Commonweal applied the same reasoned approach to the Soviet invasion of Czechoslovakia. Events there in early 1968 had "proceeded to discredit the totalitarian monolith theory of international communism. For the first time in twenty years a hundred flowers are blooming, with effects felt already in Polish, East German and Hungarian governments which are now trying to suppress or discredit similar developments within their own borders." Even the Soviet backlash later that year failed to alter editorial opinions. Rather, it led the editors to fear that conservative Cold Warriors in America would justify a continued reliance on militarism on the basis of Soviet tactics in Czechoslovakia. *Commonweal* sought an American outlook that rebuffed Catholicism's reactionary Cold War past in favor of situational analyses based on specific circumstances, people, and world events.[45]

Throughout this decade, the United Church of Christ (UCC) had also demonstrated a call for peace, demand for disarmament, and condemnation of the American Cold War mentality. This stance against militarization squares with the denomination's commitment to activism that took shape almost immediately after its creation in 1957 with a theology of human improvement that did not need the Vietnam War to inspire it into action. Adding a denominational voice to the liberal mainline ecumenical community, the UCC's left-of-center foreign policy builds upon our already rich understanding of the Christian antiwar movement.

The official publication of the United Church of Christ, *United Church Herald*, added a denominational voice to pleas for peace. This included specific references to revolutions, current wars, and the more evasive Cold War, as well as generic statements about the need for world leaders to seek peaceful solutions to all conflicts. As Louis H. Gunnemann explains in his history of the UCC, *United Church Herald* crafted within its pages much of the UCC's commitment to human improvement, a theology that naturally called for global peace. Lay people voiced this sentiment, as the example of Emily Brookes revealed in a 1964 letter to the editor. Mirroring the hostility to the Republican presidential candidate Barry Goldwater found in the *Christian Century*, Brookes explained that "his ranting about Communism in warlike terms and his attitude toward the countries in which Communism abides hardly allow for future peace between these countries and the United States. If the world is to escape atomic war, we must find ways of living together despite our different forms of government." The fear tactics of many Cold War advocates hardly swayed Brookes, who instead called for peaceful solutions. And unlike other denominations that balanced such lay rhetoric with conservative counterpoints or even defenses of U.S. policy, *United Church Herald* focused on these and similar comments to craft a general UCC position against war.[46]

United Church of Christ leaders made the same pacifist point even more forcefully. In front of delegates at the 1967 General Synod, President Ben M. Herbster called for the United States to lead efforts for global peace. Rather than a generic, staid call for such a nebulous aim, Herbster suggested what the United States had to do to achieve peace and why the world needed this effort:

> War must be stopped, or our brothers and we shall all perish. It must be stopped now; war not only in Vietnam, but Israel, in Korea, and in Southern Arabia. It must be stopped now. The arms race must be halted. We must have a world-wide treaty to banish nuclear arms—and a world treaty without China as a signatory would be a farce.
>
> Arms proliferation is not the way to security; it is the way to death. Our Lord put the matter plainly: "all who take the sword will perish by the sword."

Other denominations and leaders walked a finer line between support for Cold War policy and calls for peace. Rather than worry about isolating or angering moderate or conservative members, Herbster articulated a leftist position and framed it as the true stance of the church.[47]

Yet the Soviet invasion of Czechoslovakia in 1968 caused the United Church of Christ to reiterate its disdain for communism, even as it called for cooperation with Communist nations. Enthusiasm about Czech reforms early in the year gave way to blasting the Communist bloc for interfering in another country. A September article written in response to the August invasion reported that "after 20 years of essentially Stalinist Communism in Czechoslovakia, a 'democratic' Communist group has taken power and the country is experiencing a new surge of freedom." Like other Christian institutions, the UCC hoped for the best during this transformation and decried the Soviet's invasion as a response to it. In harsh language, *United Church Herald* editors compared Soviet actions to Adolph Hitler's combat against anyone within his realm who questioned his authority. They stated that lust for power governed such actions, or the desire to control "14.3 million human beings." While the United Church of Christ took a strong and liberal stance regarding global affairs, none of this rhetoric ignored the reality of Communist oppression.[48]

This UCC foreign policy position squared with the denomination's emphasis on a theology of human improvement. Actions and reports from the 1965 General Synod in Chicago demonstrate the broad support within the denomination for such a position. The Council for Christian Social Action was charged with providing statements to the church body as an articulation of its stand on various domestic and international issues. This body carried out the demand of the UCC Constitution that the denomination persistently address social concerns as part of its Christian calling. In 1965, General Synod delegates ratified the Council for Christian Social Action's statement on disarmament: "General Synod re-affirms its belief that war is incompatible with Christian teaching and that it is an ineffective means of solving international disputes. Therefore, General Synod supports long-term authorization by Congress for the United States Arms Control and Disarmament Agency." Before the Vietnam War had had enough time to turn Americans against Cold War containment theory and traditional hostility, the UCC had joined other liberal Christians to articulate such a position. Reacting to a serious drought and economic poverty, the Council for Christian Social Action further convinced delegates of the need for Christians to overlook ideological battles with other countries when human need came into play. The General Synod therefore "encourages the United States Government to sell wheat, other foods, medical and other necessities of life" even to Communist nations. Finally, delegates proclaimed that admitting the People's Republic of China into the United Nations was a necessity for minimizing world hostility. Again squaring with a liberal Christian elite that had articulated such arguments since the 1950s, the UCC made a bold statement in 1965 when it not only advocated the PRC's entry into the UN but also "further urges the American people to make known to their government their willingness to support positive economic and cultural programs with the People's Republic of China." The UCC desperately championed a more peaceful point of view in line with its Christian calling.[49]

While it is impossible to determine what direct effect these periodicals and the United Church of Christ had on politicians and other government leaders, they clearly worked hard to add their voice to calls for reduced Cold War tension. Studies such as Charles DeBenedetti's and Charles Chatfield's *An American Ordeal* already have demonstrated that some religious individuals and entities had qualms about American nuclear policy and militarization in the 1950s. They created organizations such as the National Committee for a Sane Nuclear Policy (SANE), which condemned the building and use of nuclear weapons, to campaign against these policies.[50] The moderate and liberal Christians we have been discussing belong to this group of dedicated believers striving to change what they saw as a dangerous foreign policy long before the U.S. escalation of the Vietnam War, tracing all the way back to the 1940s and 1950s. They added to liberal Christianity a mixture of intellectuals and middle-class people worried about the international hostilities and working to change American policy through their Christian institutions.

Even more evidence that some Christians had moved beyond traditional Cold War mentalities and concern about a Communist monolith came when they criticized the United States for its foreign policy throughout the 1960s. These Christians, mirroring other concerned Americans, thought that the United States shared blame for global hostilities and could therefore reduce tension by changing its behavior. They used the church's moral authority to make this point.

The *Christian Century* led this charge with its liberal intellectualism. Instead of blaming Communists alone for the *U.S.S. Pueblo* affair, an editorial posited that "if the *Pueblo* at any time encroached upon North Korean territorial waters in its intelligence-gathering mission, then the moral and legal claims of our government are not so unambiguous as some of its spokesmen have so righteously maintained." The periodical's domestic liberalism also led to criticizing U.S. foreign policy because funding the military-industrial complex took money away from welfare reform and other social programs. It had regularly championed Lyndon B. Johnson's Great Society programs as beneficial in the context of a humanist theology. However, the Cold War drained resources from these programs in order to pay for armaments and the military. John M. Swomley Jr., an editor-at-large, stated that the "cold war and the military-industrial complex have created and sustain each other. Their impact on the domestic scene is overwhelming." Though they were not specifically articulated as religious issues, the *Christian Century* often reported on poverty, human welfare, and economic disparity because of the moral undergirding of such concerns. Anything that took away from alleviating or correcting these problems caused consternation for the periodical.[51]

Commonweal also thought that the United States made mistakes in foreign policy. It turned frequently throughout this decade to an expert on Eastern European history to articulate reactions to changes in the Communist bloc and to shape the periodical's diplomatic point of view, Professor Matthew M. Mestrovic of Fairleigh Dickinson University. Mestrovic's articles generally made three points: they applauded satellite nation rebellions, condemned communism, and called for a changed U.S. foreign policy. In 1964, he wrote about Rumania's defiance of the Soviet Union, a good case study for the changes taking place in the Communist world at that time. Rumania's recent past provided the backdrop for Mestrovic's analysis: Gheorghe Gheorghiu-Dej and the Rumanian Communist Party came to power in 1944 with the assistance of Soviet troops. He and the party ruled with the typical iron fist associated with Communist dictatorships, including terrorism, imprisonment of dissidents, and suppression of free speech. In short, Dej relied on force to maintain power during his twenty-plus years of control. Yet by the early 1960s, Dej had grown leery of Soviet coercion and used the Chinese rift with the Soviet Union as a model for asserting his will in Rumania. In April 1964, Rumania published a rebuke against Moscow's demands and began asserting independent courses of action. Mestrovic's three points of emphasis were exemplified in Rumania's repudiation of the Soviet Union: (1) Rumania had lashed out against Soviet influence within her borders; (2) but "what has taken place, to use Maurice Couve de Murville's cumbersome but apt phrase, is a 'desatellization' of the Rumanian state, rather than a 'liberalization' of the dictatorship"; (3) this change nonetheless put stress on communism that the United States could take advantage of by reaching out to countries such as Rumania and not isolating them simply because of their communism. Mestrovic's article represented a Catholic periodical in transition regarding its foreign policy viewpoints: while communism still endangered the world, the Cold War had changed and demanded a different American response, a point of view it wanted its readers to see.[52]

Throughout the 1960s and 1970s, controversy brewed within the Southern Baptist Convention between moderates and conservatives that finally resulted in a conservative takeover in the early 1980s. While SBC views on foreign policy seldom manifested in this division, glimpses of the tension appeared when the Christian Life Commission (CLC) spoke about the United States' diplomatic policy, thereby becoming the only national SBC entity to join these liberal Christian voices. The CLC had a leadership that espoused moderate theological and political ideologies, often to the dismay of SBC lay and clergy members with whom they disagreed. Regarding foreign affairs during the 1960s, the CLC director of organization, Bill Dyal, wrote about the SBC moderate stance regarding missions and communism. In an article that focused on missionaries sending God's message to people without the baggage of "cultural transference," Dyal warned against idealizing the United States and thinking that "God is on our side." He maintained that, while "God is on his throne," this throne "is not located in Washington, D.C." Far from connecting the Cold War to a religious war, Dyal viewed it as a matter separate from church affairs. He also explained how this illegitimate linking of God and the United States undermined mission efforts because it lost people who otherwise might listen to a religious message. In other words, already in the mid-1960s and prior to America's heavy involvement in Vietnam, Dyal felt that some Americans undermined mission efforts because of their dogmatic Cold War attitudes.[53]

Much like Dyal in the SBC, AME Reverend Benjamin J. Nolen Sr., editor of the *Christian Recorder*, at times diverged from generally accepted AME Cold War mentalities, especially regarding race. Recent scholarship by historian Jonathan Rosenberg demonstrates that many civil rights leaders throughout the twentieth century linked world affairs to their fight for equality in the United States. They used global politics to push the United States toward better civil rights advocacy and to create a global fight for racial equality that transcended national boundaries. The AME contributed to this linkage, as Nolen revealed in many of his editorials. First, Nolen distanced himself from extremists bent on revolution and decried the expansion of communism: "Extremists don't represent the large majority of Negroes" around the world. This squared with the generally conservative diplomatic bent of the denomination. Yet he also pointed out that "the cries for freedom in America are joined by the surging millions of blacks across the seas; who are wearied of the tyranny and totalitarianism of the world." As communism continued to confront democracy, Nolen asserted that positive efforts toward racial equality in America would assist the United States' Cold War fight by exposing Communist oppression while revealing the ability of democracy to correct racial injustice. For Nolen and those in the AME, as with other leaders of the civil rights movement, race and global politics commingled, forcing the United States to confront its own racism and that of its allies in order to win this global battle.[54]

An emphasis on global community, American responsibility, and disarmament also appeared in United Church of Christ publications throughout the 1960s. *United Church Herald* voiced such an opinion in 1964, a time when most Americans, including other Christians (other than an influential leadership within Protestantism that had resisted traditional Cold War politics from the beginning), said little against Cold War policies because the nation still generally feared communism. Herman F. Reissig warned that "those who believe that the gigantic U.S. military establishment is a necessary response to the threat of Communist imperialism are dangerously naïve if they do not see that the establishment carries its own threat to both democracy and peace. Military men . . . are tempted to think salvation depends on an increase of the power they represent." These strong words that condemned American militarism as much as they did communism came at a time when most of U.S. society had only started to question Cold War policy, if they had done so at all. In this regard, the UCC pushed a liberal agenda based on its theological convictions against war, thus adding a strong denominational voice to the argument other liberal Christians had been making since the 1950s. The Council for Christian Social Action also led the church on this front, dedicating an entire 1965 issue of its official periodical, *Social Action*, to its desired American response to global tension. Authors and editors repeatedly called for restraint in arms development, asked for superpower summits, and lamented that war had changed "from a means of defense to a means of annihilation." Charles M. Savage, a student at Andover-Newton Theological School, used *Keeping You Posted*, a periodical published by the UCC Office of Communication, to further this line of thinking. He firmly placed this UCC point of view in the context of the denomination's Christian conviction to help *all* peoples of the world. Savage found it maddening that ideological battles between Communist and democratic nations allowed people to starve or kept necessary medical supplies from reaching around the globe. He therefore applauded Christian/Marxist dialogues for focusing on assisting people, not on religious differences. Savage stated that the world "demands greater sensitivity to the cooperation [between all nations] in confronting the problems of hunger, population, and world trade." In short, for the United Church of Christ, the Christian call to serve humanity trumped global politics or a blind backing of U.S. foreign policy.[55]

These Christians worked diligently to get their message out: the United States was not perfect and had to alter its behavior in order to better serve the world and protect its ideology. And they began this crusade long before the Vietnam War, thus indicating that these liberal Christians had joined others who have already been studied, such as the National Council of Churches of Christ, who questioned American foreign policy prior to U.S. engagement in Southeast Asia. This fact refutes the notion that the Vietnam War instigated, at least for liberals, the questioning of traditional Cold War diplomacy. In fact, they had already begun to do so—some as far back as the 1940s—before President Johnson escalated America's involvement in Southeast Asia, meaning that the Vietnam War intensified the breakdown of a Cold War consensus on the American home front, rather than spawning it. The fact that America remained a relatively conservative place may indicate to some that these voices failed. Yet they contributed to a vibrant national debate during the 1960s and clearly worked to force their constituencies to rethink the way that the United States behaved in the international arena.

Conclusion

A spectrum of beliefs about foreign policy had developed within American Christianity by the end of the 1960s, and all of them contributed a religious voice to the American cultural war about foreign affairs. *Christianity Today*, conservative Catholic periodicals such as *America*, and the Southern Baptist Convention continued to manifest a traditional Cold Warriorism that supported U.S. policy with few questions and despised all things Communist. In addition to political reasons for doing so, reports from missionaries and the fate of Christians inside Communist countries solidified their stance. These Christian entities contributed a forceful religious voice to the national dialogue by portraying communism as an evil force that Christians must combat. No understanding of American public opinion about foreign policy or the rise of conservatism during the 1960s can be complete without this analysis. First, as other studies have demonstrated, it proves that a persistent and conservative anticommunism held sway over a large portion of Americans. Second, it reveals that much of this rightward outlook relied on a Christian reasoning for opposing communism. Beyond mere political and international arguments, a moral conviction guided their diplomatic beliefs. In contrast, the intellectual voice of the *Christian Century*, liberal Catholic periodicals such as *Catholic World*, and the United Church of Christ came to denounce the militarism of American policy and hoped for more staid and less reactionary relations with Communist nations. While these more liberal entities continued to despise Communist ideology, they also built upon a liberal Christian legacy from the 1950s and despised the arms race, the threat of nuclear war, U.S. backing of oppressive dictatorships, and a U.S. foreign policy that too often bordered on brinkmanship. A theology of human improvement led them to demand a foreign policy that protected all peoples of the world, not just Americans. These more liberal entities also contribute to our understanding of foreign policy during the 1960s, especially by demonstrating a faith reasoning for changing Cold War mentalities away from the harsh rhetoric against all things Communist that existed prior to the Vietnam War's escalation. Meanwhile, moderate Catholic journals and the African Methodist Episcopal Church exemplify a muddied middle ground. Within the AME, an anti-Communist, pro-American tone mixed with questioning some aspects of U.S. foreign policy, such as its impact on race relations across the globe. And for several Catholic periodicals, support for the Cold War gave way to doubt about whether or not such a stance should continue unabated into the future.

Christian Cold War opinions from the 1960s present a complicated picture regarding the intersection of religion and foreign policy, ranging from a traditional conservatism that defended containment theory to a liberal call for disarmament and an easing of global tension. Faith played into the various stances as denominations, periodicals, and religious leaders placed their opinions in the context of their theological outlook and history. By decade's end, where some Christians saw a necessary war against Communist atheism, others saw an outdated policy that threatened global war unnecessarily. These positions by church bodies and periodicals often paralleled their unique histories and theological outlooks. More humanist theological doctrines led adherents to denounce U.S. Cold War aims, while evangelical and missionary enthusiasts sought continued American interference with Communist expansionism. While American Christians remained virtually unanimous in their disdain for communism, they differed significantly in their ideas about how to protect the United States' image and about what was best to do for other people around the world. Indeed, this very disagreement lay at the heart of perhaps the most important foreign policy issue of the 1960s, the Vietnam War.

2

Christian Responses to Vietnam, 1964–1968

Introduction

In 1968, Dr. Harold John Ockenga, pastor of Park Street Church in Boston, traveled to Vietnam and wrote an article for *Christianity Today* in response: he castigated those who called for negotiations with North Vietnam or prophesied a U.S. defeat because doing so did "a great disservice to a heroic people and a great cause." He felt that a "compromise with the VC [Vietcong]" would mean doom for everything the South Vietnamese had fought to establish, which in his mind was democracy and religious freedom. For Ockenga and many other conservative Christians, Vietnam represented a domino to protect in the midst of the larger Cold War. They clung to a traditionalist Cold War mentality and contributed to a prowar public opinion that supported Lyndon B. Johnson's war aims in Southeast Asia. Martin E. Marty, a regular columnist for the *Christian Century*, disagreed. Never one to mince words and employing his typical wry sense of humor, Marty commented on the Vietnam War and the 1968 presidential election. A leaflet he pretended to have written to drop over Vietnam asked the Vietnamese, tongue in cheek, not to "approach us about negotiations during 1968, 1972, 1976, or any other Election Years" because the political party in power had to appear strong against communism. "Surely you have enough humanity left in you to be empathetic about the embarrassment you cause us" by requesting negotiations at such times, Marty wrote. Furthermore, he went on,

> You have no idea how infuriating it has been for us to drop as much explosive power on your little nation as we did on western Europe in all of World War II, only to be told that this hardly nettles you. If negotiations are to proceed, we demand statements in advance admitting that you have been inconvenienced by our massive show of superiority.

Marty wanted the war to end immediately, demonstrating a liberal Christianity that protested the war from the very beginning. Such disparate opinions were rampant among Christians during the 1960s when it came to the United States' involvement in Vietnam, as they contributed their religious voices to the American cultural battle raging about the war.[1]

Christian America manifested the entire spectrum of opinions about the Vietnam War, from a conservative backing of U.S. policy to an antiwar campaign, and everything in between. The shift from the 1950s consensus regarding anticommunism within American Christianity emerged in part because of these reactions to Vietnam. Regardless of their position, the Christians discussed here all felt passionately about their stance, believing that it was not only right for the United States but important for Christians, too. Our focus here is on the second half of 1964, when the war began amidst a presidential election, and all of 1968, a pivotal year in the war when antiwar protests escalated and public opinion began to sour against U.S. policy in Southeast Asia. Careful study, established Cold War positions, and experiences around the globe shaped the reactions of these institutions, which offer a cross-section of the diverse American Christian responses to the 1960s Vietnam War. These entities reflected American society's grappling with foreign policy during the 1960s, and also their desire to shape American public opinion and policy toward their particular points of view.

Previous studies have already outlined some of the Christian responses to Vietnam, especially the antiwar activism of some Christians. Indeed, a mainline, relatively liberal elite clergy carried out an orchestrated and steady attack on the Johnson administration beginning in 1964 and continuing throughout the duration of U.S. involvement in Vietnam. They built upon a legacy that they had established already in the 1950s of questioning American involvement in the arms race and U.S. reliance on militarized ideologies. Most notably regarding Vietnam, this doubting of U.S. foreign policy included the creation of Clergy and Laity Concerned about Vietnam (CALCAV) and the use of the National Council of Churches of Christ to promote responsible and legal means to protest the war. Earlier work has illustrated the vital role that this part of the Christian community played in antiwar activism. Yet it hardly represents the whole of American Christian responses. Lutheran Americans, for example, debated the war internally among their ranks and included prowar advocates, antiwar protesters, and many others struggling to find meaning and a position during the first half of this war. The antiwar entities in this study protested the Vietnam War from the beginning, on the basis of their already strong questioning of Cold War foreign policy.[2]

The United States became involved in Vietnam as part of the Cold War. When the French decided to withdraw forces from the country in 1954, after almost a century of controlling Vietnam as a colony, American officials stepped in and brokered a settlement with the Soviet Union and People's Republic of China to split Vietnam at the 17th parallel, thereby keeping either side in the Cold War from achieving a decisive victory in Southeast Asia. As the areas above and below the 17th parallel later manifested into nations, South Vietnam became the United States' ally, and North Vietnam allied with the Communist nations. While the United States intended for South Vietnam to become a democratic and free nation, it never lived up to this expectation. Beginning with the regime of Ngo Dinh Diem and continuing throughout the 1960s and into the 1970s, a series of corrupt dictatorships emerged that further alienated the Vietnamese in the region and subsequently engendered local hostility toward the United States. In part, this led to the creation of the National Liberation Front, a conglomeration of various South Vietnamese factions and North Vietnamese Communists allied in an effort to oust the South Vietnamese government and therefore also America's presence in the region. For its part, the United States feared losing Vietnam to communism and attempted unsuccessfully to reform these South Vietnamese governments. In 1964, a skirmish in the Gulf of Tonkin escalated tension between the United States and North Vietnam, which U.S. officials used to justify increased military involvement in the civil war already raging within Vietnam. On 2 August 1964, the *U.S.S. Maddox* engaged with North Vietnamese forces. A second alleged attack by North Vietnamese vessels two days later spurred President Lyndon B. Johnson to ask Congress for the right to defend U.S. interests in the region, thus gaining authorization through the Gulf of Tonkin Resolution to wage an undeclared war in South Vietnam. This occurred despite the fact that U.S. officials, including the president, already knew at the time that the second attack never actually happened.

All the while, U.S. experts on Vietnam in and out of the government began a heated debate about the nature of Vietnamese communism and the danger it posed to the United States. This same debate took place among American Christians. A traditionalist, Cold War approach informed Johnson's early handling of the war, which viewed North Vietnam as part of a Communist monolith encircling the globe and thereby endangering freedom and democracy. Conservative policymakers and average Americans once again called for a show of force to stem the tide of this expansionist danger. But unlike in previous Cold War skirmishes, other parties within the academic and government communities vocally disputed this approach. They instead saw variances within the Communist world, such as the hostility between the Soviet Union and People's Republic of China. Additionally, they explained how Ho Chi Minh, the Vietnamese revolutionary hero and leader of North Vietnam, played the two Communist giants off one another and speculated that North Vietnam under Ho might actually cooperate with the United States, in a manner similar to that of Tito's Communist regime in Yugoslavia, which often defied Soviet edicts in favor of its own unique approach to communism and diplomacy, in order to gain leverage over its own affairs. They emphasized that America was interfering in a civil war and that the Vietnamese were hostile to any foreign interference on behalf of corrupt governments in South Vietnam that alienated its citizens.

Average Americans participated in this argument about the Vietnam War, too. The antiwar movement began as a coalition of intellectuals, traditional peace activists, and college-aged students who agreed that the United States should not fight in Southeast Asia because communism there did not threaten the United States while a war injured too many innocent Vietnamese. During the 1960s, this activism led to public protests, such as marches on Washington, D.C., campus demonstrations, and, increasingly, illegal measures to bring attention to the antiwar cause since Congress and the White House backed a prowar point of view. For example, students and their adult backers staged draft card burnings to lash out against the draft, which forced even those who opposed the war to go fight it. Yet a strong majority of Americans at the beginning of the war supported U.S. policy, still fearing the Cold War Communist menace and trusting that the government protected their best interests. Later dubbed "the silent majority" by Richard Nixon, they seldom appeared in public to voice their opinion but instead voted for representatives who shared it or quietly allowed the government to continue prosecuting the war. We know too little about them and their motivations: studying conservative Christianity's contribution in this regard helps to rectify this lacuna.

By early 1968, this swirling debate pulled Johnson into its fray and ultimately brought him to question U.S. policy in Vietnam and to work to bring peace to that region in the wake of the Tet Offensive in January in which North Vietnam, the National Liberation Front, and their supporters staged surprise attacks on almost every South Vietnamese and U.S. military installation and urban center. Deemed a defeat of the Communists by American military leaders because none of the efforts succeeded, the sudden show of strength by forces that Americans had been told were weakening nonetheless alarmed many in the United States, who now questioned the war and brought pressure upon Johnson to negotiate a settlement. Facing opposition from antiwar candidates within his own party, including Senator Eugene McCarthy of Minnesota and Senator Robert F. Kennedy of New York, Johnson withdrew from the presidential race and announced that he would dedicate the remainder of his time in office to seeking peace in Vietnam. Though he was ultimately unsuccessful, his dropping out of the election demonstrated the force of antiwar opinions and the angst Americans had come to feel about the Vietnam War.

Christian Americans participated passionately in this debate. They represented all of the points of view on the issue, often demonstrated through meticulous debate, theological reflection, and reliance on heritages firmly established within denominations and specific religious periodicals. The anguish of America regarding the Vietnam War was writ large on the pages of Christian America during the 1960s.

Christian Support for the Vietnam War

We already know that many conservatives in the 1960s supported the Vietnam War, but not enough about why and how. Studies have explained how conservative politicians maintained strong Cold War mentalities that demanded a protection of Vietnam, and that this conservative posturing led to political support from their constituencies. Yet we know little beyond this public, political, and often secular conversation about why they wanted to defend South Vietnam. As we seek to better understand conservative Americans who supported U.S. policy in Vietnam, we must look to Christian America for another important point of view. Continuing in their conviction that communism represented an evil force, Christians added their voice to this conservatism by seeking to limit its global influence and agreed with U.S. political leaders that this domino deserved American protection. Indeed, their Christian faith demanded it. Conservative Christians add a strong voice to our knowledge about which Americans wanted the United States to continue prosecuting the Vietnam War, and why.

Christianity Today embodied this conservative Christian outlook. In August 1964, immediately after Lyndon B. Johnson sought congressional approval to expand U.S. military involvement in Vietnam, the periodical pointed out the connection between this war and the Cold War:

America's policy of dealing gently with Communist imperialism has been costly through its postponement of a show of strength until too much is lost and even more risked. In Southeast Asia, as elsewhere, a show of strength is better late than never, and it is far better in freedom's cause than in the extension of tyranny. A firm reply to North Viet Nam's aggressive posture was long overdue.

This statement mirrored exactly that of U.S. officials when they argued for escalating American involvement in the war. The periodical here revealed its belief in U.S. Cold War policy that emphasized standing up to the Communists with military strength in order to force them to cease "their global march." Little had changed by the end of Johnson's administration. In March 1968, after the Tet Offensive had soured many Americans against the war, *Christianity Today*'s editors declared that "those who think these values [freedom and human dignity] are best preserved by an end to effective resistance to Communist expansionism seem incredibly naïve." They especially criticized church leaders who advocated antiwar activities because of allegedly false claims that they spoke for America's conscience. The periodical stated that conservative Christians needed to "challenge" these comments, ostensibly to avoid a Communist global takeover. The periodical embraced a staunch anticommunism regarding Vietnam and wanted to sway readers toward that point of view.[3]

Christianity Today connected this more secular outlook to its Christian philosophy. Editors declared that within the larger political and military turmoil of Vietnam, "there is a war being waged for souls." According to the periodical, a U.S. win meant the continuation of Christianity in Southeast Asia, while a loss doomed the region to Communist atheism. The editors often linked North Vietnamese Communists to international Communist efforts to eradicate religious belief in their nations. In November 1968, they explained that "reports pieced together from North Viet Nam indicate the Red regime is 'slowly eradicating Roman Catholicism and Buddhism from the fabric of North Vietnamese society." They used information from North Vietnamese defectors to bolster their claims. Frightful stories of atheist propaganda and the indoctrination of children intensified their prowar mentality, such as one story of children taken to a church and shown pictures of Jesus and Ho Chi Minh: "They were told to pray to Jesus for food, but after an hour, nothing had happened. When they shifted to praying to Ho, the Pavlovians brought in candy and cake." No documentation can verify this story, though ample evidence demonstrates the hostility North Vietnam had toward religion and its persecution of innocent civilians who disagreed with its government. Such tales added an important religious element to *Christianity Today*'s prowar stance, and to its moral suasion over reader opinions about the war.[4]

Jesuit *America* stood with *Christianity Today* regarding the Vietnam War. The fear of Communist atheism led this conservative Catholic periodical to commingle secular/political and religious/theological beliefs, and its editorial responses contained a hawkish tenor from the very beginning of the war in 1964. Already in August, as events leading to the Gulf of Tonkin Resolution unfolded, an editorial declared that the Communists "have been made to realize that direct provocation of U.S. forces in the Pacific will trigger instant, damaging retaliation." Firmly entrenched in the belief that only demonstrations of force quelled Communist expansionism, editors concluded that North Vietnam now knew that "President Johnson's determination to meet force with force has the support of the American people." Indeed, by November the periodical wanted an escalation of U.S. involvement in the war. Fearing that the advisory role of U.S. troops put them in harm's way without the ability to protect themselves from Communist insurgents, an editorial stated that "it makes no sense to be serving merely in an advisory capacity when U.S. troops are so obviously in the thick of the fight." This position even allowed *America* to support the U.S. policy of backing dictators if they could control a region and keep the Communists at bay. Editors explained that the new Vietnamese leader, "Tran Van Huong, in other words, has the air of a dictator. Perhaps, after all, that is what South Vietnam needs. Arguments over Ngo Dinh Diem will doubtless go on, but few will deny that the war in South Vietnam was never being lost as efficiently as during the past year of 'liberation' from the 'autocratic' Ngo family." Such voices within the American populace gave support to the Johnson administration's prosecution of the war.[5]

In line with this reasoning, *America* blamed the North Vietnamese and Vietcong solely for the war because of their expansionist ideology. The periodical explained away any evidence to the contrary because decades of believing this Cold War principle had so ensconced itself in its foreign policy perceptions. When confronted with proof that certain Buddhist factions in South Vietnam also denounced their government, the editors concluded that "the strong possibility exists that South Vietnam's Buddhist movement has been deeply infiltrated by the Vietcong." Four years later, when the Tet Offensive shattered many American hopes that South Vietnam and the United States could win the war, *America* declared that "Vietcong terrorists had carried their attacks in massive fashion into key cities and towns throughout South Vietnam in defiance of a truce they themselves called. Clearly this was not the response of a government in Hanoi that was interested in negotiating a settlement." In other words, they blamed North Vietnam alone for the failure to reach a brokered peace between the Communists and the United States and South Vietnam. Even the pope's 1968 Easter message, in which he appealed for peace in Vietnam without taking sides, failed to assuage them. Partially blaming the American peace movement, editors stated that the success of peace candidates in the 1968 presidential election and Johnson's withdrawal from it should give Americans pause. They explained that "the notion that, in these circumstances, Hanoi is about to talk with a view to reasonable compromise could turn out to be wishful thinking of the wildest sort. The nation had best be prepared." With little direct linkage to its theology, *America* embraced a conservative Catholic outlook that supported U.S. efforts in Vietnam as necessary to stopping Communist expansion.[6]

Catholic Digest squared with *Christianity Today* and *America* in supporting the United States' policy but took a much different approach in making this argument. Articles from the 1960s regarding Vietnam almost always focused on the effects of war on the children of that country, applauded U.S. institutions for attempting to alleviate their suffering, and asked for more help from Americans. As with its Jesuit counterpart, its prowar stance stemmed from its perception of what caused this problem and the belief that only a U.S. victory could solve it. As one article told readers, "The longest shadows of the warfare that has been bleeding Vietnam for 20 years fall upon the children. You see them playing in the streets of Saigon, refugee-swollen city of 1.6 million—between raids of the Viet Cong—thin, in tattered clothing." The article blamed North Vietnamese aggression and Vietcong insurgents for the violence perpetrated upon these children and for the nation's economic plight. Later, editors appealed to the government and private groups to provide aid to these children through a special clinic for them. Similar efforts throughout Vietnam drew praise as well, and calls for more funding. Again linking charity and assistance to children with support for America's effort, an article explained that U.S. forces did good things amidst the fighting, such as helping nuns operate a school for blind girls in Saigon. Without this economic and spiritual support, *Catholic Digest* worried about the future for these young women. *Catholic Digest* was concerned about Catholic operations in Vietnam and the innocent children of the nation, thus adding a more overtly Catholic link to conservative support for American actions in Vietnam.[7]

Many Southern Baptist Convention leaders also voiced support for the United States' efforts in Vietnam. While the SBC as a whole represented a myriad of points of view, much of its leadership sided with conservative Americans. In 1968, Baptist Press reported on a survey of five hundred ministers in Florida and Louisiana that demonstrated a hawkish stance. Seventy-five percent agreed or strongly agreed that the United States could not afford to lose in Vietnam, with 69 percent backing an escalation of the conflict if current U.S. forces failed to win. Perhaps more telling of their conservative stance and adamant approach to winning the war, 47 percent sanctioned the use of nuclear weapons if essential for victory and 36 percent stated that the war should continue even if it brought about World War III. The SBC secretary for the Orient articulated a more moderate position that nonetheless backed the war as necessary. He feared that Americans had started to favor only extreme hawk or dove positions instead of a "policy of patient perseverance" that he labeled moderate but that clearly involved a desire for the United States to remain in the war. The SBC leadership thus campaigned generally for a prowar platform within the denomination.[8]

H. Franklin Paschall, elected SBC president in 1967 and 1968 and pastor of First Baptist Church in Nashville, Tennessee, also supported U.S. involvement in the Vietnam War. Paschall often voiced his opinions in letters to lay members of the SBC, who wrote to him about their concern that too many Americans and Christian institutions had adopted an antiwar attitude. These letters indicate a vast amount of lay agreement with their leader's position. Fearing that "a determined effort is going to be made to have Southern Baptists join the Left-leaning-liberal Church groups in stabbing our Viet Nam boys in the back," they pleaded with Paschall to steer a different course. Paschall seldom minced words when he spoke about politics or theology, persistently backing a conservative agenda. Though better known for a failed effort at keeping the SBC from splitting along moderate and conservative lines in the 1980s, his SBC presidency often sided more with conservatives than moderates, especially concerning secular issues. Regarding the Vietnam War, he simply told one person, "If it takes 'total victory,' that is total destruction of North Vietnam to bring about negotiations for a just and honorable peace, then I am for it." He also made such statements to the media, thereby countering antiwar Christians in their fight against the war. More than mere hawkish posturing, however, led him to this opinion. In addition to backing the Cold War and wanting to resist Communist expansion, Paschall thought prowar statements better served the U.S. soldiers fighting in Vietnam. Not only did he see this support of the troops as an American duty, but he asserted that "Christians have not shown enough concern for our boys who are giving their lives for freedom."[9]

Paschall's prowar position received further support from many editors and writers of Southern Baptist Convention newspapers, as he was not alone in trying to shape his denomination's outlook regarding the Vietnam War. A mixture of foreign policy, politics, and religion informed their opinions. Dr. C. R. Daley, editor of the *Western Recorder* of the Kentucky Baptist Convention, most stridently explained the Christian reason many within the SBC had for their Vietnam War position. Using domino-theory imagery and playing on fear of Communist atheism, he stated that "Communism must be stopped somewhere, or this Godless darkness will cover the earth." The Vietnam War therefore represented more than a mere war; it pitted God's side (United States) against the devil (North Vietnam). Daley also reminded readers that "our unhindered freedom to preach the gospel to these nations depends upon containing Communism." He and others still prayed and hoped for peace. But unlike antiwar Christians, prowar SBC writers insisted that an unconditional peace without guaranteed protections for Vietnamese Christians damaged God's aims for the world and could not be tolerated. Criticizing the antiwar movement in America, *Alabama Baptist* editor Hudson Baggett asserted that "anyone who consciously or unconsciously seeks to follow the way of peace at any price courts disaster." A retired professor from Southwest Seminary voiced a similar concern. Although he questioned some tactics involved in the fighting and wished that the war had never started, T. B. Matson wrote that "we may wish that our nation had not gotten involved in it, but we do not believe we can wisely or honorably pull out of Vietnam." This mixture of foreign policy with Christian conviction in the Baptist press also led to paternalistic concern for the Vietnamese, another reason why many editors supported the war. James W. Kelly, a Baptist minister and chief of chaplains for the U.S. Navy, told the *Baptist Message* that U.S. engagement in the war provided the only "defense of an otherwise helpless people," so he could not sanction abandoning them "in their hour of need." Southern Baptist periodicals belong to the list of American institutions that backed U.S. involvement in Vietnam, in this case on the basis of a combination of political and religious reasoning.[10]

Conservative Christians even found agreement with their cause from a small contingent within the United Church of Christ, a denomination that otherwise belonged firmly to the antiwar point of view. Little of this UCC opposition appeared at the General Synod, but letters to the editor of the *United Church Herald* indicate that it existed nonetheless. A February 1968 letter summarized this position succinctly: "The U.S. is fighting in Vietnam primarily to contain Communism. We are fighting as a Christian nation to prevent Communism from engulfing a weak people. We are not fighting simply to protect South Vietnam but to contain Communism when and where it must be contained for our own good and the good of mankind." This statement embodied many of the hallmarks of conservative prowar opinions regarding

Vietnam. First, it maintained a belief in containment. The letter also depicted the Cold War in religious terms, by describing America as a "Christian nation," with the implication that communism represented atheism and even evil. Finally, U.S. paternalism revealed itself with the description of the Vietnamese as a "weak" people incapable of defending themselves and needing the fatherly United States to provide protection. Another letter more pointedly evoked the religious crusade image by asking if Americans had to obey the biblical charge to be their brother's keeper: "Assuming that the answer is yes, then as an individual and as a Christian nation we *must* be in Vietnam and places like Vietnam as long as godless Communism forces us to be." Given the long history of the UCC as traced through the more theologically conservative Evangelical and German Reformed Church and the Congregational Christian Church, it stands to reason that a conservative minority existed that disliked the UCC's generally activist agenda, especially regarding U.S. foreign policy. Though little evidence indicates that such positions were widespread within the United Church of Christ, these letters show that the UCC had at least some internal dissension regarding its Vietnam War stance in the 1960s.[11]

Conservative Christians consistently added their voice to support for the United States' prosecution of the Vietnam War. We need to add such information to our understanding of the way Americans responded to the Vietnam War during the 1960s to gain a complete picture of the culture war taking place regarding foreign policy. In addition, this information contributes another way to examine the resurgence of conservatism during that decade by adding a religious element to what others have already studied. Through religious convictions and theological reflection, conservative Christians asserted that protecting Southeast Asia from communism mattered in the context of the larger Cold War.

Antiwar Christians

Liberal Christians disagreed with the conservative assessment of the Vietnam War, in large part because, as we have seen, they did not see communism as a global monolith but rather as an ideology with different factions and countries affiliated with it. This outlook allowed them to question U.S. actions in Southeast Asia from the very beginning of Lyndon B. Johnson's escalation of the war, as opposed to others in the antiwar movement who took time to study and understand it before delving into their activism. Too, the vast amount of literature about the antiwar movement and its influence, including Christian organizations founded to protest the war, must also acknowledge the importance of traditional entities, such as periodicals and denominations, when considering how Christians contributed a religious reasoning for protesting what they viewed as an immoral U.S. engagement in a civil war. These Christians countered the above conservative, prowar point of view with an antiwar advocacy born from an already established foundation of questioning traditional Cold War diplomacy.

As with the larger Cold War, the *Christian Century* provided a strong intellectual voice to this liberal fight against the war. While much of the United States believed President Johnson when he said in August 1964 that North Vietnam had attacked the United States without provocation in the Gulf of Tonkin, the *Christian Century* questioned U.S. actions from the beginning. By December, editors wondered about the necessity for American involvement in Vietnam: "We wait for an explanation from Washington as to why we have to fight a war against North Vietnam, or to take warlike actions against that country at this particular juncture." This statement placed the Vietnam War in the context of their discarding of containment theory. No longer fearful of every form of communism, the editors sought a deeper explanation than the mere fact of combating communism. Johnson and other leaders had failed to convince these liberal Protestants regarding his foreign policy. If anything, the attacks on this policy grew worse by the end of the year and after his reelection, when editors called for a negotiated peace because "the present U.S. policy in South Vietnam solves nothing. If the administration is on the verge of adopting a new Vietnamese policy, it should be the policy not of the craven or the bully but of the negotiator seeking a political settlement." Few American individuals or institutions came out against the Vietnam War quickly and forcefully in 1964. Years of U.S. intervention in foreign lands to stop the spread of communism had immunized too many. Not so the *Christian Century*, which from the very beginning joined a Christian liberal elite that wanted a detailed explanation that seldom came and that never convinced them of the war's necessity.[12]

By the end of Johnson's administration, this opposition to traditional Cold War policy had entrenched itself within the *Christian Century* editorial offices. Four years of a futile effort in Vietnam had solidified their foreign policy perceptions away from traditional Cold War containment theory. Howard Schomer, an editor-at-large, contributed a commentary that made this point:

No true dialogue can be initiated so long as the two sides remain deaf to each other's central concern, the one unable even to hear that Hanoi is no Peking puppet and the other incapable of conceiving that this time the white man hasn't the faintest intention of settling in for decades and centuries to come. So thus far the N.L.F.-Hanoi axis wants this war more than it wants a peace which it fears the United States would dominate. And thus far Washington wants this war more than it wants a peace which it fears would increase Chinese Communist power.

Those who viewed communism as a worldwide monolith insisted that the Soviet Union and People's Republic of China orchestrated the war. As Schomer pointed out, this was hardly true. North Vietnam managed its own affairs, albeit with Soviet and Chinese financial and munitions support. Yet North Vietnam in part played the two superpowers off one another to gain more aid and shunned any attempt to control its affairs, a factor that led to armed skirmishes between the PRC and Vietnam by the late 1970s. Schomer's writing demonstrated that those at the *Christian Century* already knew this fact in 1968. While he hardly supported North Vietnam or its southern allies, neither did he adhere to an assumption that all Communists worked together to undermine the United States. The fact that these statements came from Schomer proves especially telling about the periodical's point of view because he was the most conservative of their editors and otherwise vocally anti-Communist. Yet the above stance was the lesson that he and others delivered to the *Christian Century*'s readership in order to bring into question American actions in Vietnam.[13]

Schomer's colleagues agreed with his position, further demonstrating the periodical's antiwar stance toward Vietnam. As editor-at-large J. Claude Evans stated in linking the periodical's shunning of traditional Cold War foreign policy to its Vietnam War position, "The U.S. government is still making its foreign policy decisions on an outdated analysis of the Communist threat—an analysis more appropriate to the 1950s than to the 1960s." Carl P. Zietlow of the American Friends Committee wrote an article for the *Christian Century* that further detailed this link between outmoded Cold War philosophies and the Vietnam War. He argued vehemently for peace, applauding the fact that America met in Paris in 1968 with North Vietnam to attempt to negotiate but also upset that the United States refused to recognize National Liberation Front advisors, too. Where the American government saw an illegal South Vietnamese body with ties to northern Communists, Zietlow more accurately saw a complex alliance of various Vietnamese groups, albeit with a Communist presence, that had to be reckoned with in order to achieve a lasting peace. He concluded part of his article with the further entreaty that the United States "should work for a real change in U.S. foreign policy, to prevent a repetition of the Vietnam cycle in Thailand, Rhodesia, Guatemala, and other far-flung places." Indeed, Peter Berger, a professor at the New School for Social Research in New York City, worried that the government's concealing of information from the American public regarding Vietnam might lead it to hide other foreign policy initiatives if "Vietnam proves only the first of a series of imperial adventures." In other words, if the government maintained faith in the domino theory while ordinary Americans began to question it, Berger was concerned that presidents would disguise the use of force elsewhere around the world because they continued to prosecute Vietnamesque wars. The immediate and continued denunciation of the Vietnam War throughout the 1960s from the *Christian Century* stemmed primarily from their discarding of containment theory and subsequent outlining of the complexity within the Communist world. Writers and editors viewed Vietnam as in the midst of a civil war, with the United States as an outside aggressor, an outlook it strove to teach to its readership.[14]

The *Christian Century* also had religious grounds for its antiwar position. Editorials tended to describe the war as immoral because it harmed so many innocent people. Rebuking those who advocated the war because of Communist atrocities and who condemned antiwar protesters for only criticizing the United States, one January 1968 editorial stated that "a Christian word on this or any other war must necessarily concentrate on our side so far as moral issues are concerned even as it may report the evil on the other side. We know of no way to work on the conscience of the enemy to bring about protection of the innocent. But we do have a (dwindling) bit of faith left in our political process." It continued that

> No where in the Christian tradition can we find a charter to repent for someone else; we have to concentrate on ways in which *we* are returning evil for evil. That we "know" they started the war before we escalated it does not lessen the realization that the absence of restraint on our methods of fighting that war is a blight on America, a blight open for the world to see and recoil from.

By May, editors lamented that peace talks had failed in part because the United States continued to fight the war all out, was afraid to show weakness, and clung to a false hope that America could still win: America's "feeling of optimism about the war proves to be only a symptom of our sin. For in fact nothing has happened to absolve our national guilt" in injuring the innocent and prosecuting a war that failed to meet the seven just war tenets. As outlined previously in this book. The *Christian Century* felt that U.S. involvement in the Vietnam War fell well short of meeting this Christian standard. In short, two writers explained on behalf of the periodical that "a growing consensus among mature, morally sensitive people is that the spiritual integrity of the United States, rooted as it is in the Judeo-Christian tradition, cannot be secured by our present policy in Vietnam." No argument made a stronger statement about why the periodical wanted its readers to oppose the war than such deliberations based on its religious convictions.[15]

The *Christian Century* had some SBC support for its position. Unlike the conservative SBC opinions described above, leaders from the SBC's Christian Life Commission (CLC) worked to counteract their colleagues' attempts to shape a prowar SBC stance. The CLC's antiwar position regarding the Vietnam War mirrored that of other Christian protesters and provided one signal that moderates and conservatives within the SBC would disagree more and more throughout the 1960s and 1970s. Within the SBC, the CLC offered the only evidence of a sustained, dogmatic, and adamant cry for an end to the war, regardless of the cost. William M. Dyal Jr., CLC director of organization, blasted the Southern Baptist Convention for its silence about the Vietnam War and called for protest. Indeed, he claimed that "Christendom, and especially Southern Baptists, seems mainly to sound a silent shriek. Where is the declaration under God of the costliness of life? Where is the reminder in the churches that our men *and* theirs are the creation of God for whom Christ died?" As had his prowar counterparts, Dyal framed his stance in terms of his Christian conviction; but where they saw a danger to Christianity, Dyal grieved over the loss of human life and the destruction of God's people. Writing before Christmas 1966, he proclaimed, "Let our 'silent shriek' become instead a courageous proclamation of the worth and dignity of every life." Foy Valentine, the head of the Christian Life Commission, also denounced the war because it failed to meet the criteria for a just war. Later ousted and denounced by conservatives, Valentine throughout his service took moderate to liberal stances regarding secular and religious issues. After taking over in 1960, he and the CLC championed the civil rights movement, much to the chagrin of many within the SBC. Such criticism never stopped him from voicing his Christian conviction, which included his belief that the Vietnam War was immoral.[16]

The CLC also preserved sermons in the SBC archives that buttressed its antiwar position. For these ministers, God called them to deliver their message of conscience before lay people from the pulpit on Sunday. Preaching at the Marsh Chapel at Boston University, Pastor Robert H. Hamill announced that "this total war effort adds up to a program that is bankrupt and immoral. Bankrupt because it doesn't work in Vietnam. Immoral because it contradicts the elemental human conscience." He then explained that an admission of wrongness by the United States would not damage the nation but rather "prove our greatness." Pastor John R. Claypool told the congregants at Crescent Hill Baptist Church in Louisville, Kentucky, much the same thing. Calling it a "war disease," he asserted that "we need to 'fight the good fight,' and refuse to let the spirit of war corrupt the spirit of love and truth that is God's highest gift to each of us." As had their prowar counterparts, for these pastors, the church spoke prophetically to the state when it came to the Vietnam War because they felt that responsible Christians had to speak against a war they saw as immoral. Furthermore, speaking in 1966, they demonstrate how quickly these SBC antiwar advocates came to protest the war in a public way. Using the pulpit became a forceful way to attempt to shape lay opinion.[17]

Other segments from within the denomination existed outside the Christian Life Commission that allied with them in this campaign against the war. Though war protesters within the denomination were not as numerous as their prowar counterparts, Baptist papers did reflect the presence of the antiwar attitude among their constituents. For example, the predominant SBC prowar opinion that appeared in an edition of the *Maryland Baptist* was balanced by an article by Dr. Henlee H. Barnette, a professor at Southern Baptist Seminary, who argued that militarism would not contain communism. Instead, Barnette asserted, American participation in Southeast Asia had driven more and more of the Vietnamese population into the Communist camp because of the actions of the South Vietnamese government and promises of liberation from foreign domination by the Communists. Historical research has confirmed Barnette's theory, as many South Vietnamese who otherwise remained neutral were propelled to the revolutionary camp because of imprisonment in internment camps, restrictions on religious practices, and forced conscription.[18] Barnette wrote that "communism cannot be contained by military might where the people as a whole couldn't care less about the types of government they live under, but just want to be left alone." This view echoed the sentiment of experts on Vietnam from throughout the country who tried to explain to government officials, including President Johnson, and ordinary Americans alike that the Vietnamese were fighting a civil war against foreign control, not a global battle of right and wrong between the United States and the Soviet Union. At its fall 1968 gathering, the SBC Michigan Convention asked members for prayers for servicemen and their families *and* "for responsible leaders on all sides to seek an early ceasefire and termination of all hostile activities and any further buildup of military power and advantage." While a showing of this sentiment is rare, the Michigan Convention demonstrates that blocs of Southern Baptist Convention members disagreed with their prowar counterparts. Perhaps because of its northern location amidst major universities and antiwar activity, or maybe because of its relatively small size in comparison to the conventions located in the South, the Michigan Convention made one of the few public antiwar statements on behalf of a large Southern Baptist constituency.[19]

Yet no one more adamantly opposed the war on behalf of the Southern Baptist Convention than the editor of the *Arkansas Baptist*, Erwin L. McDonald. McDonald stood out among his colleagues for taking a moderate and sometimes liberal stance on numerous issues, including foreign policy and civil rights. As we have seen, he already had engaged conservatives in a debate through his editorials about Southern Baptist Convention beliefs and behaviors during the 1960s. He thus used his paper as a platform to try to teach his readers about the follies of American involvement in the Vietnam War throughout this decade. He campaigned for this cause primarily because of his religious convictions. Believing an SBC theology that God would punish the misdeeds of humanity, he warned that "all of our material resources cannot save us and the world from the holocaust of war. Christ, the Prince of Peace, really is the only hope." He then charged Americans with acting to stop the war: "If American Christians remain silent in their day of good news, will not punishment overtake them?" He also thought that the United States acted like a trapped person in quicksand, whose panicked struggles only cause him or her to sink deeper and deeper toward death. Though he disliked communism as much as his colleagues, he stated that "some of us have not yet been convinced that communism can be destroyed by destroying people." McDonald worked passionately to shape his readers' opinions through his editorials against the war based on this questioning of traditional Cold War diplomacy.[20]

As the rest of the nation erupted into generational conflict regarding the Vietnam War, so too did the Southern Baptist Convention, though not in as pronounced or prolonged a fashion as at secular institutions or in major

American cities. Nonetheless, on this occasion college-aged members of the SBC protested the war and urged their denomination to do the same, proving that the SBC was not immune to the protest movement, even if the historical record indicates that this was an isolated event for this denomination. As we saw earlier, the 1968 national convention in Houston brought these young people to the attention of the wider church body when they organized a peaceful picket of messengers as they entered the hall. Calling themselves Baptist Students Concerned, they took up a host of issues, including racism, poverty, and the Vietnam War, hoping to convince their elders to steer the denomination in a new direction. When queried by Baptist Press about their activism, the students explained that "a crisis of conscience" drove them to lash out at Southern Baptist silence on these crucial issues of the day. Their presence failed to impact the convention as a whole, though they did dialogue with both supportive and hostile members and SBC leaders. A group of pastors even agreed to meet with the delegation. Ronald Joyner, a student at the University of North Carolina, stated that he believed "the war is fundamentally unjust and immoral. He added that if peace does come it will come in spite of the Southern Baptist Convention and not because of it." Compared to their peers around the nation, these students appear benign and respectful. But a public demonstration to a conservative church body that questioned the unrest and violence around the nation represented a bold step for these young people. They contributed a youthful antiwar voice to their lay and clergy elders who also protested the Vietnam War. As shown above, the SBC engaged in the culture war over the Vietnam War, both within itself and in attempting to broadcast its message(s) to a larger audience.[21]

Unlike the SBC, the United Church of Christ voiced its displeasure about the war in a number of ways, with a majority of its leaders and laity in agreement from the onset of America's military buildup in Southeast Asia. Already in 1965, the General Synod advocated a negotiated settlement. The UCC's antiwar platform matches its liberal activism on behalf of civil rights and the women's movement, and against societal and governmental oppression in the United States and around the globe, in line with the National Council of Churches and the liberal ecumenical movement. The UCC's opposition to war also parallels the early arguments found in the *Christian Century*. The assembly adopted the Council for Christian Social Action report that in part asserted that "only political and diplomatic methods of negotiation and discussion can find a peaceful solution" to the Vietnam War. In April 1968, the *United Church Herald* published the results of a survey that it distributed to its readership that confirmed this earlier attitude against the war. Of the

1,921 people who responded, almost 54 percent agreed that the United States should unconditionally stop the bombing of North Vietnam in order to negotiate a peace settlement and over 58 percent disapproved of the United States using "all military strength necessary (short of nuclear weapons) to achieve victory in the war." This survey also indicated that UCC members no longer supported containment theory as it applied to Vietnam or the Cold War in general when a resounding 70 percent declared that the United States should not send troops to another part of the world if a parallel situation to Vietnam developed somewhere else.[22]

By 1967, the United Church of Christ General Synod buttressed other antiwar Americans and more forcefully denounced the Vietnam War. Those assembled ratified a resolution on "Justice and Peace in Vietnam" that criticized the United States, called for a negotiated cessation of hostilities, and warned of God's judgment if U.S. leaders failed to do so. Calling the United States a "colonial power," the resolution declared that "judgment will also fall upon those who, professing the high purposes of freedom and self-determination, frustrate these very purposes through destructive and cruel means." Delegates demanded that the United States work to negotiate a peaceful settlement, in particular by working through the United Nations and with the North Vietnamese. Importantly, the statement also criticized North Vietnam for blocking peace efforts and insisted that any settlement include "justice and security for the people of Vietnam." It also warned that judgment would "reckon with those who seek to impose their will through terror and violence and who seek to establish tyranny under the guise of 'wars of liberation.'" But the resolution aimed its harshest condemnation at its own country, stating that "in sorrow and in moral anguish, we seek now to give voïce to the church's witness to justice and peace in the present situation." In other words, this American church body felt most responsible for persuading its own government away from war. It therefore started the resolution with the warning that "God judges and will judge the guilt of men and nations for the tragedy of Vietnam." The UCC president, Reverend Ben M. Herbster, added his harsh condemnations to this resolution in his remarks to the General Synod. He blasted those who urged bombing without restraint in order to weaken North Vietnam, objecting that "this is no way toward peace." Reminding his audience of God's wrath against those who take up violence as a solution, he asserted that "arms proliferation is not the way to security; it is the way to death. Our Lord put the matter plainly: 'all who take the sword will perish by the sword.'" In short, Herbster attempted to influence UCC members toward an antiwar position when he stated that "war must be stopped, or our brothers and we shall all perish. It must be stopped now; war not only in Vietnam, but in Israel, in Korea, and in Southern Arabia."[23]

UCC clergy and lay people also criticized the war because it contained too much ambiguity and too many unanswered questions. Alan Geyer articulated part of this reasoning from his leadership position as director for international relations for the UCC Council of Christian Social Action. He carefully outlined the realities of the Vietnam War, the country's history, and the difficulty of fighting a guerrilla movement. This included a balanced account about the terror inflicted upon innocent people by revolutionary advocates, including North Vietnamese insurgents and the South Vietnamese opposed to their dictatorial government. Yet he continued by revealing that the oppressive nature of the Saigon regime exacerbated the problem and made it more difficult for the Vietnamese to choose a side. He then added that the United States shared blame for these war atrocities and explained that "the legitimacy of American intervention has been gravely sullied by publicity and propaganda concerning terror and torture, difficult as it is to prove direct American responsibility for them." In short, he questioned U.S. continued participation on behalf of a corrupt South Vietnamese government in the midst of a complicated revolution, thereby also questioning a 1950s-style Cold War attitude. Geyer, a moderate on the war at that time, demonstrates the thought process that pushed some Christians from an initial moderate position to a much more liberal antiwar stance by the 1970s. J. Stanley Stevens, associate editor of *Keeping You Posted*, the UCC publication for the Office of Communication, added his dislike for U.S. involvement to the denomination's antiwar advocacy: "Never was it more evident that we sorely need a set of national priorities. We use our power—almost without restraint—to carry on a most unpopular war against Southeast Asians, but we refuse to use that power to help the miserably poor and starving in our own country. We readily spend over *two* billion dollars a *month* in Vietnam, but we find it hard to spend *one* billion dollars a *year* for the relief of the poverty-stricken in our own country." Stevens therefore questioned the national priorities of the United States and called for an end to the war. Or, as a lay letter to the editor stated, American youth "were called to that area [Vietnam] to fight for what seems to be a very obscure and unexplained reason." He further wondered "where is the proof" that Americans died in Vietnam for the welfare of the United States? Unanswerable questions drove many UCC people to their antiwar position.[24]

Yet UCC antiwar advocates did more than discuss their position at denominational meetings or through church periodicals: they also acted against the war from the very beginning. This activism included protesting, peaceful demonstrations, and illegal actions, moves that the UCC took regarding other issues as well, such as civil rights. This activism stemmed in part from its theology of human improvement, which crafted the church's response to many issues, as its public forums and statements focused on protecting and valuing life above all else. At other times, this activism merely involved a lay person actively protesting the war without public demonstration or extreme behaviors. *United Church Herald* described one such means of protest when it detailed how a pastor's wife transformed "junk mail" from a nuisance into a peaceful weapon. She took stamped cards and envelopes from these mass mailings and mailed them with a request for the recipient to "urge the President and your Congressmen to: de-escalate, halt the bombings, stop defoliation, negotiate. . . . Stop killing and maiming our sons." Others took bolder steps. As noted above, some UCC clergy, such as Paul E. Gibbons, protested the draft by returning draft cards. His colleague, James L. Mengel, received a prison sentence for going a step further. He had participated in pouring blood on draft records to protest both the war and the selective service system. He offered the following as part of his explanation:

The action in Vietnam is drastic, calling for drastic action by concerned persons. Some call my involvement in the draft-card-bleed-in bizarre. I submit that the Vietnam policy of the United States and the "die-in's" are bizarre.

My blood is interchangeable with the blood of my brothers of any skin pigment in Vietnam. The senseless waste of their blood and lives is a deep concern of mine.[25]

We know a great deal about the antiwar movement during the Vietnam War. A prolific group of intellectuals, students, and liberal Americans united to protest U.S. involvement in Southeast Asia. And we know much about the Christian participation in this faction that came in the form of public protests by famous individuals such as the Berrigan brothers, as priests, and Reverend William Sloane Coffin Jr., as well as in the form of organizations challenging conservative opinion, such as the National Council of Churches of Christ and Clergy and Laity Concerned about Vietnam. Yet adding the Christians studied here enhances this knowledge. Using a theology of human improvement and worried about the plight of all people in Vietnam, liberal Christians crafted statements and argued against American involvement in Southeast Asia in order to stem the tide of war and stop the fighting. As with the left-leaning Christians studied by others, the more moderate to liberal Christians of this study contributed to the antiwar movement. Furthermore, they offer proof that some Christians dove into their antiwar activism the minute the war escalated in 1964, not after a period of studying it or because of revelations from the front of war atrocities: they felt from the beginning that the United States had entered into an unjust war in Vietnam. They also gave moderate Americans who wanted to protest the war a "safe" and traditional means of communicating their discontent. Instead of taking to the streets or publicly blasting the United States, they could support religious periodicals, leaders, and denominations that communicated their antiwar stance to national leaders, including the president. Ultimately, this voice adds to our knowledge about all of the varying groups who led to the slow but nonetheless successful antiwar movement.

A Middle Ground

Not all Americans fit into neat categories of U.S. policy supporters or Vietnam War denouncers. Christian America also offers a glimpse into the thoughts of many Americans who had variant opinions about the war or who changed their understanding of it over time. Studies have demonstrated that public opinion about the war evolved, from general support of it at the beginning to more and more unease over it by the end of the 1960s. Opinion polls in particular demonstrate as much. But these sources and studies seldom get into the fundamental reasons for this shift. Christian Americans contributed a religious voice to these conflicted attitudes about the Vietnam War during the 1960s and help us to better understand why and how this shifting took place.

Commonweal, the lay-published Catholic periodical, provides one such example. It adopted a moderate tone that at first backed U.S. policy in Vietnam but progressed toward an antiwar position by 1968. This shift mirrors that of the American population in general, which cautiously supported the war as necessary in 1964 but which became disillusioned as the war dragged on without resolution by 1968. In an editorial written immediately after the Tonkin Gulf incident, *Commonweal* offered its belief that Lyndon Johnson had acted with restraint but that some determined response was needed:

> Preserving the general peace and deterring the North Vietnamese and Chinese Communists clearly called here for more than a stern rebuke or a complaint to the United Nations. The President, too, has ably defined the nature of the retaliation and left the next step up to the enemy. He has taken pains to portray the U.S. response as carefully calculated and restrained.

The editors included in this statement all the hallmarks of the Cold War: trust in the government, fear of communism, and a belief in containment. Yet this surety had already begun to disintegrate by November, when former *Commonweal* editor William Pfaff wrote that the Vietnamese history of resistance to Western influence and civil war made it impossible for the United States to democratize that country completely. He also stated that this "does not discharge our responsibility" in Vietnam. Pfaff explained that the heart of the matter rested with the anti-imperialist bent of the Vietnamese, a factor that Americans could not reverse. But simultaneously he called for some action and presence, not yet willing to give up on this important region in the Cold War.[26]

By 1968 *Commonweal* called for peace. After Johnson stepped out of the presidential race and vowed to conclude his administration by focusing on peace negotiations with North Vietnam, editors stated that "it is a great tribute to Mr. Johnson that he recognized both the fact and the cause, and is stepping aside in the fashion he is—not vindictively, not schemingly, but with words on his lips of peace and love among men. More could be asked of no one." This statement solidified the editors' moderate approach taken throughout the 1960s regarding Vietnam; though they had moved toward desiring peace, they still believed that the president worked for the best interest of the nation. In contrast, the editors later blasted that "the main obstacle to the start of peace talks, however, seems to be the hawks in the Johnson Administration who cling to the pipe dream that a total military victory in Vietnam is possible." This unsigned editorial demonstrated that, despite a faith in Johnson, the strain of the war had taken away the editors' blind trust in American officials to do the right thing. Rather, they concluded that a military defeat of the Communists in Southeast Asia was impossible. This conflicted opinion continued even after Nixon's election in November, when editors supported a renewed bombing of North Vietnam in order to threaten the North Vietnamese back to the negotiating table, hardly a move toward peace. Yet they simultaneously criticized that the world would see this as the United States caving in to South Vietnam's wanting a continued war: "the bombing cannot resume without appearing to the world that the tail is wagging the dog. But isn't that the case anyway?"[27]

Commonweal's coverage of the 1968 election sent further mixed signals because editors repeatedly backed Democratic candidates who maintained a peace platform. Already in January, with Johnson still running for reelection, an editorial declared that "the moral outcry against the war grows everyday, and this is heartening. Secondly, the candidacy of the talented and capable

Senator McCarthy and the still weak rating of Mr. Johnson in the polls could conceivably force a reappraisal inside the Democratic party." Throughout the year, the periodical positioned the Vietnam War as a central election issue and only backed peace advocates. After Johnson withdrew from the election, an editorial called for Eugene McCarthy, the Minnesota senator who first threw his hat in the ring as a peace candidate, and Robert F. Kennedy, who had waited to enter the race on such a platform until he witnessed McCarthy's success, to cooperate and support each other if they truly wanted peace in Vietnam. The editors feared that otherwise they would split the peace vote and pave the way for a prowar Democrat or Republican. This concern included a fear of Hubert Humphrey, the eventual Democratic nominee, because "he cannot escape responsibility for his share in the Administration's mindless escalation in Vietnam, and the Democratic party cannot be allowed to imagine that those who want an end to the war will now support any candidate identified with Johnson policies." Editors were bipartisan in such fears, also worrying that Nixon's "pledges to end the war by negotiations—and also never to impose a coalition on Saigon" canceled each other out. *Commonweal* reflects an America in transition, from harsh Cold Warriors to antiwar advocates. Though without much linkage to its theological outlook, the periodical added a moderate Christian voice to Vietnam War deliberations.[28]

This same tone of moderation and mixed signals appeared in *U.S. Catholic*. But in contrast to the more secular message coming from *Commonweal*, *U.S. Catholic* framed its argument in religious terms. Executive editor Robert E. Burns lamented what the war did to the people of Vietnam, condemning the Communists, Vietcong, and Americans for atrocities and for putting innocent civilians in harm's way. He wondered if Americans ever thought about the simpler aspects of war, apart from "life or death, blood or peace," such as the education missed by an entire generation of children because violence raged around them daily. While not a position for or against the war, this contemplation by Burns showcased his wrestling with the moral issues wound up in the fighting. Burns was also acutely aware that the Catholic Church remained silent about the war. He criticized the National Conference of Catholic Bishops because the American body only considered the war "in the most general terms" at their 1968 meeting. While he acknowledged that the maintenance of collegiality prohibited a firm stance for or against U.S. policy, he blasted that this should not preclude a statement about the means used to fight the war: "Isn't it possible for a man to believe that our Vietnam policy itself is justified and at the same time oppose our use of napalm or anti-personnel bombs in areas where civilian and military personnel cannot be distinguished? Every Catholic schoolboy is taught that a good end does not justify an unjust means." As with *Commonweal*, Burns's struggle with the Vietnam War led to a relatively moderate position for *U.S. Catholic* that neither promoted nor entirely condemned the war.[29]

The Catholic World's journey to an antiwar position reflected the same trajectory of many Americans and embodied its moderate approach to secular affairs. Its 1964 coverage by and large indicated trust in the government's handling of the escalation and belief that it was necessary, but by 1968 editors and writers called for an end to the conflict on the basis of their continued analysis of the situation. A November 1964 article by the director of the Institute of Asian Studies at St. John's University in New York, Dr. Paul K. T. Sih, placed Southeast Asia in the midst of the Cold War and called for containing communism there. He explained that "thus far the advance of East Asian communism has been halted in Korea, Taiwan, and India. The crucial line of defense at the moment is southeast Asia. In Laos and Vietnam, the struggle has grown intense since the forces of Ho Chi-minh, backed by Red China, are infiltrating in increasing numbers to the south." His article contained key elements of traditional American Cold War fears, with a Communist giant puppeteering North Vietnam, unprovoked expansionism, and a subsequent advocacy for the U.S. goal of protecting South Vietnam. Coming on the heels of the 1950s and early 1960s, Sih's view paralleled the belief a majority of Americans had regarding communism and the slow drift toward war in Vietnam.[30]

A decidedly different position appeared by 1968 in *The Catholic World*. Four years of watching the United States support corrupt dictators in South Vietnam led editor John B. Sheerin to complain that the United States was "stubbornly obstructing a movement for social progress in Vietnam" by prosecuting a war on behalf of oppressive regimes. In addition to now questioning this U.S. approach, Sheerin felt that "an independent, pro-Marxist regime will emerge in Vietnam." Here, too, a changed Cold War viewpoint emerged when he described the Vietnamese as "independent," not as acting at the behest of Moscow or Peking. Sheerin's scrutiny of the first four years of fighting led him to exclaim that "the wisest course for us is to admit our 'massive miscalculation' and try to make the best of our future relationship with Marxist Vietnam." Importantly, this statement did not support Communist regimes or condemn the United States. Rather, his editorial laid out the reasons for his antiwar position based on his reading of the circumstances, a reading that no longer relied on traditional Cold War dogma. Donald J. Wolf, a research associate in political science at the Cambridge Center for Social Studies, made a more forceful statement on ending the war. Though he understood the argument that abandoning South Vietnamese allies imperiled them and did not want to see another Communist country in the world, he maintained that the present war "cannot be justified on political grounds; *therefore* it is immoral." He based this statement on the way the South Vietnamese government inflicted harm on too many innocent people. He concluded that "none of the means available to the United States in withdrawing from the war, regardless of which is chosen, would have consequences as evil as continuing the war, even a vastly de-escalated war." As with many of its Christian counterparts, *The Catholic World*'s coming out against the war rested primarily on secular, political grounds. Yet those grounds contained a moral element that led to this position's appearance in a religious periodical.[31]

Evidence from the Southern Baptist Convention annual assemblies indicates a conflicted opinion for some in that denomination, too, despite SBC leaders from the prowar and antiwar sides trying to sway members. Starting with the 1966 national convention, the SBC each year passed a resolution that at least indirectly related to the Vietnam War. In each case, the convention issued rather benign statements that grieved the war but tacitly supported the U.S. government. The 1966 "Resolution Concerning Peace" demonstrates how the SBC made generic comments that neither overtly supported nor condemned the war: "Let us here call Baptists and fellow Christians throughout our land to renewed prayer for our American troops, for their loved ones, for our enemies, and for world leaders, that they may somehow be led of God together to find the high and honorable road to peace and gain together the wisdom and courage to walk it." This ambiguity stemmed most likely from staunch local congregational control, which made it difficult for the national body to make controversial statements. By 1967, however, Southern Baptist Convention messengers had grown weary of how many Americans spoke against the government and thus included in another peace resolution the statement that "we assure our duly elected leaders in government that we support them in developing strong and wise policies [and] in pursuing a just peace in Vietnam." While this was not a prowar statement, trusting the government in this case certainly offered a tacit support for the ongoing conflict. However, as Americans came to question the war more and more by 1968, so the Southern Baptist annual meeting applauded efforts toward peace, including the use of the United Nations, a strategy other conservative, prowar Americans disliked. Collectively, though generic in nature, these resolutions reveal that Southern Baptist Convention members trusted the government to pursue a Vietnam policy that was best for the nation.[32]

The African Methodist Episcopal Church took a middle ground about the Vietnam War as well. The AME's principle newspaper, the *Christian Recorder*, and the General Conference's responses to Lyndon B. Johnson's presidency demonstrate this complexity. As we saw in regard to the AME reaction to the Cold War, African American groups, both Christian and secular, hesitated before questioning an administration that had done more than any other in U.S. history to assist with civil rights. A denomination founded because of the social justice issue of race did not want to antagonize the president, who did much to better the protection against racism in America by marshalling civil rights legislation through Congress and then signing it into law. The *Christian Recorder* published a letter that Lionel H. Newsom sent to President Johnson in November 1967 expressing just this point. After a few African American leaders, including the Reverend Dr. Martin Luther King Jr., came out against the Vietnam War, Newsom wrote that "this letter of deep appreciation for all you have done to make our nation a true democracy is far overdue. It appears a bit ironic that the one President who has done more for Negro Americans would be attacked by several of their leaders." Though the periodical in general avoided such direct stances, Newsom later wrote that he supported the Vietnam War because he backed the president. *Christian Recorder* editor B. J. Nolen took a more cautious approach that nonetheless mirrored this line of thinking: "President Johnson seeks peace in America and in the world, and suffers possibly many unfair incriminations for his efforts. Peace is a slippery eel. When you think it is, it ain't."[33]

A similar tone appeared at the national gathering of AME members in 1968. Bishop H. Thomas Primm presented a proposal to send a telegram on behalf of the 38th Session of the General Conference, an action that the assembly passed. The telegram was sent, "congratulating him [LBJ] for accepting the invitation to Paris for Peace Talks, and asking him to use all his energies to bring an end to the war." Like Nolen's, the statement neither condoned nor condemned the war. Rather, it offered support for Johnson as he embarked on his goal of ending the Vietnam War through negotiation. Even the scholarly *A.M.E. Church Review* pointed out that the former director of the United States Information Agency, Carol Rowan, stated that Martin Luther King Jr.'s antiwar platform would produce "murmurings" that were "powerfully hostile reactions" because of American anticommunism. Newsom, Nolen, Primm, and the *A.M.E. Church Review* squared with the opinion of many civil rights leaders in this regard. Indeed, King's crusade against the war earned him the enmity of previous supporters and civil rights activists within the black community who publicly trusted the president in all of his decisions because he had supported them. As race became more and more a part of the Vietnam War conversation because African Americans disproportionately fought the war during the 1960s, this tension became more evident. But for the AME, the hope for better race relations in the nation trumped protesting the war.[34]

Other evidence indicates that the African Methodist Episcopal Church cannot be labeled as prowar, either. In a comment about civil rights, rioting in America, Vietnam, and global tension, one commentator demanded that everyone work harder to make the world a better place for young people, who "did not make the world they live in; they inherited it from us." This statement included a call to work for peace. Though generic, it hardly places the AME in a prowar camp. *Christian Recorder* also printed material that defended pacifists because the World Council of Churches, to which the AME belonged, stated that "pacifists cannot be called cowards or disobedient to the commands of Christ." Here, the social justice stance of the denomination came to the fore, in advocating for respect of all points of view, regardless of one's own.[35]

If anything, the AME struggled to understand these mixed messages in the context of the larger and global Cold War, in which the denomination supported U.S. policy. At the 138th Annual Conference of the Indiana District, a report on the state of the country explained this dilemma. After listing the Vietnam War, the Soviet invasion of Czechoslovakia in 1968, and other hot spots around the world, this committee stated that "all of these events in distant lands take their tragic toll on the state of our nation. The millions of dollars spent on death and destruction and the maintaining of the 'balance of power' drastically curtail programs designed to elevate our own problems here in America." In other words, the cost of global security hindered social welfare programs in the United States that the committee supported. The cost of lives also alarmed the committee members: "Each year our young men march off to war, many of whom never to see their loved ones again." Yet despite these general condemnations, the report simply outlined these factors without explicitly calling for an end to the Vietnam War. Rather, it cried in the wilderness for change from all nations involved. *Christian Recorder* editor B. J. Nolen added his voice to this vague pondering, stating that "even the past World Wars did not bestir man nearly as much as the Vietnam war does these days. The far off battlefields of North and South Vietnam have frustrated the world no end. The young people of the world are now expressing a deep horror for the battlefields of the world." Like his Indiana colleagues, Nolen contemplated global war and its meaning for Americans without offering solutions or a direction to follow.[36]

This cautious approach also characterized the way most people in the AME discussed the home-front debate regarding the Vietnam War throughout 1968. In articles, reports, and motions, the denomination supported freedom of speech and the right of dissent without specifically placing itself amidst the fray. Karl A. Olsson wrote such an article for the *Christian Recorder*. In a careful deliberation that neither supported nor condemned the war, Olsson deplored the treatment of returning soldiers, who too often faced harassment from their nonmilitary peers, and at the same time explained that the United States had always had citizens question its involvement in war. Stating that this hardly developed because of the Vietnam War, he wanted readers to accept such controversy without dismissing the protesters out of hand. Yet he also quoted the Bible and Paul's admonition for people to obey authority. Olsson accepted debate as an important American tradition but disliked physical confrontations with soldiers who followed the dictates of their country and wanted demonstrations to take place within the confines of the law. Olsson found an analogous voice in the 1968 Michigan Annual Conference. The Committee on the State of the Country explained to delegates that "our Constitution protects the right of protest and dissent within broad limits whether in Detroit or to oppose the war in Vietnam. Despite the limits which the requirements of an ordered society impose, the protected weapons of protest, dissent, criticism, and peaceable assembly are enormously powerful." Again without endorsing one side over the other and reflecting what many Americans felt, this conference applauded the debate about the war as important for the United States.[37]

We already know that Americans were conflicted about the Vietnam War during the 1960s. Exploring these religious voices helps us to understand what led to their opinions, and what forced change over time. For these Americans, Christian convictions informed their thinking and altered their perceptions of the Vietnam War. Gaining a better grasp about what this middle group articulated and why helps us better comprehend all of the forces at play in the midst of America's cultural deliberation over the Vietnam War.

Missionaries and Vietnamese Points of View

These more generic discussions became more powerful when Christian Americans added to them first-hand accounts about the Vietnam War. As with missionary reporting from other parts of the globe, some Christians had access to knowledge unavailable to most Americans, when missionaries and other Christians "on the ground" in Vietnam reported personal stories and eyewitness accounts to their colleagues in America. This information intensified opinions for both those who supported American policy and those opposed to it.

Nothing solidified *Christianity Today*'s backing of the Vietnam War because of its Christian convictions better than the eyewitness accounts from missionaries. Such a pragmatic concern tells us something that we have not before learned about the Americans who supported U.S. involvement in Southeast Asia. The periodical reported regularly on mission efforts throughout the world and the importance of evangelical outreach to Christians everywhere. Missionaries believed that they lived a theology of saving people from eternal damnation by bringing the message of Christ to them, a Christian's responsibility according to many evangelicals. Although war disrupted this task and went against Christian ideals, for editors and writers the actual deeds of Communists against believers doing God's work led them to support the Vietnam War. Discussing conditions throughout Asia, editors decried the fact that missionary observers had "found scant ground for optimism. Not only has one-third of the globe fallen under Red banners, but Christians in Asia are outnumbered and outfought in the greatest onslaught since the Muslims wiped out Christianity in North Africa thirteen centuries ago." Evidence from missionaries in Vietnam added to this perception. War-torn areas often led indigenous people to missionary outreach because they sought asylum, shelter, food, or a message of hope amidst despair. It therefore sounded encouraging when Dr. Kenneth C. Fraser, vice-president of the Christian and Missionary Alliance, stated in 1964 that five new churches had been built recently despite the war. But the threat of violence from Communist forces tempered this enthusiasm, as demonstrated by a 1968 attack on a mission compound in Ban Eke Thuot, 150 miles east of Saigon. During the Tet Offensive, *Christianity Today* stated that a Vietcong attack killed six missionaries when they bombed the center and nearby homes. Horror stories intensified readers' already solid fear of Communists: after the night assault, "when daylight broke, the two men [missionaries] decided they would appeal to the Viet Cong to get Carolyn [a 41-year-old missionary] to a hospital. They were shot dead on the spot." Carolyn Griswold later died, too. Such stories entrenched the periodical and its readers in their theological grounds for opposing the Communists in Vietnam and pushed them toward greater support for the American war effort.[38]

Much like *Christianity Today*, writers for the conservative Catholic *America* grounded their position in information coming from the church in Vietnam. Associate editor John McLaughlin, S.J., made this case in a column that detailed the Catholic Church's struggles under Communist regimes. As he explained, "Many of the Jesuits now living in Saigon have seen the Communists at close range, chiefly in China, where they lived until their expulsion." This referred to the fact that the People's Republic of China had expelled hundreds of Christians from the mainland when they took over, including Catholic missionaries and priests. Those allowed to remain in China saw the church's power hindered by the government, religious freedom stripped from society, and an attempt by authorities to hand pick Catholic leaders instead of allowing the Vatican to do so. McLaughlin further explained that these priests and Catholics who had fled to Vietnam now wanted a stronger effort by the United States to win the war because "no other way will work with the Communists." Additionally, McLaughlin had traveled to Vietnam and there met with a group of approximately twenty U.S. Air Force Catholic chaplains, who shared the opinion that only a war could protect the church in Vietnam because the Vietnamese Communists would force it underground, as had the Chinese. They described to him the terrorist tactics of the Vietcong and the horror of holding young soldiers as they died. McLaughlin and these chaplains regarded the Communists as responsible and backed the U.S. effort in order to safeguard Christianity, and specifically the Catholic Church, in Vietnam. While one may question the narrow view of blaming the Communists entirely, it is also crucial to understand that the motivation for *America* in supporting the Vietnam War went well beyond blind jingoism.[39]

Missionaries in Vietnam steered many opinions toward a hostile attitude about communism within the Southern Baptist Convention, too. The SBC began mission work in Vietnam in 1959 amidst increased U.S. support for the Diem regime, a presence they maintained throughout the Vietnam War despite the danger faced daily by those in remote locations as far away as along the border to North Vietnam. They focused on humanitarian endeavors and converting the Vietnamese people to Christianity. But in the process, they came to fear what communism would mean for that region if North Vietnam won the war. Most comments that made their way back to America by those serving in Southeast Asia firmly backed the United States and contained a mixture of politics and Christianity, expressing fear about the possible loss of democracy and at the same time knowledge that communism would doom their conversion efforts. James F. Humphries went so far as to declare that "we are willing to give our lives alongside American servicemen if necessary to guarantee" freedom for South Vietnam. Freedom to him meant the current South Vietnamese government. Humphries knew the danger communism posed, which therefore caused this strong stance.

The domino theory played into his thinking as well: "Without American help, Communism will take this country, Asia and the rest of the world." The call to carry the Gospel around the world also factored into SBC opinions. The treasurer for the Southern Baptist Mission in Vietnam, Herman Hayes, explained that "if we left we would be saying these people do not need the Gospel. When Communists take over, the privilege of preaching the Gospel ends." For SBC missions, communism mixed church and state together with its atheist stance, therefore requiring the same from Americans. For many, the late 1960s intensified these prowar feelings, as missionaries experienced Communist raids and offensives.[40]

Christian Americans who had mixed or changing opinions about the Vietnam War, such as *Commonweal*, used information from Vietnamese Christians to inform their opinion, too. The Catholic Church had the longest-standing and most permanent Christian presence in Vietnam. The first American-backed regime in South Vietnam under Ngo Dinh Diem had close ties to the church because of his own Catholic faith, and France's domination of the region had brought the Catholic Church with it. As the war heated up in September 1964 and Nguyen Khanh consolidated power with U.S. backing, the periodical pushed for America to protect the Catholic minority in Vietnam. This, in part, explained its early acceptance of Johnson's Vietnam policy. Editors wanted the United States "to press for some parallel concern for the Catholics and other Vietnamese who have been the victims of Buddhist aggression" now that protection for that group had been allegedly gained. Even after editors had by and large come to question U.S. involvement in Vietnam, the Catholic Church there continued to give them pause. They knew, for example, that North Vietnam had moved against its Catholic citizens and outlawed many religious practices. The journal therefore asked Christians throughout the world to remember fellow believers inside Vietnam and "acknowledge the Church in Vietnam as very much alive; on the other hand, they must do all in their power to pursue dialogue with Communism, giving praise where praise is due, and criticizing where there are faults." Here, too, *Commonweal's* moderate tone came to the fore; while pointing out the damage done to the church in Vietnam, editors simultaneously asked for cooperation with Communists in order to keep open avenues of communication with Catholics there. The Catholic Church's presence in Vietnam clearly complicated the issues for *Commonweal*. Though it gradually came out against the war, protection of the church and its members weighed heavily in editorial thinking.[41]

Liberal Christians also used such first-hand accounts to inform their antiwar opinions. The *Christian Century* based its moral outrage against U.S. actions in Vietnam on reports from Vietnamese people. This inclusion paralleled the journal's more worldly outlook about all issues, making sure that the most important viewpoint, the Vietnamese, played into editorial positions. For example, a 1968 editorial reported on the visit of the Buddhist poet-monk Thich Nhat Hanh. He toured the United States under the auspices of the Fellowship of Reconciliation, often grounding his comments in the opinions of Vietnamese peasants who, he explained, were neither Communist nor anti-Communist but rather "pro-Vietnamese." Hanh insisted that no outside force "can win a military victory in Vietnam unless it has the support of the peasantry. He [Hanh] points out that just now the Vietcong garner most of that support, not because of the arguments of the Communist core leadership . . . but because the people see in it the one champion of independence." His outlook mattered to the editors, who made it a central platform of their antiwar position. The periodical also published articles by Tran Van Danh, a journalist representative in the United States and Canada of the Vietnamese Overseas Buddhist Association. In response to the Tet Offensive, for example, he wrote that

> for at least six hours on the New Year of the Monkey (1968), South Vietnam was in fact liberated. For six hours, American power was imperiled. And in those six hours the "bourgeois gentlemen" of Saigon, for too long corrupted by U.S. money, woke up to the realities of their country. They saw for the first time the face of their liberators, the peasants of Vietnam.

Once again, a Vietnamese voice castigated the United States and demonstrated internal hostility to its presence in Vietnam. *Christian Century* editors therefore drew on this insider information to formulate further their antiwar position.[42]

Americans relied on a myriad of sources when formulating their opinions about the Vietnam War. Christian institutions had first-hand knowledge from which to draw because of the Christian presence in Vietnam in the form of missionaries, the Catholic Church, and other eyewitness accounts.

Conclusion

Christian America's opinions about the Cold War lay at the heart of their disagreements about the Vietnam War. Conservative Christians maintained a traditional Cold War fear of all things Communist and therefore supported the Vietnam War as necessary for stopping Communist expansion. *Christianity Today, America*, and *Catholic Digest* published material expressing these views, and found parallel thinking among many people in the Southern Baptist Convention. Yet too few studies have included an analysis of what led them to this position, thereby giving us an incomplete picture of American society's view of the war from a conservative perspective during the 1960s. A strong antiwar voice came from the *Christian Century, U.S. Catholic*, and the United Church of Christ, institutions that denounced the Vietnam War from the very beginning because they had already cast aside any faith in the domino theory. Whereas most histories of the antiwar movement in relationship to the general American population indicate a slow shift against the war during the 1960s, these Christians denounced it at once, joining their liberal Christian colleagues from other organizations that had been blasting U.S. foreign policy since the 1950s, and jumped into the antiwar fray immediately in 1964. Still other entities saw mixed opinions or slowly altered ones regarding Vietnam in the 1960s. The African Methodist Episcopal Church at times questioned the war but shied away from any dogmatic denunciation for fear of alienating President Johnson and thereby undercutting his support for the civil rights movement. *Commonweal* and *Catholic World* cautiously backed U.S. involvement in Vietnam at the beginning but were persuaded by antiwar voices and the events in Southeast Asia by 1968 to turn against it. Christian reactions to Vietnam in the 1960s, in other words, present a very complicated picture, one that mirrors the rest of American society.

Their views of the Vietnam War contained both secular opinions that seldom related to theology and, ironically, at the same time deeply imbedded positions that related to their faith and history. In order to more completely understand both church history and American popular opinion during the 1960s, this analysis of Christian America's involvement in this culture war provides a glimpse into what motivated people both secularly and religiously to view the Vietnam War the way they did. Christianity spoke with an impassioned voice throughout the 1960s regarding the Vietnam War specifically and foreign policy generally, a fact that persisted into the 1970s. Without taking to the streets or going beyond traditional means of voicing their opinions, Christians of every stance regarding Vietnam contributed to the national conversation about the war. And their faith was central to this discussion. Christianity played a vital role in shaping public opinion in all of its manifestations, and in reflecting how and why Americans felt the way they did about the war.

Christianity Confronts Cold War Nixon Policies, 1969–1973

Introduction

In June 1970, messengers to the Southern Baptist Convention's annual gathering signaled a continued conservatism in their foreign policy outlook. Coming at the end of a violent few years in U.S. history, with the assassination of leaders such as Malcolm X, Martin Luther King Jr., and Robert Kennedy, urban rioting and burning, the eruption of Chicago during the 1968 Democratic National Convention, and antiwar protests that met with prowar demonstrators and turned into brawls, this convention offered messengers a chance to articulate their view of the problems to the rest of the nation. Though it allowed for the possibility of "dissent when it is done in an orderly manner," the SBC's "Resolution on Extremism" found daily evidence in America of "internal destruction and violence" and worried that this domestic risk weakened the nation to the point that adversaries could damage it. Messengers therefore voted to urge the president of the United States to continue working toward peace and "to contain radical extremists as well as the encroachment of conspiratorial communism at home and abroad." Communism was still viewed as an expansionist force, and they trusted their president to maintain vigilance against it. Delegates to the 1971 United Church of Christ General Synod disagreed. Instead of a world full of Communists, they saw a dangerous arms race and demanded that the United States do more to reduce global tension. They resolved that the United Church of Christ "develop public understanding of the issues of arms limitation and of proposals of disarmament, so that support may be engendered for the Strategic Arms Limitation Treaty talks and other disarmament efforts." The General Synod also blasted the excessive amount of U.S. military spending. In "deploring the excessive military budgets of the past decade," it implored its constituency and the government itself "to urge consideration of alternative budgets that reduce U.S. military budgets by as much as one half, and emphasize the conversion for peaceful development of the U.S. economy." The conservatism of the Nixon administration sent these liberal Christians on a crusade to end the decades-old military buildup that had occurred under the auspices of the Cold War.[1]

The 1970s ushered in a new president, reduced tension between the United States and Communist giants, and simultaneously continued Cold War anticommunism and fears. And once again American Christians commented on the world around them from both secular and religious points of view. The schizophrenic nature of U.S. foreign policy—from détente on the one hand to a continuation of the Vietnam War and persistent efforts to stop "the spread of communism" on the other hand—meant that Christians had to grapple anew with the Cold War and American diplomacy. As with the 1960s reaction to both the Cold and Vietnam wars, these opinions most often squared with the historical legacy of their given publication or denomination with respect to both secular and theological understandings of the world. Their positions provide a glimpse into the passionate and articulate voice of Christian America regarding foreign relations and, at the same time, demonstrate that the mixed opinions probably muted the overall Christian influence within the culture war because of this very diversity, despite ardent attempts to shape public opinion.

Christian Americans still had plenty of topics to address when it came to communism and religion during this decade. Throughout the world, Communist governments continued to attack religion when they came to power. This included Soviet suppression of Baptist dissent, monitoring of the Russian Orthodox Church, and a crackdown on church bodies in satellite nations if they worked against the Communist government. The People's Republic of China, too, persisted with religious persecution. This manifested itself most prominently during the late 1960s/early 1970s in the Cultural Revolution, when thousands of young people marauded throughout China claiming to purify the nation by eliminating institutions of higher learning and any remaining signs of religious faith. While the harshest and most extreme moments of the Cultural Revolution had dissipated by the early 1970s, the suspicion against religious belief continued and the state maintained laws against organized churches. Refugees from a variety of Communist nations gave first-hand testimony to the plight they faced if discovered worshipping or even reading a religious tract or the Bible. Revolutions throughout the world, especially in Asia, Africa, and Latin America, further provoked this continued Cold War fear; Communist movements everywhere attacked the church as part of the establishment and therefore alarmed Christians in the United States.

Yet reactions indicate that Christians did not all see this Communist threat in the same way. Previous examinations of the post–World War II Christian community have revealed a majority opinion in favor of U.S. Cold War policy. This approval included a mixing of civic and religious elements and hostility to communism everywhere. However, this patriotic faith began to fractionalize by the 1960s, as we have seen, and broke apart completely by the 1970s. When Richard M. Nixon became president in 1969, he implemented his own brand of foreign policy that played into this debate. For example, he earnestly championed his negotiating with the Soviet Union over the arms race with the Strategic Arms Limitation Treaties. In November 1969, the United States and Soviet Union began a series of meetings to limit the military buildup by both nations. SALT I, signed in May 1972, limited antiballistic missile sites and froze ICBMs (intercontinental ballistic missiles) and SLBMs (submarine-launched ballistic missiles) to their current levels. However, it failed to address other areas of concern, such as long-range bombers or the development of new weapons. Negotiations for SALT II began soon thereafter but did not reach an agreement until 1977. Liberal Christians applauded Nixon's efforts with the SALT talks but felt that they did not go far enough since they allowed for too many loopholes. Conservatives examined them cautiously, afraid of any compromise with communism. Many others stood somewhere in between, with a fear of the USSR but hope that such diplomatic ties really could bring world peace. Clearly, the dominant Christian voice of support for the government from the 1950s had given way to a diversity of Christian opinions by the 1970s.

Nixon's emphasis on détente further pulled Christian Americans into the foreign relations arena, with its promise to reduce tension between the United States and the Union of Soviet Socialist Republics and the People's Republic of China. Nixon and historians often cite these efforts as his diplomatic triumph, especially visits to both Moscow and Peking. In addition to opening a crucial dialogue, the United States shipped grain to the Soviet Union during the early 1970s because of famine and paved the way for the PRC's entry into the United Nations, after having blocked the Communist government since its inception in 1949 in favor of the exiled Chiang Kai-shek regime. On the one hand, Nixon deserves credit for this initiative; on the other hand, the USSR and PRC had just as much to do with it, and Nixon's motivation was not completely altruistic. In part, he used the friendlier relations with both nations to drive a wedge between them. The USSR and PRC had held enmity toward one another since the PRC's creation, including a border dispute and disagreement over who truly led global communism. Knowing that each side would distrust the other's relationship with the United States, Nixon and his security advisor and later secretary of state, Henry Kissinger, manipulated détente to highlight this division with the hope that it weakened the Communist world. Christian America had a variety of reactions to this strategy. Some applauded it, some disliked its Machiavellian nature, and still others worried that Nixon did not do enough to demand religious liberty within the Communist countries during his visits.

Current understandings of church life during the 1970s reflect precious little about how Christians viewed foreign policy. It is true that they had other concerns with which to contend during this time. Mainline Protestant denominations dealt with a decline in membership and focused a lot of energy on ecumenism, evangelical fundamentalists spent a great deal of energy mobilizing to enter the political realm through grassroots initiatives, and the Catholic Church continued to implement, argue about, and respond to Vatican II. The emergence of religious pluralism in America meant that there was much in the religious world to draw attention away from international affairs. The swirl of activity from the 1960s, including protests, intense scrutiny of foreign policy, and a constant mantra about the state of the world, had died down somewhat by the 1970s. Christian voices tended to focus less commentary on Cold War issues than they had just a few years earlier. But they *did* articulate their opinions and helped to reflect and shape American perceptions by framing them in the context of both their heritage and current theological outlooks.

Patriotic Faith

Conservative Christians during the 1970s still clung to their opposition to all things Communist and focused on repression of religious belief around the world in support of their position. With a more conservative and Republican president in office, they supported official U.S. hostility toward the Communist world and applauded Richard Nixon as firm but reasonable, given his efforts toward détente. In other words, Communists were unreasonable and dangerous, while the United States represented God's will, leading conservative Christians to a patriotic faith in their country. The noted scholar and activist for religious freedom in America, T. Jeremy Gunn, has described this factor as government theism, or the notion that the United States represents God's will. A study of conservative Christians during the 1970s solidifies Gunn's thesis.[2]

For *Christianity Today*, news about Europe solidified its anti-Communist leanings, especially when this news collided with its theology of outreach and proselytizing. Editor-at-large Carl F. H. Henry reported in February 1972 about conditions in Eastern Europe, where Communist governments had stifled religion for a number of years. Yet he found hope because "young people are said to be more open now than in past years because of the continuing vacuum left by atheistic Communism in the lives of the masses." He was especially thankful that "Communism has failed to eradicate religion—not surprisingly so, in view of man's created nature and the inability of material things to satisfy his spiritual needs." Henry saw in this continued yearning for spiritual guidance proof of the Holy Spirit's persistent influence on the world and wanted evangelicals to participate in spreading this message. This did not, however, alleviate his fear of Communist tyranny, especially against religion, and so he reminded readers that "not only does it aggressively propagandize against Christianity, but it discriminates against those who align themselves with the churches by depriving them of managerial posts and by limiting university opportunities for their children." *Christianity Today* further emphasized this mixture of anticommunism with evangelical hope in an interview with Dr. B. P. Dotsenko, a top Soviet nuclear scientist who converted to Christianity and in 1973 taught at Waterloo Lutheran University in Canada. A Mennonite, Dotsenko in his interview sounded the refrain of Communist brainwashing against religion that gave way to a longing for religion when the Communist ideology failed to manifest a more perfect society. Dotsenko stated that the lessons of Christianity "sank deeply. . . . The Great Commandment spoken by Jesus somehow frightened me. If these words were true, then all the teaching of Communism was false from the roots." *Christianity Today*'s persistent anticommunism during the 1970s cannot be understood unless placed in the context of its evangelical outreach. Salvation for humanity rested in spreading the Gospel, and communism's oppression of religion hindered these efforts. Not surprisingly, its coverage of global communism therefore contained this mix of fear about the ideology and evidence of Christ's continued triumph over it. And in claiming Christ for their point of view, editors wanted to sway public opinion toward its foreign policy outlook.[3]

According to *Christianity Today*, the Soviet Union still lay at the heart of communism's atheist worldview. Despite reduced tension with this Communist superpower under Richard M. Nixon's administration, the periodical blasted the USSR and called for vigilance against it. Here, too, a mixture of Christian hope mingled with outright fear tactics. Edward E. Plowman, the periodical's news editors, demonstrated this dichotomy when he explained that "after more than fifty years of atheistic indoctrination and outright harassment, religion hasn't gone away as Lenin predicted it would. Indeed, evidence indicates a recent upsurge in spiritual activity." But Plowman also warned of communism's campaign against faith. Here he and other editors described a holy war without naming it as such: their comments in support of U.S. policy came more from their concern about the inability to Christianize the Soviet Union and other Communist nations than from concern about governments. This stands to reason, coming from a Christian periodical; yet it revealed in their thinking a religious war against communism being waged by the periodical and by the United States. In other words, it exposes their belief in a government theism, where they championed a United States that fought on behalf of God, not just the American people. Associate editor David E. Kucharsky explained that "to be sure, thousands of churches are open every Sunday all across the Soviet Union. Many are crowded. But the Communist authorities enforce strict regulations against evangelism and Christian education. Those elements are indispensable to a virile church." The church persisted underground, the state combated it, and *Christianity Today* thereby commingled international relations, politics, and religion in its pages to convey a patriotic backing of U.S. policy.[4]

In fact, *any* religious repression concerned the periodical. The Soviet Union had gone after Russian Jews from the very beginning, imprisoning them on false charges, closing their businesses, and outlawing Jewish religious customs, such as the baking of matzoh for Passover. When the Soviets heavily taxed Jewish citizens attempting to flee the country in order to stem their outward flow, the world Jewish community reacted with shock and mobilized a campaign against these oppressive tactics. This activism inspired Christians who disdained Communist oppression of religion, too. Backing the American Jewish Congress's call for Congress to halt preferential trade status with the Soviet Union until they reduced this taxation, *Christianity Today* denounced the Soviets: "Communists may despise the capitalistic money economy, but anyone who has ever tried to travel in the U.S.S.R. or to engage in any financial transactions with a Soviet-bloc trade partner knows that Communists love capitalistic hard currency and will resort to almost any expedient to acquire it. Thus the astronomical exit tax on departing Jews." The lines between theology and politics, even between *Christianity Today* and U.S. policy, had completely blurred because of religious oppression in the Soviet Union.[5]

And the Soviet Union did not stand alone in *Christianity Today's* criticism, as the People's Republic of China (PRC) received the same treatment. At times, the periodical sounded the familiar refrain of anticommunism and the danger that the government posed to its citizens without a specific reference to religion. Having questioned the admittance of the PRC into the United Nations, for example, editors watched for opportunities to demonstrate the hypocrisy of Red China's behavior after being admitted by the early 1970s under Richard M. Nixon's spirit of détente, a strategy he hoped would further factionalize the Communist world. Editors pointed out Chinese anti-democratic tactics when the PRC, now able to veto UN actions as a member of the Security Council, in 1972 blocked the admittance of Bangladesh as a member nation. In 1971, Bengalis in East Pakistan declared an independent nation of Bangladesh, having rebelled against the military dictatorship of West Pakistan. The Pakistani government, supported by the United States because of bases in that nation from which the United States flew spy planes over the Soviet Union, slaughtered many of the insurgents, while India, after recently signing a friendship treaty with the Soviets, intervened on behalf of the rebels, who eventually won. The PRC backed West Pakistan with economic and military aid, though it privately cautioned that the repressive military action West Pakistan took doomed its efforts and publicly never spoke against the Bangladesh independence forces, which would have countered Chinese Communist ideology. China's reasons for this middle ground were complex: they concerned a fear of Soviet intervention in Asia that might lead to actions in Tibet and consternation about the possibility of Indian dominance in Southeast Asia and its subsequent alliance with Pakistan, a U.S. ally that further played into détente with America. Blocking the UN admittance of Bangladesh played out this knotted foreign policy. Bangladesh was not admitted into the United Nations until 1974, when circumstances had changed profoundly. So China's blocking of Bangladesh's admittance in 1972 prompted *Christianity Today* editors to write that they found it "ironic that mainland China's first veto in the United Nations should be used to keep out the newly independent nation of Bangladesh. One should think that a government that for so long considered itself—not without reason—unfairly deprived of international recognition would be among the leaders in backing Bangladesh." Revealing their reason for caution about the PRC as well as the USSR, the evangelical periodical maintained its Cold War hostility toward international communism in the messages it delivered to readers.[6]

As with the Soviet Union, proof of religious oppression in China that defied *Christianity Today*'s Christian calling particularly rankled editors. Carl F. H. Henry once again outlined much of this reasoning for readers. The editor-at-large described China as it existed in 1972, devoid of religious life because of the 1960s Cultural Revolution. He wrote how guards had burned

Bibles, destroyed institutional churches, and converted Christian buildings into museums and political centers. The Cultural Revolution had maintained a hostility toward religion into the 1970s, thus making the PRC an enemy of Christianity. But again paralleling treatment of the Soviet Union, Henry stated that "although no visible church remains, mainland China indubitably shelters an invisible church"; Christians "are at best an isolated, harassed, and lonely remnant, deprived of corporate community and witness. But they attest the inability of Communism to satisfy all the needs of man. Jesus Christ remains an incomparable treasure for multitudes who would rather risk their bodies than lose their souls." His statement contained all the hallmarks of Cold War holy war: a dangerous enemy, an atheistic threat, and the yearning for deeper religious meaning that kept the Christian spirit alive. Of course, this viewpoint tacitly assumed that the United States embodied the opposite spirit, as a Christian nation struggling to protect religious freedom around the globe. The very next month, Henry returned to a doom and gloom attitude in reporting on Christian evangelical believers who fled China and described scant religious faith there, a dictatorial state that imprisoned those who openly believed, and a scarce number of churches anywhere. The People's Republic of China pursued its atheistic agenda, thereby squashing Christian belief and driving it underground. This policy diametrically opposed the calling of the evangelical magazine to spread the word of God, thus making the two natural enemies. *Christianity Today* combated its opponent through its printed word and by articulating a faith in government theism on behalf of the United States.[7]

Depicting something perceived as even more dangerous, Dick Hillis wrote an article for *Christianity Today* that described the worship of Mao Zedong that had supplanted all other faiths in the People's Republic of China. This reverence for Mao moved the nation in evangelical eyes toward a more dangerous idolatry than even atheism. Hillis was the director of Overseas Crusades, an organization he founded in 1950 after serving as a missionary to China since 1933 and being expelled during the Communist takeover. His article meticulously detailed the crimes of Mao's regime, the innocent people killed and imprisoned, and the danger of communism. It focused much of its attention on atheism and the state's campaign against the church. But Hillis found most alarming the fact that "the largest political party in the world has set out to deify him. He is the only god that millions of people have ever known." He detailed how Mao's image appeared throughout the nation and how people were forced to thank him for food, shelter, and clothing. Hillis's most pessimistic assessment of this situation came in the only response he knew was available to *Christianity Today* readers: prayer. He explained that prayer "may be 'the most' you can do, for prayer is the greatest weapon God has entrusted to man." Hillis solidified for readers the PRC's danger: not only did it oppress religion and eliminate missionaries, but it attempted to create a new worship of Chairman Mao that undermined everything evangelicals believed.[8]

The Jesuit *America* added a Catholic voice to this conservative backing of a patriotic faith. If anything, 1970s world conditions confirmed for the periodical that its traditional Cold War outlook should not change. When the Bangladesh revolution commenced, editors insisted that the Chinese had supplied arms to the revolutionaries and fomented the entire episode, despite evidence now pointing to the fact that it was an internal independence movement. Even the Sino-Soviet feud played into *America*'s faith in Communist expansionism; its reports highlighted that the two superpowers collided over which nation could best lead this global initiative. Where other Americans used the dispute to debunk the myth of a Communist monolith, the conservative Catholic periodical reported on a *Pravda* article, in which the Soviets pointed out that the PRC sought "to dominate Asia," to prove the persistence of expansionism. The editorial stated that "Peking's bid to seize the ideological hegemony in Asia" angered Moscow with good reason: because of its truth. Two years later, another editorial persisted with this outlook. It stated that the Chinese marshaled the "Third World" to oppose the Soviet Union and United States, with the idea that these nations would look to the PRC for leadership. Nothing profoundly new or unique characterized this point of view from the Jesuit periodical. It contained nothing religious and simply carried traditional Cold War fears into the 1970s. Yet it did so on the basis of contemporary events and continued knowledge of the danger that communism posed to Catholicism, as can be gleaned from other articles from that era that also indicate the journal's willingness to go against this anti-Communist doctrine if it concerned human need.[9]

An *America* report on the condition of the Catholic Church in Czechoslovakia further reminded readers about the plight of the church in Communist lands. After the Soviet invasion of that nation in 1968, hard-line Communists regained control and once again went after the church, both Catholic and Protestant, because of state atheism and fear that it harbored insurgents. *America*'s editors explained that Czech radio had specifically singled out the Catholic Church for "'interference' in the 'political and social life of the country' and warned that if they did not stop 'the State will take action.'" In other words, editors explained that the Communist attack on religion in general and the Catholic Church in particular persisted, a reality that signaled the end of religious freedom in that nation. Yet while this and other reports highlighted religious persecution in a variety of Communist countries, *America* did not simply espouse a knee-jerk anticommunism. Unique circumstances spurred an alternative viewpoint, as the example of Cuba demonstrates. Cuban Catholic bishops had been pleading for three years for the United States to lift the economic blockade because it injured innocent civilians and did little to the government itself. *America* concurred. Editors wrote in 1972 that the embargo "hurts the Cuban people rather than their leader and hinders the cause of inter-American unity." Regarding Cuba, *America* agreed with its moderate and liberal counterparts because it concerned human need and the Catholic Church, not simply politics. While its staunch anticommunism continued with other subjects, faith, Catholic leadership, and the plight of innocent people could change editorial policy and what it wanted to convey to readers to shape their opinions.[10]

The Southern Baptist Convention added a denominational voice to Christian traditional Cold War viewpoints. Ironically, the denomination that historically tied itself to a staunch defense of the separation of church and state often backed government theism when it came to the Cold War. One writer for *Baptist and Reflector*, Herschel H. Hobbs, criticized the dialogue that had started to take place between Christians and Marxists during the 1960s and 1970s in the hope of finding shared philosophies and thereby lessening the tension between these ideologies. Often these conversations emphasized the common interest in meeting basic human needs, a concern both biblical in basis and at the heart of socialist principles. Hobbs wrote that the comparison between Christianity and communism failed. Using a passage from Acts 4:32, he stated that, indeed, "Christian faith and love in action" led to assisting those in need and to sharing resources, while "Communism calls for a *forced* pooling of all economic resources." In other words, he highlighted the oppressive nature of communism versus the free will inherent in Christianity. Underneath this statement lay the persistent fear of communism based on its dictatorial methods. The National Baptist Association similarly reminded people that Communists wanted to conquer the world, including the United States, in this instance by encouraging American youth to wear the peace symbol. Though specious in its history, the article as published in the *Baptist Beacon* alleged that it was a satanic symbol and "a central part of the national symbolism of Communist Russia." Getting young Americans to wear it therefore provided evidence to this author that communism had infiltrated the United States and sought to weaken its Christian principles, a sign in the eyes of this writer that religion and the U.S. government had blended together. It became the duty of SBC periodicals to therefore educate their readerships about these dangers and to remain vigilant by supporting U.S. Cold War efforts.[11]

Time and again, the actual repression inflicted upon the world by Communist governments provided evidence to conservative Baptists to support their Cold War hostility, especially when this repression hindered religious observations. When the 12th Congress of the Baptist World Alliance met in Tokyo, Japan, in 1970, Baptist Press released news about two Scandinavian Baptist newspapers that pushed for the assembly to speak against the treatment of Christians inside Communist borders. The Southern Baptist Convention in this instance stood in solidarity with others around the world in worrying about the arrest of Christians, the closing of churches, and communism's atheistic agenda. Baptist leaders from around the world offered further proof. The president of the Nigerian Baptist Convention, E. O. Akingbala, stated that communism in Nigeria "is an undercurrent movement. Communism is atheistic; we fear it. Life in a communistic state [would be] worthless; and denial of God—denial of freedom to worship—we fear more than the civil war just past." As with the 1960s, the proven actions of Communists to foment civil war and purge the world of religion supported the Southern Baptist Convention in its continued stance on the danger of communism going into the 1970s. For them, no change in containment theory or faith in the domino theory was needed because the Communist menace had not changed. They wanted SBC members to remember this fact, too, and thereby vote and act in an appropriately conservative, anti-Communist manner, with a patriotic faith in U.S. actions.[12]

At the heart of the Southern Baptists' fear of communism lay the treatment of religious believers within Communist countries, particularly those in the Soviet Union. As had *Christianity Today*, when a large block of Russian Jews attempted to leave the country in the early 1970s because of religious persecution and to go to Israel, the Southern Baptist Convention missionaries in Israel took up their cause. Once again SBC missionary outreach gave them inside access to what went on around the world. After meeting with the few whom the Soviets had allowed to leave and with family and friends of Russian Jews living in Israel, the Baptist Convention in Israel pleaded with the USSR to allow them to leave without payment. Such handling of people gave reason for those in the Southern Baptist Convention to suspect the Soviet Union, but proof of other believers in the USSR gave them heart. Pastor George W. Hill of Calvary Baptist Church in Washington, D.C., invited

Alexander P. Eustafiev, the press counselor for the Soviet Embassy, to speak at his church in order to connect his congregants with those around the world. Eustafiev spoke of seeking common ground that could better relations between the United States and Soviet Union and told those gathered that "in his own family there are several 'believers,' especially among older aunts who are members of the Russian Orthodox Church." This visit both encouraged and worried Southern Baptists; they found hope because Christianity survived inside the Soviet Union but despaired that it appealed predominantly to the elderly, without the ability to reach out to youth. Either way, the treatment of religious believers inside the Soviet Union solidified the Southern Baptist Convention's hostility toward communism.[13]

This linking of religion and the Soviet Union meant that many within the Southern Baptist Convention commented from their positions of religious authority on foreign policy, thereby mixing U.S. Christianity and politics in an obvious way. This fact underscores how seriously the SBC took the Cold War because the denomination historically championed a strict separation of church and state. Dating back to its colonial roots and the state oppression many Baptists had endured historically, the SBC took up religious freedom as fundamental to its existence. The separation of church and state principle often prompted a strong SBC patriotism because this nation protected their faith. Because the fight against the Communist bloc included a religious war, however, this belief in the separation of church and state did not include conversations about the Soviet Union or People's Republic of China. In these conversations, government theism took hold within the SBC.

The SBC president in 1969 and 1970, W. A. Criswell, visited Richard Nixon in the White House along with other religious leaders at the behest of Billy Graham in order for the president to better explain his announced trip to China. Many religious leaders had balked at his outreach to an atheist nation and wondered why his agenda did not include a conversation with the Chinese about religious liberty. Graham, the president's friend and confidant, organized this meeting in August 1971 to alleviate their concerns. This strategy worked for at least one participant, as Criswell emerged from the briefing with a changed opinion. He explained to the media that Soviet armaments in the Middle East and Vietnam posed a greater danger to the world than the PRC and that he believed that Nixon's trip would factionalize the Communist nations and weaken their global influence. Not only does this reveal Criswell's continued hostility toward the Soviet Union; it merges the church and the state in that these religious leaders felt called to the meeting, listened to the president, and afterward promoted his foreign policy in their comments to the press and to their religious constituents. Nothing that Criswell stated directly linked his reaction to his faith, yet he attended as the SBC representative and Graham had orchestrated the meeting because Christian leaders had questioned White House diplomacy. Nixon, Graham, and Criswell united to try to shape SBC opinions toward supporting the president's diplomatic efforts.[14]

Other Southern Baptist Convention leaders and lay people discussed foreign policy as it related to Asia, with comments about a variety of countries that displayed a similar mix of hope and concern. For example, prior to Nixon's announced détente with China, the periodical for the Baptist missionaries, *Commission*, worried about the PRC's atheism but applauded the number of believers who had fled China and lived in Taiwan: "As the Communists put the torch to the mainland to see if they can indeed burn down Chinese society, other fires were burning in Taiwan." This same dualistic approach applied to North and South Korea, where SBC missionaries feared the north and assisted those living in the south. Applauding South Korea as a U.S. ally with forces in Vietnam, *Commission* contrasted the two nations by explaining that "the north is still veiled in the semi-secret vacuum which communism demands" while in the south "a vibrant and alert Republic of Korea moves rapidly toward becoming one of Asia's strongholds of freedom." Once again church and state intermingled, because freedom meant religious liberty and the right for the SBC to operate missions, while communism led to an enforced atheist agenda. Missionaries to Thailand voiced similar concerns. As nearby nations embroiled themselves in civil wars and Communists worked to conquer Vietnam and Cambodia, American missionaries in Thailand worried about the future of that nation. One citizen of Thailand who had come to the United States for her college degree explained that the biggest danger lay along Thailand's border with Cambodia, where Cambodian Communists "sought to convert to Communism" the people with whom they talked. Yet her Baptist faith and relationship with America offered a hopeful future for the SBC. Other reports described Thailand's fight to ward off Communists. Efforts in this campaign included "accelerating economic development," using propaganda about the way Communists treated people once they took over to sway citizens against communism, and, because the Thais revered their monarchy, explaining that the Communists would eliminate it.[15]

Conservative Christians articulated a patriotic faith during the 1970s, further proving T. Jeremy Gunn's theory that a government theism had taken root in the United States as a result of the Cold War. Belief in traditional

Cold War ideologies since the 1950s led them to disdain communism and trust that the United States best defended the world from this expansionist ideology. Religious persecution by Communist countries solidified this outlook. We must study these conservative Christians in order to gain a complete picture of American society as we seek to best understand foreign policy opinions during Richard Nixon's administration.

A Country Gone Astray

Liberal Christians countered these conservative voices with a completely different analysis of U.S. foreign policy. Patriotic faith went too far in their view; instead, they asserted that the United States had gone astray in its militarism and fear of all things Communist. This argument built upon a fear that patriotic faith was akin to idolatrous culture-worship, a lesson learned from the confessing churches in Germany during World War II, emphasized by theologians such as Reinhold Niebuhr already in the 1950s, and subsequently taken up by the Protestant mainline ecumenical movement. By the 1960s, therefore, although none of the representatives to be discussed supported any Communist nations, they insisted that, as Americans, they only had the power to alter what their own country did internationally. These Christians divorced themselves completely from traditional Cold War ideology, on the basis of their change of opinion from the 1960s and a dislike for the foreign policy of Richard M. Nixon. To that end, they went on a crusade to denounce America's jingoist approach to foreign policy and called for disarmament with a theology of human improvement that led them to insist that even détente did not go far enough to reduce global tension.

After Nixon won reelection in 1972, *Christian Century* editors took aim at his conservative policies and expressed pessimism about the next four years. In a backhanded compliment about his détente with the USSR and PRC, an editorial stated that "he must work to bring unity [to the nation]. Perhaps he will do so, reversing his domestic style with the same skill he has shown in international affairs with his spectacularly successful trips to the Soviet Union and the People's Republic of China." The opinion piece expressed sincere hope that Nixon would work, as he had promised in his campaign rhetoric, to heal the nation's divisions but did not believe he actually intended to do so. In addition, even with some agreement with Nixon's reaching out to the two Communist giants, editors worried that this led Americans to believe that the president and United States had "firm control of the world." Associate editor Cornish Rogers felt differently, thinking that because of détente, "we have been let off the hook. There are no external pressures to force the U.S. to live up to its creeds; and with beefed-up police forces and modernized techniques for domestic control, the government can safely ignore internal pressures for reform." Cornish insisted that with the repression of dissent within the United States, the Vietnam War, and other trouble spots around the world, Americans could not simply trust that Nixon had control of foreign policy because of friendlier relations with two nations. He wanted to remind readers about this important fact and thereby influence their opinions toward an opposition to Cold War politics as usual.[16]

The *Christian Century*, too, responded to the successful independence movement in Bangladesh. But where *Christianity Today* and the Southern Baptist Convention criticized the PRC, an article by James Armstrong came down hard against the United States' support for West Pakistan. Armstrong, a bishop of the United Methodist Church, wrote that he saw Nixon's trips to Moscow and Peking as major accomplishments but that "the cynicism of the administration's foreign policy was revealed when hundreds of thousands of peasants in Bangla Desh were being slaughtered by soldiers from West Pakistan." Armstrong claimed that Nixon ignored this atrocity to appease "his new friends in Peking," not because of firm or moral foreign policy leadership. Instead, the "President sided with the brutal dictatorship in West Pakistan, betraying our longtime allies and the world's most populous democracy, India." In short, he described this move by the United States as one of "inconsistency and total bankruptcy." Armstrong felt that the United States could only live up to the standard and ideology that it espoused if it did so consistently, from region to region, from circumstance to circumstance, unlike its previous modus operandi during the Cold War. A Christian reading of foreign policy demanded such continuity and honesty. Siding with a dictator against an independence movement went against this moral conviction, and Armstrong could not disassociate this U.S. stance from its better relationship with the USSR and PRC merely to applaud those efforts. He campaigned as a Christian for an even more radical change in the United States' diplomatic outlook.[17]

Whereas the *Christian Century* usually censured Richard Nixon's foreign policy, it crafted a more nuanced understanding of other nations, including Communist states such as Cuba. An article by William Jeffries, director of peace education for the southeastern region of the American Friends Service Committee, demonstrates this complexity. After traveling through Cuba, he wrote that "we had heard many bad things about the Castro regime, chiefly from its most vociferous detractors, and now that we have seen that regime in operation we must say that there is much truth in these unflattering reports." His account then commented on the lack of freedom of speech, restrictions on the press, a strong military presence in daily life, propaganda in the schools, and numerous political prisons on the island. Jeffries also described the horrid economic conditions under which most Cubans lived. Yet he cautioned against reactionary hatred toward the nation: "it is a mistake to think of the Castro regime as an unmitigated evil. In order to have a realistic view of Cuba today and to formulate a realistic, decent policy toward it, we must know about the constructive things that are going on there." He then detailed its positive attributes, such as housing for everyone, universal health care, solid education, and industrial output. Jeffries desired a reduced tension between the United States and Cuba because it would make the world safer for both peoples. Editorials about the island nation sounded a similar refrain. Again denouncing Nixonian diplomacy, editors wondered if the United States truly wanted a better relationship because it insisted on maintaining a military presence at Guantanamo Bay: "Surely it is understandable that the Cubans would look upon Gitmo with disdain; to them, it symbolizes not only the U.S. domination of the past but also a current danger to the island's independence." While not backing the Communist regime, this realistic approach demonstrates the *Christian Century*'s typical delineation of foreign policy opinions: at times in a religious context and often devoid of it, editors and writers examined all sides of the issue but focused the desire for change on the United States because they had influence in that realm. This approach informed the way the periodical sought to educate its readers against the outdated Cold War model of despising all things Communist.[18]

A parallel overview of the People's Republic of China during the 1970s appeared in the *Christian Century*. Hwa Yu wrote a regular column for the periodical that described Chinese life in realistic terms. He often focused on describing issues and realities that went against American stereotypes of both traditional Chinese life and its existence under communism. Without condoning or ignoring repression there, Yu painted a more complex picture of the nation. In one article, he wrote about local life and the fact that it actually represented a more fierce democratic system than those of many Western nations because of resident participation levels. Neighborhood and street committees were elected locally, except for a party representative, and constituted the basic unit of local government. These elected representatives attended meetings at various government levels and intimately knew the concerns of the local villages. While this system of representation operated within the more dictatorial Communist system, Yu explained that it gave a voice to a wide array of citizens, in contrast to the American stereotype of a total dictatorship that issued edicts from the top of the Chinese government. Yu also commented on the reverence for Mao, as did *Christianity Today*, but rather than isolate this reverence as worship of him, he explained the concept as a movement and why many Chinese were drawn to it:

> The Maoist vision is both messianic and eschatological, fixed on the end of the present age and the advent of a new age to be brought about by people's spontaneous uprisings in each country, and on the establishment of socialism and proletarian hegemony to replace present systems of exploitation. China's role in this historical movement is seen as inspirational and supportive rather than provocative.

Yu admitted the component of Communist expansionism contained in Mao's vision, but rather than issue a visceral condemnation, he reasoned about why this appealed to Chinese citizens. His article contained both the positives and negatives about the situation, the typical stance of the periodical toward Communist countries as it crusaded to alter American Cold War perceptions.[19]

The same intellectual attitude toward Communist countries materialized when the *Christian Century* commented on Christianity within their borders and the repression of religious faith. The printing of an article by a "special correspondent" from within East Germany reveals how the periodical dealt with the church there. Editors allowed for the anonymity of the writer in order to keep his identity hidden from Communist officials, who might arrest him if they read his thoughts about religion and his denunciation of some Communist policies. Here, they agreed with more traditional Cold War hostilities toward communism. The author described a church that was beholden to an oppressive state but that still lived out Martin Luther's legacy of leading society and commenting on wrongs within it, walking a "dialectical tightrope of serving a Communist-ruled community by means of constructive criticism." Christians there had little power, made no overt claims to it, and were forbidden from having a mass following. At the same time, this writer stated that "their authority depends solely on the validity of their ideas and on their own spiritual integrity. They are a gift to their own nation and to world Christendom." When it came to Christians inside Communist borders, the *Christian Century* more readily condemned communism. Oppression and denial of faith went against its liberal theology of freedom and openness. Despite the persistence of Christian communities within East

Germany, and although applauding their fortitude in commenting on religion and politics, the mainline Protestant journal found little good to say about the treatment of Christianity there. Even as it crafted a more liberal foreign policy outlook for its readers, the editors and writers understood the complexity of the situation and the danger faced by many Christians.[20]

Christian Century reporting became even more condemnatory when it came to religion inside the Soviet Union. The arrest by Soviet officials of many believers, often merely because of open proselytizing, angered the liberal mainline periodical and brought calls for reform within the USSR. Editors and writers never believed Soviet propaganda about the freedom of religion or the claims that people did not go to church because they had no faith in Christian institutions. As with *Christianity Today*, the imposition of a tax on Jewish people trying to leave the Soviet Union provided one source of proof of Communist tyranny. Calling this tax a "gross violation of the fundamental human right to leave one's country freely," two writers denounced this policy. Within these ruminations were expressions of concern about the oppression of religion that led so many Jewish citizens to want to leave. In July 1970, a correspondent from Kent, England, reported on arrests of Baptist dissidents within the Soviet Union. Michael Bourdeaux wrote of "a new wave of arrests of Baptists." Baptists had come under particular scrutiny in the Soviet Union because they refused to kowtow to the state and often spoke publicly against it. This led to incarcerations and even killings because of poor prison conditions or forced labor that was so harsh it killed people. In addition, Soviets often charged Christians with the vague accusation of "corrupting youth," which meant that they publicly spoke of Christianity or tried to lure people to its appeal. The *Christian Century* lashed out against this policy and explained that it stemmed from Soviet hatred for religion and not from a real violation of the law. Indeed, editorials and articles had nothing good to say during the 1970s about Communist countries and the way they treated religious believers. Instead, they exposed injustices and blasted Communist atheism. Yet these condemnations did nothing to mute the periodical's censuring of U.S. policy, which it also felt was flawed and too militaristic. Instead, they reveal the complexity with which the *Christian Century* viewed global diplomacy as it fought to convince Americans and their leaders to change the harsh anti-Communist policies of the past.[21]

The same liberal Christian outlook came from the United Church of Christ, which had campaigned for a number of human rights and liberal causes since its founding in the 1950s. In 1971, the UCC embarked on a campaign that it called "Whole Earth–Whole People," which aimed to contribute efforts toward human liberation, to eliminate world hunger, and to alleviate poverty. The essence of this initiative best embodied UCC theology and its human focus. The program was very much in line with the denomination's Christian conviction to help those less fortunate, and rhetoric about it contained indications about where the UCC stood regarding the Cold War. The adoption at General Synod of the goals and objectives for this program included a call for Americans to see themselves as part of a global community not easily divided into Cold War camps. If the UCC intended to belong to a Whole Earth–Whole People, this had to include those in Communist countries. The fourth objective therefore asked for the church and country "to define and apply United States power in ways that are appropriate to the development of an international community which is grounded in the concept 'Whole Earth–Whole People.'" In other words, isolating half the world because of governmental affiliations with the Soviet Union or People's Republic of China defied this objective. David M. Stowe, executive vice president for the UCC Board for World Ministries, further asserted this in a column for the UCC's official periodical, *A.D.*: "The world is intrinsically one. We have one environment in which we flourish or perish; to ward off nuclear suicide, we are building a world in law and political arrangements; we rejoice in a spreading world culture."[22]

A desire to participate in this global community further led the United Church of Christ to issue calls for peace. Though generic, the repeated emphasis on this important Christian principle in the midst of the Cold and Vietnam wars emphasized the United Church of Christ's fight against world tension and desire for all people to live in harmony. To make this point, *A.D.* printed a prayer written by the famous preacher Harry Emerson Fosdick, reflecting on the tomb of the unknown soldier. This 1930s prayer pleaded, "O my country, stay out of war! Cooperate with the nations in every moment that has any hope for peace. Enter the World Court. Support the League of Nations. Contend undiscouragingly for disarmament." The editors reprinted this amidst Cold War disarmament talks, the Vietnam War, and global fighting in general as another way to cry out for peace. *A.D.* furthered this call in an Advent Calendar of prayers that it published in December 1972. It asked UCC members on December 6 to pray as follows:

> Harder than we've ever prayed for anything before, O God, we pray for the end of war, of all bombing, of the fire of snipers, and of the dislocation of homes. Sheathe our swords lest we Americans die by them in conscience, if not in body. For the words of the "Prince of Peace," soon to be born again in our midst, are heavy in our ears.

In terms more pointed against 1970s Cold and Vietnam war policies, it prayed on December 9 for "the President of the United States, that he may do everything possible to honor the cry of people for peace." These prayers for peace offered more than generic Christian calls for this ambiguous concept; they directly challenged U.S. foreign policy, demanding that the United States live up to a Christian calling and advocate for the end of war. In this way, the UCC strove to sway public opinion against a conservative foreign policy. In contrast to conservative Christians, they held no sentiments toward a patriotic faith that backed everything that the United States advocated during the Cold War. Instead, the denomination crusaded for a change in U.S. Cold War policies.[23]

The official United Church of Christ periodical echoed this plea for disarmament that challenged traditional Cold War politics. In May 1970, editors wrote against antiballistic missile (ABM) deployment as a hindrance to arms reduction but also published an article in favor of ABMs. The UCC debate over ABMs emphasized the reflective nature of UCC foreign policy opinions because it included both sides of the issue, yet each denounced the arms race. Milton H. Mater, an Army Reserve officer, included statements in his article that supported the government and opposed communism, including an insistence that antiballistic missiles were positive military spending because of their defensive nature. Yet this moderate UCC voice also proclaimed that "the immorality of basing our defense solely on retaliation by nuclear destruction against helpless people is so obviously un-Christian that it is a wonder our nation ever agreed to such a policy. We should have been clamoring for a means to defend ourselves against nuclear attack so that we would not be forced into a position of threatening murderous retaliation." The editorial page countered this when it denounced the fact that the United States had built new ABM sites in the midst of the SALT treaties because "before financing more missiles, we ought to be aware of the unsavory effect such action will have on SALT." This issue displayed the varying opinions of UCC members yet the simultaneous agreement to denounce the arms race. *United Church Herald* editors, writers, and readers wanted the United States to emphasize disarmament; any militarization that hindered disarmament became a target for their criticism when they wrote to shape reader opinions toward their viewpoint.[24]

UCC comments about Red China and Cuba offer examples of how this hope for a reduction in Cold War hostilities applied to specific circumstances, according to lay and clergy members. The UCC had advocated throughout the 1960s allowing the People's Republic of China into the United Nations, applauded when this finally happened, and approved of President Nixon's historic opening of relations with the Communist nation in the 1970s. The 1969 General Synod had anticipated this change when it "recommend[ed] that the Council for Christian Social Action form a Committee on a New China policy for the 1970's." The denomination saw the possibility for reduced Cold War tensions because of cooperation with the PRC. Despite this hope, the UCC also lamented the Cultural Revolution and government oppression suffered by citizens in Red China. In other words, the United Church of Christ condoned the new relationship between the United States and China that developed under Nixon while still seeing the danger posed by communism to the citizens of China. However, this unique relationship with China led others in the UCC to wonder why it applied to only one country: "If Richard Nixon can finally discover China, maybe we can get somebody or other to discover Cuba." Huber F. Klemme made this statement because "the U.S. policy of intransigent opposition and isolation has multiplied the suffering of the entire people" of Cuba needlessly. Writing this as part of a study group on U.S.-Cuban relations for the Council for Christian Social Action, Klemme concluded that "no good ends are served by this estrangement, and both peoples are losing the advantages of close humanitarian and cultural ties." In other words, the UCC wanted a more consistent foreign policy that acknowledged differences within the Communist world and that allowed for reduced tensions between the United States and Cuba on a par with the new China approach. The United States was not always correct, and the UCC worked to educate its members about that fact. In 1973, the General Synod connected this belief regarding Cuba to UCC calls for a global world within a Christian context, void of political boundaries:

> Because our Lord commends the peacemakers;
> Because to us is entrusted the message of reconciliation;
> Because we believe that all persons are members of the family of God;
> Because governmental policies have caused hardships and estrangement between the peoples of Cuba and the United States;
> Because contacts between our countries are improving in spite of fundamental differences in government, philosophy, and policy; and
> Because we believe the United States policy and attitudes toward Cuba should move toward the reconciliation of existing differences;
> In Christian concern the Executive Council, acting for the Ninth General Synod of the United Church of Christ, therefore respectfully urges the governments of the United States and Cuba to resume diplomatic relations and to work for friendship, trade and mutual assistance.

The United Church of Christ by the 1970s had a consistent voice regarding foreign policy. No longer swayed by traditional Cold War hostilities, the denomination cried out for reduced tension and applied this principle consistently, whether in discussing disarmament or in addressing U.S. relations with particular nations.[25]

Where conservative Christians maintained a patriotic faith in the United States' foreign policies, liberal Christians vowed to change the United States' reliance on militarism. A mere faith in the government had disappeared for these Christians, at least as of the early Cold War, if not before. Nothing throughout the Cold War altered this resistance to such idolatry, a position further solidified by their perceptions of foreign policy during the 1970s. Instead of seeing America as God's chosen nation, they argued that its reliance on confrontation and antagonism made the world less safe. As Christians, they crusaded to shape the opinion of Americans toward a more reasoned stance that championed disarmament and modeled the peace called for in the Bible. To be sure, they condemned Communist nations for their atheism and oppression of innocent citizens. But this fact did not lead them to see America as perfect; they saw the nation's flaws, and worked through Christian convictions to change it in a more intensified way.

Changed Opinions

Some Christians changed their foreign policy outlook during the 1970s, in contrast to staunch conservatives and liberals who came into the decade with firm convictions and merely solidified them under Nixon's presidency. These Christians had ended the 1960s with a stance against all things Communist by falling in line with more conservative Christians who supported U.S. foreign policy with a patriotic faith. Yet further reflection during Richard Nixon's administration gave them pause. They gravitated away from total trust in the government and aligned themselves with liberal Christians who added a religious voice to the opposition to America's militarized Cold War philosophy. In this regard, they teach us something about why some Americans would also come to condemn the Vietnam War, on the basis of a new analysis of Cold War diplomacy.

The Catholic periodical *Commonweal* paralleled the trajectory that scholars have already outlined for American society overall in regard to Cold War opinions. During the 1960s, the American public slowly drifted from a Cold War posture of trusting the government toward questioning its reliance on containment theory. By the 1970s, editors and writers no longer implicitly trusted government officials and came to question U.S. diplomacy. When Cambodia degenerated into civil war in 1970, *Commonweal* seized upon it to articulate this new vision. Lon Nol, a pro-American general, overthrew the neutral Prince Norodom Sihanouk government, which eventually paved the way for the Communist Khmer Rouge insurgency. While traditional Cold War advocates emphasized that this latest violence proved the domino theory, *Commonweal*'s lay editors disagreed. Rather, they pointed out that Peking and Hanoi hardly supported Sihanouk, whom conservatives had labeled a Communist sympathizer during his reign, and bickered with one another over Communist leadership in the region. Such confusion caused editors to insist that readers "take out that set of dominoes you had stashed away" because the theory no longer applied, the world had become too complex to fit into such neat and stereotypical boxes. Further evidence of its move away from moderation came in this editorial's final assessment of the Cambodian situation as it related to the United States: "Is America winning? Is America losing? By what criteria? No one can answer. What we *are* doing is bleeding, killing, dying, destroying—intervening in quarrels that should not be our business, embittering them, sometimes even initiating them." This type of clear repudiation of American foreign policy moved *Commonweal* decidedly leftward, reflecting a trend others have found in American society at that time but giving us more of an explanation as to why they did so.[26]

By 1972, *Commonweal* articles about foreign relations denounced U.S. Cold War policy completely and shrugged off all moderation. Even after the 1971 Strategic Arms Limitation Agreement by the United States and Soviet Union, Ramsdell Gurney Jr., an assistant professor of history at the University of Santa Clara in California, wrote that "an arms race spirals on with ever increasing stakes and risks." To him, the agreement did not go far enough. He blamed the United States in large part for this problem because "for the last two and a half decades the impetus and initiative for the arms race has come primarily from the United States." He noted this position because the agreement banned only certain weapons, while the United States protected its numerical advantage in bombers and future military weapons, which were not covered by the agreement. Gurney's assessment placed the periodical firmly in favor of disarmament and in a camp that opposed the continuation of the arms race. Editors took a similar stance regarding Cuba. While still disdaining Castro's dictatorship, they complained that "for the U.S. to react [to Cuban communism] by playing the bully towards Cuba year upon year is to demean itself in the international community." Rather, *Commonweal* hoped for an easing of tension between the nations, at least in the form of normalized diplomatic relations. In addition to also wanting a review of the travel ban and use of the military base at Guantanamo Bay, editors asserted that "the first urgency is the dismantling of the trade embargo, an immorality whose effects are largely to penalize the poor, the sick, the aged and the very young." To them, traditional Cold War hostility toward all things Communist no longer should apply to U.S.-Cuban relations, and they strove to sway reader opinions toward their new outlook. The adding of a moral argument lent a Christian component to their understandings of foreign policy.[27]

Yet this posture hardly signaled that *Commonweal* viewed international communism any differently than with the hostility it had traditionally held toward it. Its altered view affected only visions of U.S. actions and policy. When Josip Broz Tito in Yugoslavia purged an insurgent movement within his nation and accepted Soviet military and economic assistance to do so, a frequent contributor to the periodical quickly denounced Tito's anti-democratic tactics. A professor at Fairleigh Dickinson University, Matthew Mestrovic, wrote that "the internationally alarming facet of Tito's growing reliance on the military and the secret police and the concomitant power struggle for succession is that it offers the Soviet Union the long-awaited-for opportunity to bring Yugoslavia back into its fold." Tito's retrenchment and purging of foes demonstrated Communist repression and the use of intimidation par excellence. *Commonweal* took note. While it had moved toward a liberal outlook and no longer accepted U.S. reliance on containment and vilification of all things Communist, neither did it ignore the oppression still faced by people within the Communist bloc when it worked to persuade readers toward a new foreign policy understanding.[28]

Executive editor Robert E. Burns of *U.S. Catholic and Jubilee* viewed the Cold War similarly to *Commonweal*, especially in discarding traditional Cold War domino/containment theories from the 1960s. An article he wrote in denunciation of the Vietnam War best illustrated this take on the larger Cold War. He focused most of his wrath on American actions in Southeast Asia. However, he also blasted U.S. Cold War policy. For example, Burns questioned why the Nixon administration used the language of Communist expansionism to justify its actions in Vietnam when it had recently "bribed" the Soviets with grain assistance and the People's Republic of China with a withdrawal of support for its enemy, Chiang Kai-shek, as part of détente. If America could cooperate with the Communist giants, Burns insisted that this invalidated the domino theory. Additionally, he asserted that "we now know that when in 1964 the C.I.A. was asked to evaluate 'the domino theory,' its reply was that this theory was false, that very little was likely to change outside of Indo-China as a result of a Communist victory within it." Burns had little to say about the context of his Catholicism in making these arguments, but neither had *Commonweal*. As with other liberal Christians, the immorality of American actions alone prompted Christian response without the need for explanation. Regardless of why, *U.S. Catholic and Jubilee* added its voice to liberal Catholicism's changed foreign policy opinions by the 1970s in the way it attempted to shape reader beliefs.[29]

Even one conservative Catholic periodical indicated that the importance of Cold War rhetoric and anti-Communist hostility had dissipated by the 1970s. *Catholic Digest* in the 1960s had represented one of the most conservative voices among Catholic periodicals. Its Cold War opinion denounced all things Communist and supported U.S. foreign policy without question. Yet during the 1970s, the periodical included virtually nothing about the Cold War, communism, or foreign policy in general, except for commentary about the Vietnam War. This shift suggests that the consistently high level of concern about Communist danger had dwindled, though some information reveals that it did not disappear. The periodical included information about outreach, missions, and humanitarian aid going to a few Communist lands and even more going to areas with current civil wars that included a Communist component. These reports clearly blamed the Communists for such uprisings. But with little else to expose their current opinion, historians must assume that Cold War tension had been reduced enough by détente and the changed 1970s circumstances that it no longer sat on the front burner for all Catholic periodicals.[30]

A somewhat more conflicted and moderate tone appeared in *Catholic World*, which changed its editorial attitude regarding the Cold War drastically from the relatively liberal outlook of the 1960s. But as with its perceptions of the world during the 1960s, the Paulist fathers' periodical applied theology and the church directly when making statements. A brief biography of Vladimir Lenin sounded a traditional anti-Communist mantra because of Soviet atheism. Nikita D. Roodkowsky, assistant professor of Russian literature and history at Newton College of the Sacred Heart, wrote a vehement denunciation about how the Soviets aimed to purge the nation of all religion: "The fierce religious persecutions of the churches which started in 1917 and continue to this day stem from Marx's and Lenin's theomachy (struggle against God). The whole of Soviet culture is nothing but the result of this drive to create for the first time in the history of the world a civilization without God." When viewed in the context of religion, communism was condemned by *Catholic World* as harshly as it had been throughout the

Cold War. Yet other articles questioned the United States' global outlook. A professor at the University of Dubuque Theological Seminary, Dr. Carnegie S. Calian, wanted America to concern itself more with global poverty and hunger. Rather than maintain a strictly militarized outlook, he thought that "nations like ourselves must find ways to alleviate poverty in the world at a price other than that demanded by communism." Though still harshly anti-Communist, compared to conservative Catholics, *Catholic World* took a moderate approach to the 1970s Cold War because it called for reform from both Communist countries and the United States and always wrote in the context of its Christian calling. In this way, it reflected a portion of America torn about how to view foreign policy during the complex 1970s but beginning to question the actions of the United States.[31]

Not every Christian entered the 1970s already decided on how to approach foreign policy. As these Catholic periodicals demonstrated, some Christians moved their opinions away from conservative anticommunism and toward a more liberal, antimilitarized perspective based on a new analysis of global events. Joining other Americans who altered their understanding of diplomacy during this decade, these Christians added a moral voice to the reasons given as to why this change was necessary.

African Methodist Episcopal Church

The African Methodist Episcopal Church adds a distinctive voice to Christian views of foreign affairs during the 1970s. On the one hand, it maintained a conservative anticommunism, denouncing its atheist policies and oppression of people around the world. Yet the denomination simultaneously questioned Richard Nixon's diplomacy as too threatening, thus causing members and leaders to cry out for peace. This conflicted viewpoint made the AME voice dissimilar from those of the other Christians we are examining.

In a variety of articles on an eclectic array of topics, the *Christian Recorder* revealed that the African Methodist Episcopal Church's anticommunism had changed little during the 1970s. In the 1960s, the United States had engaged in a vibrant debate over whether or not "God is Dead," as German philosopher Friedrich Nietzsche famously claimed. Countless theologians and Americans disputed claims that a technological, scientific rationalism had replaced the need for religion in the United States. James H. Foster wrote an article making this point for his denomination in which he included hints about the continued anti-Communist AME bent. He outlined Karl Marx's irreligion and therefore, in part, blamed this "God is Dead" controversy on the Communist doctrine that "religion is the opiate of the masses." While not the point of his article, Cold War ideology slipped into his commentary. J. A. McQueen made the same point in an article about a number of contemporary American social problems and the church: "It seems that there is a lack of the proper moral perspective on our times. In the meantime, we dare not lay all this seeming moral dilemma on the church. And we cannot put it all on Communism. However, there is a communistic influence in this country." Editor B. J. Nolen reminded readers on a different occasion that "in most Communist nations the prerequisite for any kind of 'religious freedom' is that the church and church people stay out of politics." He made this statement in an article about the importance of people considering their faith when going to the voting booth in the United States. Indeed, these subtle references to communism most commonly manifested the denomination's anti-Communist point of view because they came in completely different venues, from different authors, and were used to confirm a point that had nothing to do with communism, all with the assumption that readers would simply agree with the negative portrayal of communism. In another example, an article about whether or not rock music was demonically inspired, the writer provided context for the argument by firmly stating that "Satan is the mastermind behind Communism." These writers clearly reveal an embedded fear of Communist expansionism, even into the United States, as they wrote in order to persuade readers to see this point of view.[32]

When projected onto the world stage, this anticommunism led to fear of the United States' Cold War rivals and, relating specifically to its Christian outlook, a concern for global mission work. At the Indiana Annual Conference in 1972, the Committee on the State of the Country reported to delegates about the persistent Cold War threats that haunted the nation: "South East Asia, Red China, and the Soviet Union could be a threat to the United States." They also asserted that "Atomic War has produced a sense of stress." This type of language demonstrated that the 1950s/1960s Cold War understanding of the world held sway for many Americans going into the 1970s. It remained an integral part of the nation's life, according to this AME district. In addition to these more entrenched Communist opponents, colleagues in Michigan pointed out the revolutionary unrest throughout Latin America during the early 1970s and warned of a "Communistic struggle over government control" there. The AME reflects a persistent conservative worldview for some African Americans during this decade.[33]

Writings about missionary activity in Communist lands provided the Christian context for why the African Methodist Episcopal Church felt this way. Spreading the Gospel through mission outreach and revivals lay at the heart of its Methodist theology, thus drawing the ire of its members toward Communist nations that inhibited this crucial part of the Christian life. Editor B. J. Nolen told *Christian Recorder* readers that "one half of the world is now closed to Christian missionaries. China, the Soviet Union and other Communist nations make up a considerable part of that half." The foreign policy concerns of the United States thereby became a worry for the AME, too. As with other Christians, AME members could not easily separate the Cold War from their religious faith. In another article, the woman's page of the periodical explained to readers about the danger South Korean Christians faced if North Korea invaded that country. Here again American diplomacy mixed with the church's faith life. If Communists from the north took over South Korea, it spelled doom not just for democracy but also for the Christian missionaries and outreach facilities throughout that nation. While none of the AME reports contained the dogmatic opinions of the conservative Christians we have seen previously, they do connect the political and religious in important ways to suggest that more was at stake for AME members when they discussed the Cold War than mere political freedom and democracy.[34]

AME comments on the USSR reveal all of the above concerns aimed at one country: a general anticommunism, a fear of Communist expansionism, and a particular condemnation of oppression of religious belief. When Paul Robeson died, the *Christian Recorder* obituary hinted at how it felt regarding his pro-Soviet points of view. Paul Robeson was a Columbia University-trained lawyer who left that field and became a famous actor, singer, and black rights activist. Throughout his life he also defended the Soviet Union because it worked against racism. Where some in the black community saw a passionate defender of civil rights and supported his free speech privileges when he sympathized with the Soviet Union, others saw a dangerous person swept away by Communist ideology and an un-American individual. *Christian Recorder* editors emphasized the latter when they stated that Robeson's "political views cast a deep and somber shadow over his life and over his career. He was an open admirer of the Soviet Union." The AME periodical thereby revealed the subtle yet palpable anticommunism embedded in its opinions that it used to sway reader opinions.[35]

When tension around the globe flared up, this mentality often led to blaming the Communist superpower for threatening global peace. The 4th Episcopal District in Michigan stated in one report its fear of world conflict when referring to tension in the Middle East. In addition to the Israel-Arab standoff, it claimed that the Soviet Union's use of troops and advisors there threatened to escalate the situation. Other reports about the Soviet Union added the threat to religion posed by that nation. In a report about the Russian Orthodox Church, B. J. Nolen stated that "while the Communist takeover in Russia was a severe blow, the Church of Moscow survived and in recent years has made its presence felt in Orthodox circles." This note contained the hope so often manifest in American Christian reports about religion in Communist countries when proof of the church's survival reached Western sources. Yet it also reminded people that the Soviets had attempted to cripple Christianity. When Richard Nixon visited Moscow, the secretary-treasurer of the AME Sunday School Union took the opportunity to further comment on this reality. A number of Christian groups complained to the White House that it remained too silent about religious freedom in the Soviet Union. They wanted the unique chance for the president to speak directly to Soviet premier Leonid Brezhnev to urge him to defend Christians in his nation. H. A. Belin Jr. therefore explained that

> the Kremlin theoretically guarantees freedom of religion but in fact denies it to many Christians. Some languish in prisons for their beliefs. Many others are inhibited in the practice of their faith and discriminated against in education and employment. Yet precious little has been done in the free world to mobilize responsible opinion in their behalf. Our indifference has been downright appalling.

Here again the AME aligned with many of its conservative Christian counterparts in viewing the Soviet Union as the most notorious of Communist countries threatening American security and Christianity, inside and outside of its borders.[36]

Such similarities to conservative Christians, however, hardly characterize the entirety of African Methodist Episcopal Church comments regarding foreign affairs. In other areas the church body fell more in line with the social commentary of the African American community as a whole, a characteristic not manifested in white Christian entities. For example, the nation focused a great deal of attention on young people during the 1960s and early 1970s, often fearing their hostility toward adult authority, antiwar protests, riots, contempt for traditional social mores, and general unrest. The generational conflict ruptured the African American community, too, as the civil rights movement evolved into the black power movement and the young lost patience with the politics of accommodation and working through the political process. Yet few black leaders or organizations dismissed the youth as readily as their white counterparts, often because they understood their angst and irritation with the slow improvement in race relations in America. A distinctive blend of anticommunism and backing of America's black youth therefore materialized in the *Christian Recorder*. In an article aimed at AME youth, a writer explained how the radio Voice of America broadcast into Communist lands, generating interest among Soviet youth in rock and roll, jeans, and other aspects of U.S. culture. The item then called American youth to influence Soviet peers with "Bible study, church attendance, a life of prayer and a testimony for Jesus Christ." Without giving a blueprint for such action, the commentary demonstrated both the denomination's anticommunism and its faith in American youth. Rather than decry their disinterest, it called them to arms and expressed faith that they could respond positively. Editor B. J. Nolen more explicitly praised young people when he stated that "the bulk of American youth despite all the brainwashing, is a bunch of intelligent young people able to read between the lines and see events amazingly accurate. They no longer swallow the anti-America diet dished out by the one-worlders." He felt that by September 1972 American youth understood the danger of communism and supported their nation. No other denomination's or periodical's commentary on youth linked it to communism, as did AME discussions. With a unique faith in the younger generation, writers trusted that America would continue to fight the effects of communism on Christianity around the globe and wanted readers to do so, too.[37]

Further distancing the AME from conservative Christian counterparts, a distinct calling for human unity in AME foreign policy opinions appeared during the 1970s. This complexity stemmed from the Christian longing for peace, as manifested, according to the AME, in Jesus' command to love one another. All war and violence was antithetical to their Christian outlook. Although this theology was by no means unique to the African Methodist Episcopal Church, no other conservative Christians so explicitly made this part of their theology a cause for qestioning otherwise pro-American, anti-Communist statements. The 88th Session of the Chicago Annual Conference in 1970 made this very point: "While the church gives sanction to armed preparation and military training as a defense against attack and for the elimination of evil, it must proclaim that war is unchristian and peace is the goal of the church." Though it avoided taking a position on any particular Cold War issue, hot spot, or diplomatic relationship, the statement emphasized that "we do claim to have the mind of Christ in terms of trying to live peaceably with all men. We propose that the energies previously and presently used for military conquest be just as aggressively used to bring about peace and reconciliation among our fellow human beings in troubled lands." This rhetoric prompted other AME entities to applaud specifically Richard M. Nixon's efforts toward détente because it offered a nonmilitary solution to Cold War antagonisms. While the church body, and African Americans in general, had much less attachment to this president because of his lack of (or outright disdain for) civil rights commitment, it did highlight these steps toward reduced tension with the two Communist giants, not because it agreed with his foreign policy or politics but because détente matched a more Christian approach to diplomatic relations.[38]

The African Methodist Episcopal Church adds a unique voice to Christian reactions to foreign policy. In the 1970s, AME support for the president had softened. While black America had trod lightly in criticizing Lyndon B. Johnson, that concern disappeared under Nixon, a more cautious politician who at times openly condemned important race issues such as busing to desegregate schools. Yet this domestic disagreement hardly meant that the AME had turned away from its conservative outlook regarding the Cold War and communism. Throughout the 1970s, a persistent condemnation of communism appeared in its periodicals, church resolutions, and leader statements. Quite often, this subject transcended racial boundaries because commentary about communism seldom linked the subject to American race. The denomination reflected a conservative African American point of view. Nonetheless, the African Methodist Episcopal Church did long for peace and proclaimed that longing to be the true desire of Christians everywhere.

Conclusion

As in the 1960s, perceptions of the Cold War varied among Christians in the early 1970s. Conservative Christian voices, including those of *Christianity Today* and the Southern Baptist Convention, maintained a harsh anti-Communist belief because of the danger communism posed to missionary work and a conviction that Communist nations advocated repressive expansionism. They were joined by conservative Catholic journals, such as *America*, that also disdained communism and thought that events in the first part of the 1970s justified the United States' long-held hostility toward Communist nations for wanting to rid the world of religion. They arrived at a patriotic faith in their country based on their theological convictions, thus wedding themselves completely to a government theism under Richard

Nixon. They are an important addition to our understanding of the conservative resurgence during that era. In contrast, the *Christian Century, Commonweal, U.S. Catholic,* and the United Church of Christ carried opposition to the arms race and concern about the threat of a nuclear holocaust into the 1970s and called for America to work to reduce global tension. They often combined this fear with condemnation of U.S. backing of dictators simply because those dictators sided with America against Communist nations. In short, they persisted with their crusade against the United States' reliance on traditional Cold War hostilities. The African Methodist Episcopal Church continued with a sharp criticism of communism while at the same time demanding that the United States work more diligently for peace. A complex picture thus emerges when studying American Christian reactions to foreign policy under Richard M. Nixon's presidency and its reflection of U.S. public opinion.

The 1970s found Christian America still engaged in the culture war over foreign policy, as the Cold War burned hot and communism remained an important and contentious issue. Christians couched their response in terms of historical outlooks on the world and in the context of varying theologies. As we seek to understand public opinion about foreign policy during this decade and the reaction to Richard Nixon's foreign policy, Christian America offers an interesting glimpse into a myriad of perceptions often otherwise lost to the historical record because not all of these individuals vocally protested or took to the streets in action. While some did and have been discussed in other research, many others wrote letters to editors and articles to one another, crafted and voted on resolutions, and used the power of denominational numbers or periodical platforms to attempt to sway opinions. In addition, American Christianity teaches us how faith shaped foreign policy outlooks. Conservative Christians feared communism and saw little reason to soften their position regarding it. Liberal Christians condemned the United States and Communist nations together for their hostility and militarization. And still other American Christians sat somewhere between these polar opposites, grappling with pragmatic concerns about both Communist tyranny and the danger of maintaining a hostile posture by the United States. Theology and politics played a role in these reactions, sometimes exclusively, sometimes together. In thus reflecting American society, such Christians also demonstrate how some organizations worked to shape opinions toward their worldview. Indeed, this same mixture of opinions and reasoning also influenced Christian reactions to the Vietnam War during the Nixon administration.

Christian America Responds to Nixon's Vietnam Policies

Introduction

Elected in 1968 partially because he pledged to seek peace in Vietnam, Richard M. Nixon became a lightning rod for Christian debates about the Vietnam War during the 1970s. Establishing a policy that came to be known as "Vietnamization," Nixon insisted that he would not abandon the U.S. ally in South Vietnam until it could prosecute the war on its own and thereby protect itself. This stance and a desire to maintain U.S. credibility and prestige in the Cold War led to Nixon's assertion that he sought "peace with honor," not peace at any price. History has demonstrated that, in reality, Nixon wanted Vietnamization and the striving for peace with honor merely to delay the collapse of South Vietnam so that it would not appear as if the United States had lost a war under his watch.[1]

For conservative Christians, Richard Nixon became a trusted ally in the White House in their bid to protect the world from communism. They supported many of his policies, including those in the areas of race relations, law and order, and diplomacy, thus becoming a key Republican constituency and already foreshadowing the rise of the Religious Right under Ronald Reagan. In contrast, liberal Christians fought this rightward trend within American Christianity, joining liberals throughout America in denouncing Nixon and calling his integrity into question. They were a part of the American movement opposed to all things Nixon, starting with his foreign policy and moving eventually into his role in Watergate.

Understanding these Christian voices from the 1970s alters our knowledge about that decade in fundamental ways. First, we see that conservative Christians had already moved toward Republican politics by 1969 because of their support for Nixon, beginning with his stance on law and order, gravitating to his position on race relations and other domestic concerns, but also including his foreign policy. Second, we see a liberal Christianity that fought in vain against this move to the right, and in doing so helped to keep the antiwar movement alive at a time when many historians suggest that it had begun to fade. Nixon inspired this activism on their part. And in seeing the movement of some previously conservative Christians toward this antiwar platform, we gain a better sense for how and why Americans came to oppose the Vietnam War on the basis of religious sensibilities. All of these Christian voices contributed an important voice regarding the cultural battle over the Vietnam War.

Two particularly volatile weeks in 1970 prompted Christians of all stripes to weigh in with their opinions about the war. Nixon announced on 30 April that he had authorized the bombing of Cambodia, an illegal expansion of the war, according to his critics. Conservatives, however, understood the military reasoning. North Vietnam, the National Liberation Front, and their allies used what became known as the Ho Chi Minh Trail through Cambodia to supply forces in South Vietnam without risk of a confrontation with the U.S. military. The effectiveness of the threat of the Ho Chi Minh Trail led military leaders to push for eliminating this supply line with force, which Nixon condoned. Liberals, moderates, and conservatives, including those in Christian America, erupted into debate about whether or not Nixon was justified in this action or had violated the law. A protest led to violence against student demonstrators on 4 May 1970 at Kent State University in Ohio. The demonstration led to tension between student activists and the National Guard, which, under circumstances still not entirely understood, fired into the crowd, killing four unarmed people, two of whom were merely passing between classes. Prowar Americans decried the student protesters as un-American and out of control, while antiwar critics blasted the government and unjustified killings. A few weeks later more students were killed at Jackson State University in Mississippi, leading to more anger, disagreement, and angst within popular responses to these violent confrontations on the home front.[2]

As for Vietnam itself, the civil war raged on, with the South Vietnamese, United States, National Liberation Front, and North Vietnamese fighting amid various factions and divisions. Things became worse and worse for the South Vietnamese, however, as Nguyen Van Thieu desperately clung to his fading power. If not for U.S. military and economic support, his corrupt and dictatorial regime would have fallen long before. Thieu ruled with an iron fist and incarcerated or killed anyone in South Vietnam who dared question his government. The United States backed him because they saw little other choice: they feared that only this type of government could keep that country from "falling" to the Communists. Yet amid the persistent combat, Nixon, primarily through Henry Kissinger, negotiated with the North Vietnamese for a settlement to the war. Talks waxed and waned, were on and off, and the United States tried to leverage for a better situation by bombing, offering a cease-fire to get North Vietnam back to the table, and then bombing all over again. North Vietnam bided its time, knowing that increasing American domestic pressure against the war and the hostility of many South Vietnamese to their own government would eventually pave the way for a Communist victory. In January 1973, the United States and North Vietnam finally came to terms and brokered a settlement that removed U.S. combat troops from Vietnam and protected the right of South Vietnam to exist. Nixon proclaimed that the settlement represented "peace with honor," while the North Vietnamese and their allies in the South viewed it as temporary, until they could remobilize to reunite the country as a Communist nation.[3]

Historiography about Christianity during the 1970s offers a mixed bag of issues and opinions about Vietnam and other matters. Scholars have well established that the antiwar movement benefited from a persistent Christian presence throughout this period, some Christians working within the system to persuade government leaders and their constituents against the war and others mobilizing forces for public protest and draft card burnings. These antiwar advocates had also campaigned against the arms race and nuclear proliferation. Little is known about Christians who backed the war, though my previous study of Lutheranism indicates that many within the church supported the president and U.S. involvement in Southeast Asia as necessary for protecting that nation and Christianity. Conservative evangelical leaders, such as Billy Graham, also viewed the war as imperative in the global struggle against communism. Other concerns of the time absorbed Christian attention and wove in and out of reactions to the Vietnam War, such as the decline in mainline Protestant membership and attention to ecumenism among liberal and moderate Protestants versus a resurgent conservatism among other bodies and within fundamentalism. For Catholic America, a struggle to understand Vatican II and its meanings dominated discussions, dividing this community among liberals, moderates, and conservatives, both politically and theologically, in new ways. As noted historian Jay P. Dolan states, "Catholics no longer agreed on an answer to the question of what it meant to be Catholic." Social hot topics from the 1960s persisted into the 1970s, too, such as the civil rights movement, feminism, and generational conflict, all on contested ground with a myriad of Christian reactions. These circumstances account in part for the diversity of reactions to the Vietnam War.[4]

The United States came out of the 1960s and entered into the Nixon era still confronting a divided nation, much of the division stemming from the

Vietnam War. Christian America often reflected this divisiveness by voicing firm convictions about the various issues. In doing so, Christians not only reflected society but also shaped opinions, offered solutions, and contributed to the fray in positive and negative ways. We must analyze the way Richard Nixon's presidency affected the course of American religious history because of his Vietnam War policies. Conservative Christians' backing of the president guided them increasingly toward the Republican Party, while liberals felt lied to and criticized him at every turn, foreshadowing their intense denunciation of him during the Watergate crisis. Still other Christians changed their mind about the Vietnam War, demonstrating how religious arguments against it finally started to sway more and more people by the 1970s.

Conservatives Back Nixon's "Peace with Honor"

The presence of Richard Nixon in the White House altered the way conservative Christians approached politics, in part because they maintained a traditional Cold War faith in the domino theory. With a Republican president, they found a voice in the White House with whom they agreed on a myriad of issues, including Nixon's strong anti-Communist credentials. They therefore worked diligently to support his policies and ward off the ever-increasing calls to end the Vietnam War immediately because they desired Nixon's "peace with honor." In taking this stance, they publicly sided with the Republican Party. As other research has shown, they began to align with GOP policies on race and law and order, or more generically because of their overall conservative domestic policy. But conservative Christians also gravitated toward Republican politics because of Nixon's handling of the Vietnam War, another factor that became a key reason why more and more conservative, evangelical Christians crafted a coalition that became the Religious Right and a core component to Republican constituencies in the late twentieth century.

Christianity Today completely believed Nixon's rhetoric about both Vietnamization and peace with honor. For a periodical that persisted in a strong anticommunist agenda and continually pointed out Communist oppression around the world, this position made sense. Editors and writers distrusted the North Vietnamese, as they did the Union of Soviet Socialist Republics and the People's Republic of China. When considering the lack of progress in peace negotiations between the United States and North Vietnam, therefore, they blamed the deceptive Communist tactics of North Vietnam for thwarting sincere U.S. efforts. To them, the United States protected its ally and sought a fair treaty while the Communists desired a false peace that actually paved the way for a complete, hostile takeover of all Southeast Asia. When the treaty was finally signed in January 1973, the periodical proclaimed that Nixon had indeed achieved "peace with honor." Spreading the Gospel around the globe still included combating communism and its atheistic threat everywhere. *Christianity Today* positioned itself among Christian entities that came to believe that Nixon's conservative foreign policy, and Republican Party stances in the area of foreign policy, best protected their international interests.

This conservative blaming of Communists for the Vietnam War materialized every time *Christianity Today* wrote about the failed peace talks between the United States and North Vietnam prior to the accord of 1973. Though editors did wish that Nixon and the United States would take more decisive action and not simply react to North Vietnamese maneuvers, they accused North Vietnam time and again of undermining negotiations. Their reaction to the 1970 U.S. bombing of Cambodia reveals this point: "No one should have been surprised when they [North Vietnam] aimed this blow against Cambodia. First, it was calculated to test the United States to see if it would intervene. Second, they knew that non-intervention would imperil the military position of the United States and South Viet Nam." Editors maintained that North Vietnam's entry into Cambodia first meant that the Communists created the problem, forcing a Nixon reaction. This view subsequently justified in their minds any response that Nixon implemented to protect U.S. interests. This editorial attitude from 1970 remained the same two years later. Explaining why the war continued, editors wrote that "there is no reason why an agreement in Viet Nam could not have been reached long ago were it not for Hanoi's intransigence. The United States would not have resumed bombing North Viet Nam if Hanoi had not invaded South Viet Nam."[5]

Some of this Nixon-backing came from evangelist Billy Graham, one of the founders of the periodical and a close friend of the president. The most famous revivalist preacher of the postwar era, Graham gained fame and adherents in part because he warned that the Cold War and existence of communism signaled the approaching end times. This staunch anti-communism continued through much of his career, as he gained the trust of several presidents and became an advisor to numerous administrations. Graham followed a convoluted odyssey regarding his view of the Vietnam War. He publicly asked for support for the president and his foreign policy under both Johnson and Nixon, as well as linking the Vietnam War to his avid Cold Warrior's mentality. At the same time, he attempted to distance himself from the divisiveness by making generic comments about war being a punishment from God, expressing pessimism upon returning from visits to Vietnam about the war's viability, and reminding his followers that peace should be the ultimate goal of humanity. This ambiguity, along with accusations that he was prowar, prompted the preacher to issue a statement, which was printed in *Christianity Today*. Claiming that he had "avoided expressions as to who was right and who was wrong," Graham declared that "I have never advocated war! I deplore it!" In at least an indication that he held sympathies for the American side, however, he continued that "everyone knows that President Nixon and I have been personal friends for many years and that I believe him to be motivated by a desire for peace." Graham believed Nixon and pushed to bring readers to further trust in the president through his personal relationship. While not using the words "peace with honor," Graham's rebuttal to his critics still left the impression that he supported presidential policy in Vietnam. Coming from a renowned evangelist, such pronouncements certainly were likely to have swayed some conservative Americans to also back the president.[6]

Christianity Today's reportage of the Vietnam War during the 1970s reflected American society in a key way: it had grown weary of discussing the war, avoided addressing many pivotal moments in the war's progress and in Americans' reactions to it, and searched for any way possible to move forward from the division and debate that had characterized the war. In 1970, for example, the periodical never mentioned in any way the Kent State University or Jackson State University shootings. Coming from a journal that regularly wrote about current events, this lack of reporting was stunning. It suggests that for these evangelical leaders, nothing good or new could come from a continued engagement with the prosecution of the Vietnam War and fighting about it at home. Yet editors did justify Nixon's bombing of Cambodia, an escalation of the war that had triggered the springtime campus protests, indicating at a minimum that they disagreed with the students' point of view. Perhaps editor-at-large Carl F. H. Henry put it best when he opined about a movement by denominations and other churches to seek more members and spread their brand of religion. He saw this 1973 campaign as "a time of renewal for the nation no less than for American evangelical Christians. In the aftermath of the Viet Nam war, a new opportunity exists for national unity and stability, and its best guarantee lies in the renewal of moral and spiritual sensitivities." For too many Americans, the negotiated peace between the United States and North Vietnam that generated the withdrawal of U.S. troops signaled the end of the war in January 1973. Henry shared this perception, despite the fact that America continued to prop up the South Vietnamese government with military and economic aid and the fact that a civil war still raged in that country. After the longest war in U.S. history, this periodical shared most of America's wish to simply move on and forget what had happened on the other side of the world. Yet, at the same time, we must not lose sight of *Christianity Today's* conservative backing of Nixon's Southeast Asian policies. Too often, studies focus on the increasing angst in America about Nixon's foreign policy, without acknowledging that many Americans continued to support him. The stated views of *Christianity Today* and religious leaders such as Billy Graham demonstrate that some Christians still believed that South Vietnam was worth protecting.[7]

Fellow evangelicals in the Southern Baptist Convention agreed with their colleagues at *Christianity Today*. As he did when writing about any foreign policy matter, Hudson Baggett used the *Alabama Baptist* as a platform for articulating a prowar SBC stance. His comments about Vietnam during the 1970s accused North Vietnam of concealing its presence in South Vietnam, Cambodia, and Laos and insisted that "military force is all that will deter such rulers" as those in Hanoi. He continued to explain that "critics who claim that we should not use force to stop the Communists are advocating a policy which will lead to Communist expansion and domination." His opinion remained the same in 1972 when he stated that Communists never adhered to their part of treaties and would not do so in Vietnam. In Baggett's mind, this double crossing made it imperative that the United States fight to protect its interest in Vietnam and not believe any peace overtures. In responding to antiwar critics, he asked, "Why shouldn't the American people want something better than agreements that are meaningless in resolving the Vietnam War?" Baggett and his colleagues also backed the president's Vietnam policies, though history has lost many of their voices; and in doing so, they had one more issue to use as they strove to move conservative southern Christians toward the Republican Party.[8]

Hudson Baggett had plenty of conservative company from within the Southern Baptist Convention. After the death of the four students at Kent State University, the editor of the Tennessee Baptist Convention's *Baptist and Reflector* backed the president's law and order campaign. James A. Lester acknowledged the "tragic loss of life" but stated that it "serves to remind us that governmental decisions and constitutional legal interpretations can not be made on college and university campuses." Americans had to trust the government and due process to protect the United States. A captain in the

U.S. Navy and former prisoner of war also criticized the American antiwar movement within the pages of the *Baptist and Reflector* because it inhibited the Vietnam War. After a few Americans visited North Vietnam as a delegation attempting to find common ground in order to negotiate an end to the war, Captain Howard Rutledge took exception to this nonofficial envoy that had defied its own government. He called those who had visited Hanoi "treasonous Americans" because they gave heart to the Communists and in his eyes turned the POWs into negotiating leverage, thus prolonging their incarceration. The frequent appearance of such opinions in Baptist papers reveals a prowar attitude that trusted the Nixon administration and maintained a hostile attitude toward all Communists. It both reflects the way conservative Americans felt about the war and demonstrates one way in which they worked to shape public opinion into the 1970s, when history otherwise asserts that Americans had grown weary of the war.[9]

Southern Baptist Convention presidents from the 1970s also supported Nixon's policy in Vietnam because they felt that it protected America and Christians around the world. The fact that the national convention elected such conservative individuals supports the notion that the SBC was largely a conservative group of people. After Carl Bates was elected SBC president in 1970, the pastor of First Baptist Church in Charlotte, North Carolina, was asked about his view on the Vietnam War. In response to the news that President Nixon had authorized the bombing of Cambodia, Bates stated that he thought "President Nixon must be one of the most courageous men in the world" for doing what he thought would lead to a U.S. victory, despite the unpopularity of this move. Former SBC president W. A. Criswell articulated a similar position in 1971 after visiting the White House with other Christian leaders. Though Billy Graham had organized the meeting to address Nixon's announced visit to the People's Republic of China, Criswell also stated that "America will not allow Southeast Asia to fall to the Communists." He, too, had faith in Nixon's conservative Cold War approach to Vietnam. SBC presidents therefore wanted to shape SBC members toward a prowar point of view.[10]

Similar reactions to the January 1973 peace treaty between the United States and North Vietnam rang out in the Southern Baptist Convention regional newspapers. Not only did they demonstrate a generally prowar attitude; they also reveal a segment of the American population that very much trusted the Nixon administration's pledge that this treaty brought peace with honor, and the guarantee of South Vietnam's safety. Signaling the fatigue that Americans felt toward the war, *Baptist Message* editor James F. Cole also emphasized that "most Americans are truly grateful" despite a lack of evident jubilation. His colleague at the *Christian Index* did sound jubilant when Jack U. Harwell stated that "President Richard M. Nixon and all involved are to be commended for finally bringing to pass" a peaceful settlement. James A. Lester sounded a refrain of sorrow that the war had occurred in the first place, but backed what the United States had done: "The impact, side effects, sorrow, personal loss, and financial loss will be long felt and remembered by the entire nation for many years. It was perhaps necessary; none-the-less tragic. We are grateful that our national leaders were able to negotiate this settlement. We pray that it will be a lasting one." J. Troy Prince of the *Alaska Baptist Messenger* took the opportunity to criticize antiwar protesters for not trusting that the government had sought peace in good faith when he wondered if those who had marched in Washington, D.C., against the war "will have another meeting to celebrate the cease-fire?!" Most editors of Baptist newspapers demonstrated society's conservatism; they rejoiced at peace, believed that the administration had had to wait this long to get it in order to safeguard South Vietnam, and therefore applauded the president on this occasion.[11]

A clearer depiction of Southern Baptist Convention conservatism emerges when one examines resolutions relating to the Vietnam War passed throughout the early 1970s. If the SBC split between moderates and conservatives surprised many as it developed by the end of the decade, the general denominational tone regarding Vietnam should have alerted many to how far right many in the SBC had aligned themselves. In 1970, messengers pleaded for peace and described the war as "a long and lonely" one. But after maintaining that the Bible urged people to live in peace, they also declared that "Scriptures plainly teach respect and honor for governmental officials," in this case the president of the United States. They therefore resolved to "give full support to the Commander-in-Chief of our nation in those efforts to bring about a just and honorable peace." Messengers maintained the same position two years later, stating that the war's end "should be reached with the attainment of the announced objective of the United States, namely to preserve the independence and self-government of the people of South Vietnam and the return of the American prisoners of war." Nixon's propaganda about why he had to continue the war resonated with the Southern Baptist Convention, where members generally believed that he wanted to preserve South Vietnam and that the war was necessary for U.S. security. The Louisiana Baptist Convention agreed with the larger denomination when they resolved in November 1972 to "commend President Nixon for his role in seeking a just and honorable settlement" to the Vietnam War. And national messengers felt vindicated with the ultimate peace treaty signed by the United States. Their faith in the president never wavered, but grew as a result of the negotiated settlement. The 1973 Southern Baptist Convention therefore resolved to once again "commend President Nixon for his efforts in bringing honorable peace to Vietnam and his continued efforts to insure peace in Southeast Asia." The denomination's actions provide a snapshot of some Americans who supported President Nixon and his Vietnam policies. These conservative Christians were publicly affiliating with the Republican Party, even if they avoided stating as much. Inspired to do so because of Nixon's stance on the Vietnam War, they counteracted the many Americans who had come to denounce the United States' involvement in Southeast Asia.[12]

For conservatives, this backing of Nixon's policy for Southeast Asia also stemmed from worry about the fate of Christians in that area. The fact that Communists oppressed Christians in Vietnam further intensified their hope for a U.S. victory because only a defeat of the Communists could secure a continued Christian outreach to that land. *Christianity Today* editors explained this consideration in a July 1970 editorial: "One of the most tragic but least known aspects of the war in Viet Nam is the suffering inflicted upon Christian workers there." The article then detailed the murder by unknown assailants of a pastor in the Central Highlands. This attack on the church lay at the heart of *Christianity Today*'s prowar leanings; as the editors explained,

If such cruelties are committed in the face of American military might, what can be expected when forces of restraint are withdrawn and the brutal aggressors are left to their own devices? To compound our distress we have but to think of world opinion with its seemingly increasing insensitivity toward this kind of evil—unless it is perpetrated by "American imperialists."

Amidst the suffering and danger, news editor Edward E. Plowman furthered this reasoning with tales of success for Christian missionaries there. The devastation of the land led many inhabitants to seek spiritual answers or hope in the midst of despair, leading many to the Christian god. Missionaries told the periodical first-hand of such encounters: "Conversion accounts abound. One of the best known is about a young man who passed a church on his way to carry out a robbery. He heard shouting and crying, went inside to investigate, and was converted." Such stories played out the calling of evangelical believers, a missionary zeal threatened if Communists controlled that country. While many secular political and diplomatic opinions guided *Christianity Today*'s Vietnam stance, the religious was equally, if not more, important.[13]

The Southern Baptist Convention concurred with such concern for missionaries and Christians in Vietnam. First-hand accounts of Communist atrocities and the danger to Christians in the region shaped a prowar attitude for those living and serving in Vietnam. For many, it simply came because they saw the positive things the United States did there. George W. Cummins, the director of the Southern Baptist Home Mission Board's Chaplaincy Commission, visited Vietnam and returned to report that "the road our servicemen are blazing in Vietnam today is paved with new hospitals, new orphanages, new homes." This building and allowing for missionary work led him to back the war effort. Often, missionaries placed the blame on Communists for needing such relief efforts. As another SBC visitor to Vietnam explained upon returning, "Forty percent of the population are displaced persons who have been forced to leave their land and villages and move to the larger cities, where there is a higher security and protection from the Vietcong." Even after the United States pulled its forces out of the war in January 1973, missionaries hoped that the South Vietnamese government would endure with U.S. backing in order to allow for Christian outreach. While worrying about what might happen in Vietnam to Christians after the U.S. withdrawal, the Southern Baptist Foreign Mission Board maintained a presence there and used "every available means to minister to human need." The SBC Foreign Mission Board secretary for Southeast Asia echoed this sentiment, explaining that "the transitional period between war and peacetime in Vietnam may present new opportunities for evangelistic work." Missionaries had a unique perspective from which they viewed the war. Their relief and recovery brought them into contact with the positive side of what U.S. forces did and exposed the brutality of the war, which they blamed on the Communists. Hoping to continue their Christian outreach, they supported the United States and South Vietnam as the only guarantee for the survival of their evangelism.[14]

Conservative Americans generally trusted Richard M. Nixon and therefore his pledge to bring "peace with honor" to Vietnam. While much literature about this period in American history outlines the changed foreign policy opinions of Americans because of the Vietnam War, evidence suggests that this shift was not universal. These conservative Christians believed that the president had succeeded in protecting the United States and South Vietnam from communism with the January 1973 peace treaty. This point of view exposes an America too often ignored in accounts about Christianity and foreign policy during that period: staunch backers of the government who continued to fear communism and thought that the Vietnam War *proved* the domino theory correct. Furthermore, in their close alignment with Nixon's Vietnam War policy, we see another factor in the way conservative Christians began to lean toward Republican Party politics already in the early 1970s.

The Immorality of Nixon's Policies

Despite this vocal conservative advocacy for Richard Nixon's handling of the Vietnam War, other Christians denounced the president from the moment he took office in 1969 and never trusted that he genuinely worked for peace. Thinking him high on propaganda and low on actual results, liberal Christians criticized his policies at every turn and employed a theology of human improvement to make their case. Despite evidence in other studies that shows the antiwar movement tapering off by the 1970s, these Christians continued a consistent mantra against the war and therefore in opposition to the president. Nixon had caused some Americans to question his morality long before anyone had ever heard of the Watergate building in Washington, D.C., some as far back as the 1950s.

The *Christian Century* castigated the Nixon administration for continuing to prosecute what it had from the beginning called an immoral war. The mainline Protestant periodical forged ahead as an intellectual forum for Christian America and printed editorials and articles that espoused an antiwar ideology. Much of this writing started with the changed philosophy it took toward the Cold War, where a perception of a monolithic Communist threat had given way to seeing a complex ideology with variances throughout the globe, including Southeast Asia. Nixon's promise of peace with honor and persistent backing of a morally bankrupt regime in South Vietnam brought the wrath of the journal down upon the White House, even after the peace treaty that withdrew American forces from Vietnam in 1973. The *Christian Century* disdained what it called an immoral war against a smaller nation by an imperialist invader, campaigning to the bitter end to sway public opinion toward this perception, which included a negative characterization of the president.

The *Christian Century*'s lost faith in containment theory provided the first stone in its foundation for supporting the antiwar movement against Nixon. Where conservatives saw a Communist threat and another domino about to fall, editors here saw a civil war in Vietnam that at its heart had to do with self-determination and foreign domination. Associate editor Cornish Rogers pinned part of the problem on President Nixon for failing to grasp this new reality because "what he intends to do is to freeze the world as it is now."

Both the Lyndon B. Johnson and Nixon administrations in part justified the Vietnam War with the Cold War argument of stopping the spread of communism. As part of a larger intellectual community in America that by the 1970s seriously questioned domino theory dogmas, the *Christian Century* no longer allowed that that rationale justified any military engagements, especially in Vietnam. It fought to teach readers this new reality through editorials and frequent articles.[15]

Richard M. Nixon further drew the wrath of the journal for his actions as president, unlike the finer line walked by the *Christian Century* in the 1960s, when it had at least agreed with Johnson's domestic policies. Whether it was race, welfare, women's rights, or a myriad of other issues, the interdenominational periodical always found itself in opposition to the president. From the onset of his presidency, Nixon completely shunned liberal Christian ideas and input, making it clear that he would court the evangelical vote while brushing aside mainline Protestantism and its ecumenical leadership. This attitude and approach made it easier to suspect him regarding Vietnam. In fact, not only did editors and writers disagree with his foreign policy; they alleged sinister motives for his adopting the stance he did and had a hard time believing what he said—all of this long before the Watergate scandal that eventually disintegrated his administration. They accused Nixon of lying to win the 1968 election when he promised that he had a plan to end the Vietnam War. Four years later as he ran for reelection and the war persisted, United Methodist Church bishop James Armstrong wrote, "That was four years ago! Since then, 20,000 American men have died; more bomb tonnage has been dropped than the total during the preceding 15 years; more American tax dollars have been spent than during all of those 15 years. And the war has been expanded into Cambodia." Simply put, the president could not be trusted.[16]

Nothing galvanized *Christian Century* editorial opinion against the Vietnam War and the president more than his revealing in April 1970 that the United States had bombed Cambodia and that the war had spread to Laos. This illegal action, regardless of the military reasons presented by the government to justify it, proved to the periodical that the administration never had had a plan for peace and was only giving negotiations lip service. Dismissing anything that the White House said, editors stated that it should not have surprised anyone that the United States involved itself in regions outside of Vietnam because evidence of such activity had been known for several years. If anything, they hoped that the reportage would turn more Americans against the war and start the long process toward a U.S. withdrawal. By June, they matter-of-factly asserted that "U.S. operations in Cambodia must be halted immediately. While Senate deliberations over the invasion grind on interminably, it is encouraging to have had a majority of that body for the very first time in the long course of the disastrous Indochina war reject the policy of a President seeking authority to extend the war." This referred to the Senate rejection of a proposal endorsed by Nixon to authorize sending troops into Cambodia in the wake of the announcement that the United States had attacked the Ho Chi Minh Trail earlier that spring. Once again, the periodical worked diligently to sway reader opinions toward its point of view. Its antiwar crusade persisted until the fighting had ended.[17]

True to their word, the peace accord of later that month brought no rejoicing to the editorial offices of the *Christian Century*. Associate editor Jill Drum Floerke demanded that the peace movement continue despite the U.S. withdrawal because the repressions of South Vietnam and America's backing of that government continued nonetheless. Citing the professional aid worker Don Luce, she agreed with him about the need "for a continuing follow-up in regard to U.S. involvement in Vietnam—for example, to protest our continued supplying of military hardware and to watchdog the Saigon regime to bring about the end of the repression." Unlike many other Americans, including many other Christians, the *Christian Century* understood that the war continued after January 1973, with economic and military assistance from the United States. According to Floerke, this propagated American guilt and immorality. The first editorial that appeared after the White House announced the peace settlement summarized the periodical's opinion best:

> The peace that has finally come can be described in many ways, but the one word that cannot apply is "honor." And that is precisely the word President Nixon has used and the word the public has accepted without complaint. An eerie feeling emerges as the peace begins—a feeling that what is concluding is not a war in which millions died, but a bad performance, a one-sided game, or something equally unreal that no longer affects us personally. It is the culminating horror of a series of horrors that the war's conclusion is described as "honorable" in much the same way other adjectives refer to toothpaste as "bright," automobiles as "powerful" and cigarettes as "mild." Such words provide a façade covering something no one believes in order to trigger a shallow emotion of self deception.[18]

Commonweal, the Catholic lay periodical that in the 1960s had moved from cautious support of the war toward a questioning of it, by the 1970s took a firm antiwar stance that also focused the blame on Richard M. Nixon.

They, too, campaigned against America remaining involved in the war until it came to an end and questioned the president's honesty long before Watergate, as had most within the antiwar movement. The April 1970 announcement that the United States had bombed Cambodia propelled editors to denounce the president. With bold language, they responded that "it was a ruthless, offensive act, extending and intensifying the war." To drive their point further, they compared American tactics in Vietnam to those used by the Communists to suppress people: "The land invasion of Cambodia and the air invasion of North Vietnam follow as logically from the twisted premises of our nation's leaders as did the invasion of Czechoslovakia [in 1968] from the twisted premises of the Kremlin." Worse, they, too, viewed the Cambodian bombings as illegal and as an escalation of the war that the president had promised to end. After the death of the students at Kent State University, editors in part faulted the president:

> President Nixon and Vice President Agnew cannot wash their hands of responsibility in the death of four students at Kent State, despite Mr. Nixon's attempts to confuse the issue at his televised news conference. The immediate cause of the Ohio tragedy was panic, bad training, and incredibly poor leadership on the part of the National Guard; the more remote but nonetheless real cause was the exacerbation of public opinion about campus anti-war demonstrations to which Mr. Nixon and Mr. Agnew have notably contributed.[19]

Commonweal again mirrored the *Christian Century* almost exactly when it reacted to the peace accord between the United States and North Vietnam. When Henry Kissinger first hinted at a settlement in fall 1972, editors stated, "This war was prolonged by the illusion of American omnipotence and the illusion that we're justified in using *any* means to attain our national goals. A true peace cannot be built on the illusion that we have attained those goals with honor." The journal did see the possibility for peace as something "for which to be prayerfully grateful." It would end a war, after all, that editors and writers in the lay Catholic periodical had fought against for some time. However, it feared that Americans misunderstood the reality of it: "First this is not a peace; it is a fragile cease-fire, which, among other limitations, has not halted U.S. bombing in Laos. Secondly, there is nothing in the cease-fire of honor for the U.S., nor should there be, nor could there be." They asserted that the lying of presidents, support for corrupt governments in South Vietnam, and too many wounded and dead on both sides eliminated all honor. In addition to joining other antiwar Americans in fearing that the nation would put the Vietnam War behind them too quickly, editors emphasized that they felt the United States had lost the war, regardless of presidential rhetoric to the contrary. The Vietnamese people failed to conform to U.S. ideology or wishes and "all the U.S. manages to do is to get out of a land and a situation it should never have gotten into in the first place." *Commonweal* presented a Catholic lay opinion that seldom linked its faith or theology to its Vietnam War platform or explained the reason why editors and writers addressed the issue. A journal dedicated to providing national and international news from a Catholic perspective saw the link between its religious calling and its denunciation of the war as obvious, especially given that the journal undergirded its antiwar argument with an implication that the United States fought an immoral war. It did not taper off its arguments against the war or grow weary of the protesting simply because the fighting had gone on for so long; rather, the periodical castigated the president and persisted with its righteous indignation against America's policy in Southeast Asia.[20]

The reaction to the U.S. bombing of Cambodia also highlights the way the United Church of Christ viewed Richard Nixon's prosecution of the Vietnam War. As chair of the International Relations Committee of the Council for Christian Social Action, George W. Shepherd Jr. declared that "President Nixon has unleashed the Generals to invade a neutral nation," thereby creating an "unlimited Indo-China war." This provided for him a perfect example of why the UCC had to fight against American involvement in the war: "People of good conscience and faith cannot remain silent as we make this unparalleled move into a wider war." Former UCC copresident James E. Wagner added his "complete revulsion and outrage at these moves." Lay people articulated the same displeasure. A single father who marched in peace rallies with his children and actively protested the war criticized an article that his children had brought home from school that defined "Vietnamization." He lamented that "the article doesn't tell that Vietnamization means invading Cambodia and Laos and bombing North Vietnam." In his questioning of what the school taught his children, he also criticized U.S. policy in Cambodia and its subsequent illegal expansion of the war. Even into 1973, UCC lay and clergy members deplored the bombing. In the General Synod's resolution about Cambodia, delegates stated that "there is no moral basis to continue bombing in Cambodia" and urged "Congress to cut off funds for all U.S. military operations, direct or indirect in, over and from off the shores of Southeast Asia." As many Americans tried to forget what the United States had done in Vietnam because U.S. troops had stopped fighting there, UCC delegates reminded the nation that the war continued and that the United States still illegally bombed neutral nations. This denomination's antiwar crusade would not stop until the war had really ended. And much of this antiwar campaigning was linked to a profound mistrust of President Nixon that had started for members of the UCC the moment he took office.[21]

These Christian antiwar entities also framed their argument in a religious context, usually with a theology of human improvement or articulation of the war's immorality. The antiwar opinions of *Christian Century* writers and editors centered on an angst that the United States had embroiled itself in an immoral war. Whether they focused on religious references or more basic reporting and editorializing, here lay the reason why the *Christian Century* so persistently and dogmatically spoke against the Vietnam War and the president of the United States. Roger L. Shinn, the Reinhold Niebuhr professor of social ethics at Union Theological Seminary, provided an article that articulated the moral dilemma the nation faced because of the Vietnam War in the context of the 1972 presidential election. First, Shinn decried the fact that "not everyone admits that this has been an *immoral* war." He then criticized that Nixon's address at the Republican Convention in Miami promised "'never to stain the honor of the United States of America'" but never said anything about "My Lai, burned villages and napalmed children. The President's stance was that expediency might commend withdrawal, but that morality required the courageous decision to persist." Shinn hardly believed this posturing and worried about a nation unwilling to admit having made an error and therefore change its ways. Though it was difficult for a society to do so, he stated, "a people who believe in a God of justice and mercy might" alter course if they later deem earlier events as wrong. Shinn feared, however, that Americans had come dangerously close to viewing themselves as barely distinguishable from God. Too much faith in the nation and trust in all of its decisions had created an immoral climate that justified the Vietnam War and ignored war atrocities committed by it. Through this ideology, the journal reflected views that drove many Americans to an antiwar position.[22]

The *Christian Century* editorials page echoed this sentiment time and again throughout the 1970s. It repeatedly called the war immoral and detailed example after example to prove this point, including My Lai, injured and killed civilians, Kent State University, and a deceitful president. When Henry Kissinger announced in fall 1972 that he neared a peace settlement with the North Vietnamese, the sin of the war prohibited editors from trusting these words, hoping for their truth, or thinking that they erased national guilt. They stated that "of one thing we feel certain: if peace does come, it is not likely to inspire dancing in the streets or jubilant celebration of any kind. The sense of shame is too overwhelming for that." Its pessimism proved true immediately after, as November ground into December and gave way to early January 1973 without a peace treaty. Editors declared that lashing out at the president or becoming numb hardly mattered because "neither lethargy nor blind fury will bring about the redemption of a nation that has lost its soul because it does not have the moral capacity nor the available leadership to acknowledge a tragically wrong national policy of self-defeating imperialism."[23]

Yet not all writers held an entirely pessimistic attitude toward the United States ending its military engagement in Southeast Asia. Martin E. Marty took space in his column in the *Christian Century* to applaud the antiwar movement for struggling those long years to be heard by the government and American people. Admitting that "no one knows just what direct impact the movement in its prime had," he believed that Americans had eventually come to agree with it. At the least, Marty asserted, "I do know that people of conscience witnessed when they had to—to the nation where they could, and to each other in often unnoticed ways—and that something of enduring worth occurred." Here again the spiritual aspect of the *Christian Century*'s antiwar activism came into play. Marty's uplifting of the peace movement thanked it for living out a calling and listening to an inner conscience despite government attempts to thwart it and accusations of un-American behavior. Though it is still difficult for historians to verify quantifiably, they have proven Marty correct: though it was a long process with little immediate reward, the historiography has demonstrated how the peace movement influenced government policies and finally contributed to the U.S. withdrawal and January 1973 peace treaty. The *Christian Century*'s platform for publishing liberal, intellectual Christian thought sought to pull more and more Americans toward this antiwar point of view.[24]

U.S. Catholic and Jubilee, published monthly by the Claretian Fathers at St. Jude Seminary in Momence, Illinois, agreed with its Protestant colleagues and couched its antiwar statements in a religious context, thus sustaining an approach to the Vietnam War that it had begun in the 1960s and that took a variety of shapes but placed theology at the center of its condemnation. The violence particularly concerned editors and writers. Having discarded the domino theory as irrelevant to Southeast Asia, the periodical questioned why the United States clung so tenaciously to prosecuting the war and wanted to allow for Vietnamese self-determination, even if that meant communism. At the heart of this argument lay the belief that war and violence were evil. Robert E. Burns, executive editor, wrote, "But we can be sure that violence will continue until enough of us are convinced that all violence is evil. Until enough of us are repelled by a boastful 'body count' that tells us gleefully how many 'gooks' or 'slopes' were killed in Cambodia last week. Until enough of us are horrified by people who call themselves Christians justifying killing." Burns saw the morality problem as an American one. It is not that *U.S. Catholic and Jubilee* ever presented support or even tacit approval of communism; they never did. Rather, they worked to influence their country and understood that they could only persuade leaders and civilians in the United States. Seeing the war in the context of good versus evil, and placing the United States' stance with the former, this Catholic periodical continually denounced the Vietnam War, pushing its readers to see it through the lens of morality. We must emphasize the carefully crafted moral argument of such periodicals. Theological reflections buttressed this opinion for the Christians studied here.[25]

In addition to general condemnations about the war's immorality, stories and examples of Catholic participation in the antiwar movement motivated *U.S. Catholic and Jubilee* to condemn the war. St. Ann's Chapel in Palo Alto, California, provided the periodical with inspiration for how the church could blend with the antiwar movement to make a difference. The congregation allied with at least twelve other churches from various denominations to create the Bay Area Sanctuary Caucus. The churches provided food, shelter, counseling, and other support for military service personnel who refused to follow orders to go to Vietnam because they conscientiously objected to the war. A November 1972 article described how St. Ann's became involved in harboring one nineteen-year-old sailor from Detroit, Richard R. Larson. He had initially joined the navy because he came from a military family and supported his country. A tour of duty off the coast of Vietnam changed his mind, as he "began to feel as though he was doing the bombing himself, even though he was only a fireman." Larson was the first person protected by St. Ann's. He stayed there and at two other churches for four days, until the navy apprehended him, court-martialed him, and sentenced him to thirty days in the brig before giving him an honorable discharge as a conscientious objector. This story provided an example of what individual congregations could do to combat the Vietnam War. In this way, the periodical had moved from a more cautious analysis of the Vietnam War in the 1960s to a forthright denunciation of it in the 1970s, all the while placing its opinions in a Catholic/religious context so that readers could learn about the moral context of their antiwar argument.[26]

As it had since coming out firmly against the war in 1968, *Catholic World* also placed its antiwar platform in a theological context. Published by the Paulist fathers, the periodical disdained the war because its total prosecution killed and injured too many innocent people and destroyed the entire land of Vietnam. The cost outweighed any benefit despite their dislike for communism and what it did to the Catholic Church around the world. Editor John B. Sheerin wanted Americans to "scrutinize the bleak moral background of the whole American involvement in a frightful war that has killed hundreds of thousands and ravaged a whole country without benefit to God or man." To him, the loss of life in the Vietnam War hardly justified any gain; not believing Cold War rhetoric about a demonic Communist Other, Sheerin denounced the war because of the sin inherit in any fighting. *Catholic World* also asserted that Christian stewardship of the earth and its environment mandated an end to the fighting. James B. Kelly, vice president for academic affairs at Adelphi University, criticized defoliation, harm to birds and animals, and other environmental problems directly caused by U.S. actions in Vietnam. He outlined how this hurt poor farmers and endangered the earth environmentally. Ultimately, Kelly wondered how such actions could be taken by a nation claiming to liberate a people. The auxiliary bishop of Detroit, Thomas J. Gumbleton, more directly attacked the war on moral grounds in fall 1972. He insisted that any Catholic should have discerned by that time that "America's continuing participation in the bloodletting and destruction in Vietnam, Laos, and Cambodia is without moral justification" because it was "contrary to the reverence for human life that is an essential Christian attitude." Once he had articulated that he hardly endorsed the Vietcong or North Vietnamese and recognized their atrocities, he made the now common remark that he could only sway those in his country and under his immediate influence to see the error of U.S. ways. He measured the war against the "Gospel of Jesus Christ" and "Christian morality" and found it wanting. U.S. actions in particular struck him as imperialist and misguided. Nothing in Catholic theology allowed for such a war. He thus solidified *Catholic World*'s antiwar theology and leadership during the 1970s as it strove to shape Catholic perceptions about the Vietnam War. Here was another voice using a theology of human improvement to denounce the war.[27]

Some members of the Southern Baptist Convention continued to disagree with their conservative colleagues and morally denounced Nixon's handling of the war, too. The Christian Life Commission had fought against the war during the 1960s, and the war's continuation into the 1970s particularly rankled them. Foy Valentine, the head of the CLC, most poignantly continued this antiwar mantra and criticized his denomination for not sharing his antiwar passion. He denounced the Vietnam War at every opportunity and articulated an anti-Nixon platform because he felt lied to by the president. Even after the negotiated peace of January 1973, Valentine told those in his denomination that he thanked God "for the prospect of truce, however tenuous, in Indochina." Rather than celebrate as if the war had ended in the United States' favor, he saw it as continuing and further urged that "the emotion-laden events of recent days challenge Christians everywhere to commit ourselves anew to work for what the Prince of Peace called the 'things that make for peace.'" Valentine worked hard to shape his denomination toward an antiwar point of view despite failing in this effort. Valentine had some backing from other SBC clergy for this position. Frank Stagg preached a sermon at Crescent Hill Baptist Church in Louisville, Kentucky, that blasted the Vietnam War right after Richard Nixon was inaugurated in 1969. He clearly felt called to denounce the war from the pulpit, thus making it a secular, foreign-policy issue that demanded Christian attention. Where his prowar counterparts saw the Cold and Vietnam wars as religious battles against evil, Stagg thought that the Vietnam War went against Christian principles. He questioned the connection made by many conservatives to Vietnam being a war between right and wrong forces: "I do not believe that there is in Vietnam a simple war between good and evil, as a Baptist minister told the President. I do not believe that national security is being served. I believe that it is imperiled." He especially criticized that the United States was "killing" the Vietnamese people and "destroying their country." Here again we see Christians deriding Nixon from the beginning of his administration because of what they perceived as an immoral handling of the Vietnam War. Religion mixed with politics to create another source of opposition to Nixon's policies.[28]

The United Church of Christ's position also included a strong religious reasoning. Under Nixon, the actions of the General Synod and statements by UCC leaders became more vehement in their antiwar protests and condemnatory in their rhetoric. This attitude fit well with the overall context of the UCC during this decade, as it consistently fought in America and around the globe for social justice for the underprivileged, for example, supporting the grape boycott on behalf of American farm workers, advocating for federal welfare programs, and denouncing imperial moves by Western nations that impoverished indigenous peoples. Since its founding in 1957, the UCC had crafted a reputation for championing social justice issues and global peace initiatives. Despite a persistent minority dissent to its antiwar platform, the United Church of Christ continued this tradition into the 1970s when it lambasted U.S. actions in Vietnam as unethical, un-American, and un-Christian. Of all the denominations examined here, the UCC did the most to try to shape public opinion toward an antiwar platform based on morality.

Resolutions, statements, and reports from the General Synod conventions in 1969, 1971, and 1973 best reveal this religiosity. Voicing its displeasure with the Vietnam War time and again, the General Synod tried to change the course of American history by persuading its own church members, politicians, and Americans at large toward an antiwar point of view. At the beginning of his administration during its 1969 convention, UCC delegates cautiously "express[ed] appreciation for President Nixon's desire to negotiate an end to the Vietnam war. We approve his declaration that the conflict must be terminated through political rather than military means." This position squared with that of other antiwar groups and people, both from within the Christian community and without, that at first hoped Nixon had told the truth when he pledged during his 1968 presidential campaign to end the war. In anticipation of Nixon's stalling to end the conflict, the 1969 resolution went on to say, "however, . . . the speed with which these steps are being taken is insufficient." The General Synod announced that "through pulpit and forum, ballot and media," it would fight against this war and finally resolved to "urge the President of the United States of America to declare an early cease-fire in Vietnam and to accelerate withdrawal of United States troops." Already in 1969, despite the initial hope of the resolution, the General Synod voiced the UCC's reluctance to believe Nixon and demand for the war to end immediately. The UCC took a strong stance early in his administration, thereby joining other antiwar Christians and secular groups in showing a dislike for Nixon from the moment he took office, not as a result of Watergate but in part because of his foreign policy in Southeast Asia.[29]

By 1971 at the next General Synod, delegates escalated their hostile rhetoric about the war and toward the administration. In a statement on "Peace and United States Power," delegates took issue with all sides of the Vietnam War, including the North Vietnamese, South Vietnamese, and National Liberation Front. But they aimed their most condemnatory comments at the United States because the UCC felt most responsible for its own government: "far more serious, the U.S., a highly technological society, conducts war on the rural, agrarian societies of Indochina under policies which seem designed deliberately to inflict severe damage on civilians." Though they did not place their criticisms directly in the context of just war theory, the killing and injuring of innocent bystanders in the Vietnam War by the United States enraged the UCC more than anything. In a 614 to 23 vote, delegates also resoundingly passed an antiwar resolution that contained severe denunciations of the U.S. government, its citizens, and even members of the United Church of Christ: they acknowledged "our own guilt by electoral consent and inattentiveness to legislative process for the involvement of the United States in what has been widely judged to be an immoral war." The resolution, however, emphasized that it supported the United States and issued this antiwar treatise "out of a love for our country." Another action item more pointedly criticized the Nixon administration and U.S. actions in Vietnam in the context of Christian morality when it "renounce[d] the strategy of partial United States disengagement from a war that is being immorally protracted under the mask of a racist 'Vietnamization,' supported by residual United States forces, war materials, and funds." General Synod then issued a demand for a peace conference led by the United States and a total withdrawal of U.S. forces from Southeast Asia. Indeed, it took over five pages, three resolutions, and countless hours for the Eighth General Synod of the UCC to voice its hostility toward the Vietnam War. Calling U.S. participation in the war "a revulsion to conscience," delegates also resolved to give "thanks for the witness of all those who have opposed with nonviolent civil disobedience the use of United States power in the war in Indochina." The UCC became a prophetic voice against the Vietnam War, crying out against its government and working for change through its constituency.[30]

One prophet from within the United Church of Christ in particular used his position to advocate for peace and placed this position within the denomination's humanist theology. UCC president Robert V. Moss had denounced the war from its beginning and publicly censured U.S. involvement in Southeast Asia. In his address to the 1971 General Synod, he endorsed the fact that the United States had begun to withdraw its forces from Vietnam, but disliked the fact that American officials and citizens alike couched this policy in terms of "saving American lives" and not in terms of saving "human lives." His Christian calling demanded a concern for all peoples of the world, not just those from the United States, when he proclaimed that "in the eyes of God, the life of the Montagnard peasant in the central highlands of Vietnam is as precious as that of my son and your son who have been called upon to fight there." Serving as the mouthpiece for the United Church of Christ, his closing address applauded the denomination for its prophetic voice and urged all members to continue fighting against the war:

> Where has there been more sincere and agonized grappling with the issue of the Vietnam War and America's responsibility for peace than we have done in this Synod? Our almost unanimous vote to end the war and to end the deception of the American people on war aims is a clear and triumphant expression of our faith, and of our love for our country.[31]

The United Church of Christ's official periodicals from the 1970s, *United Church Herald* followed by *A.D.*, and the editor of both, J. Martin Bailey, added another consistent antiwar voice to the denomination's theological argument. Throughout the 1970s, the UCC publications served both as mouthpieces for its antiwar platform and as the primary media source by which to get this message to its constituency. This continued a legacy established in 1957 at the creation of the UCC in which the periodical shaped and articulated the denomination's theological point of view, which first examined how Christians could best work on earth to improve conditions for all people. One editorial, after demanding a "cessation of all combat missions by American forces" in Vietnam, stated that "we should accompany the moratorium on missions in Vietnam with a moratorium on missions to the moon. Apollo 13 splashed down in an ocean that may be dead in a few decades. The life-support systems of billions of human beings on earth are in danger. We've got a problem *here*. We must secure life on earth before reaching for the stars." This statement fit the United Church of Christ's consistent call for social justice and care for all peoples of the earth, including those in Vietnam, as they sought to change American opinions. A carefully constructed theology of human improvement was behind the periodical's antiwar platform when it campaigned with readers to end the war.[32]

The Christians who represented a left-leaning point of view boldly proclaimed antiwar positions and frequently condemned the Nixon administration. Even more importantly, they couched this argument in a secular/military analysis of U.S. failures in Vietnam, in a denunciation of traditional Cold War diplomacy, *and* in a delineation of the immorality that led U.S. leaders to continue the war and that characterized its prosecution. Discarding the domino theory, angry at a president who lied to the American people, and "numb" from fighting against an immoral war, liberal Christians campaigned for the peace movement because of a calling to do so. Here we find Christians who denounced Nixon from the beginning of his presidency because they mistrusted his motives and disdained his policies in Southeast Asia when a theology of human improvement informed their opinions.

Changed Opinions: Conservatives and Moderates Join Forces with the Antiwar Movement

Not all Americans entered the 1970s with one point of view and came out of it with the same one. As with many other citizens, some moderate and conservative Christians changed their position, from support of U.S. involvement in the Vietnam War during the 1960s because of its Cold War context to a denunciation of the war in the 1970s. This change was in part due to a feeling by the end of Richard Nixon's first term in office that America had erred in its prosecution of the conflict.

America, which had steadfastly defended the Vietnam War during the 1960s, migrated toward a new understanding of it by the 1970s. The Jesuit periodical, on the one hand, continued to blame the Communists alone for the civil war and global unrest in general. This sustained the Cold War fear of Communist expansionism, manifest in the Southeast Asian conflicts and North Vietnamese attempts to control that region. When Nixon failed to achieve peace by 1970 and the war crept into Cambodia, *America* blamed the North Vietnamese for stonewalling negotiations out of alarm that its dominance over the region would suffer. Editors theorized that a peace treaty that established a protected South Vietnam concerned North Vietnam because its leaders knew "that its wider ambitions for Southeast Asia may well be at stake." Central to these reports lay the persistent belief that communism worked to reach around the globe and that North Vietnam belonged to part of a monolith orchestrating this endeavor. When the fall of 1972 brought with it a cease-fire and paved the way for the January 1973 accord, *America* still worried about North Vietnamese promises not to take control of Southeast Asia. A November editorial warned that the United States, Soviet Union, and PRC had responsibility to control the North Vietnamese and protect the South from such aggression because the superpowers ostensibly controlled the Communist world.[33]

Indeed, *America* repeatedly stated that any peace in Southeast Asia must include a U.S. pledge to protect South Vietnam as an independent state. Many Americans worried about the fate of South Vietnam and its people once the United States pulled out of the region. Whether because they believed that South Vietnam protected U.S. interests in democracy and the Cold War or because of fear for the people if the Communists took over, *America* and other secular and religious bodies wanted some assurance that the world would not abandon them. This created a central premise for Nixon's pledge to establish "peace with honor": his promises included that the United States would not completely abandon its South Vietnamese allies. When the peace treaty between North Vietnam and the United States became official, *America* believed that Nixon and Kissinger had preserved the rights of South Vietnam, something crucial to their backing of the accord. On the one hand, they commended Nixon and his security advisor "for their efforts in achieving this settlement." On the other hand, they asserted that the United States "ought to make that investment in Vietnam's future not only from enlightened self-interest but from recognition of some fundamental human obligations" toward the people in South Vietnam who had sided with America. Here their Christian outlook mingled with international affairs: "even if we had never waged over that earth a war costing us annually between $3 billion and $6 billion, we should still be obliged to help the Vietnamese for we are men and women and so are they. But we are rich and they are not." This cautious approach therefore became the way that *America* tried to sway Catholic opinion about the war.[34]

Such statements indicate a fact more clearly expressed elsewhere in *America* during the 1970s: the periodical had come to openly question U.S. policy in Vietnam. By 1972, in fact, articles and editorials sounded antiwar despite the cautions and caveats listed above. Mary McGrory wrote simply that "the war has corrupted and destroyed many institutions. The military has been an obvious casualty. The moral sensibility of the country is another, and may take far longer to repair." McGrory gave the religious context for why the Jesuit news magazine commented on international affairs: in this case, she and others feared that American war actions eroded morality beyond repair, a situation that demanded attention from the church. Although they stuck to demanding that a peace treaty protect South Vietnam, editors further drifted against the war in December 1972 when Nixon resumed bombing North Vietnam because he felt that the cease-fire had failed to force them to the bargaining table. Editors stated that "we have expressed our belief in the past that attempts to bomb the North into submission or into accepting our terms show no signs of effectiveness and are, moreover, morally indefensible at this stage of the war." Editors, too, linked such opinions to their Christian convictions, calling the bombings immoral because they injured civilians and hindered efforts toward peace. They demanded that the bombings end because "the shame we have been forced to bear before the world during the season of Christmas must not carry into the new year." These statements should not be perceived as parallel with those of other antiwar Christians, however. They certainly criticized the U.S. government and its indiscriminate bombing of North Vietnam. But elsewhere the editorial reiterates that South Vietnam had to be protected, and the general tone belies a dislike for the North Vietnamese. Nonetheless, the editorial signals a sharp turn from the generally prowar attitude and trust of the government that *America* espoused during the 1960s. This switch no doubt affected readers, too, who relied on the Jesuit periodical for gaining a Catholic context for their worldview. While *America* shied away from the harsh condemnations of Nixon leveled by other antiwar Christians, it nonetheless signaled that his policies in Southeast Asia had even lost some conservative support. The journal wanted to lead more Catholic Americans to question the war.[35]

Catholic Digest, too, manifested a subtle shift in its 1970s approach to Vietnam. As we have seen, during the 1960s, articles and reports about Vietnam focused on children to highlight the danger to them, to emphasize the need for outreach and monetary support, and to affect readers emotionally. This emphasis continued during the 1970s. Yet where the 1960s statements hinted at Communist brutality and tacitly supported the United States, 1970s commentaries merely described the horrors of war without taking sides. Kevin A. Devine wrote such a treatise when he described offering mass to a group of soldiers in Vietnam. He detailed the men's fatigue, grime, and general weary attitude to depict war's reality even away from the battlefront. But Devine was most struck when one soldier stated that he had read *Catholic Digest*'s call for people to donate money because it took but a few dollars to become a foster parent: "'I've got the money, but it's all in military script. How can I convert it into a money order to mail to a kid who needs it?'" Devine continued that "after 14 months in combat, I considered myself hardened. But I was so choked up, I found it difficult to answer this grunt in the jungles of Vietnam whose only worry was a hungry child somewhere else." For the writer of this article, such a story humanized the war with its moral tale about the soldier's concern for an unknown child. It never claimed to support or condemn the war. Rather, it told readers that moral stewardship knew no bounds, even in the most deplorable of circumstances.[36]

The African Methodist Episcopal Church changed, too. It lost the moderate tone it had taken in the 1960s toward the Vietnam War and, with a few exceptions, came out firmly against the war during the 1970s. With the Democrats out of the White House, the AME Church became more resolute in sharing its opinions about foreign policy because it held no sympathy for Nixon, who at best had a mixed record on race relations. Nixon wanted his administration to include a legacy of civil rights support, and he did attempt to address economic disparity and other issues for black Americans. At the same time, Nixon appealed to more racist elements in America by rolling back integration initiatives, especially with a public campaign against school busing. In part because Nixon did little to support black rights movements and key issues, by the 1970s church assemblies, the *Christian Recorder*, and AME leaders denounced the Vietnam War publicly. As with their other foreign policy reactions throughout these two decades, some of this denunciation mirrored that of other Christian responses while at other times AME statements more deliberately placed its opposition to the war in a racial context.[37]

The African Methodist Episcopal Church's primary periodical took the lead in articulating an antiwar position for the denomination, thus trying to lead its readers toward an antiwar point of view. In articles and editorials, the *Christian Recorder* outlined the reasons for members of this church to speak out against U.S. actions in Southeast Asia, especially in connection with the younger generation. The expansion of the fighting into Cambodia and the subsequent National Guard shooting of the students at Kent State University and police shootings at Jackson State University in spring 1970 provided a solid example for why writers took an antiwar stance. The pastor from Bethel AME Church in Portland, Oregon, Alfred Lee Henderson, not only condemned these events but declared that they demanded impeachment of the president. Stating that the shootings "unleashed the murderous and diabolical forces of evil upon our society," the minister went on to say that the students protested something they "consider destructive to the moral fiber of American principle." The church had to speak out to protect the right of dissent, especially when forces worked against it for immoral aims. When a group of church leaders from a variety of denominations wrote a letter to Richard M. Nixon to object to the Cambodian bombing and the shootings, AME bishop John D. Bright signed the letter of protest on behalf of his denomination. The *Christian Recorder* credited student protesters with propelling their church elders into such important action. A church body long attuned to fighting injustice saw itself as a voice crying in the wilderness that needed affirmation and backing. The periodical buttressed this encouragement with a report on the 16th Connectional Youth Congress of the AME Church that met in Indianapolis. In July 1970, the gathering resolved that "the youth of the A.M.E. Church are stating nonsupport of the war in Southeast Asia, and [demand] immediate withdrawal from Southeast Asia."[38]

Christian Recorder editor B. J. Nolen added his voice to the AME Church antiwar cry as well. He, too, had changed his approach from a more cautious deliberation in the 1960s to an antiwar position in the 1970s. In giving an overview of national events during the first six months of 1972, Nolen highlighted that "religious opposition to the war in Indo-China continued strong," thus affirming that dissent should include church voices. A September editorial more forcefully asserted that global Christianity had to campaign actively for peace. Though he admitted that churches at times could promote or even cause conflicts around the world, he stated that their true charge should be to challenge militarism. Nolen asked, "Can religion become a force for peace rather than an added 'demonic dimension' of war?

Religious leaders have been working to give an affirmative answer to this question." He also applauded the fact that "in the United States, churches have been in the forefront of the peace movement, concerned particularly about the war in Indo-China but also making efforts for peace in other trouble spots." In other words, Nolen felt that a Christian calling for peace must transcend Sunday morning and become activism in order to convince governments, including the United States in Vietnam, to resist the use of force whenever possible.[39]

Antiwar resolutions from AME district conferences added yet another voice to the denomination's activism. The resolutions and reports combined a belief that the war had become unwinnable with a Christian calling for peace. The Michigan Annual Conference studied the desire of the Vietnamese to fight the war and found it wanting. This unfortunately rare approach of examining the indigenous people led those on the Committee on the State of the Country to report that the Vietnamese soldier "will never win the war by proxy it seems, unless we stay in Vietnam forever. Our backing of the Vietnamese Government is a poor substitute for the allegiance of its own people." In other words, this AME conference maintained that the United States should cease fighting on behalf of a South Vietnamese government not wanted by its own people. In Indiana later that year, colleagues on the Social Action Committee wanted "to point out one important fact. These conflicts not only seem to be tearing the American society in half, but they have the affect of splitting the world down the middle." Thus, in addition to questioning what the Vietnamese wanted, this study outlined how the war damaged the United States and simultaneously fueled global tension, another reason for AME Church members to advocate for a withdrawal of U.S. forces. The First Episcopal District's New York Annual meeting combined these two factors to articulate its antiwar platform. First, the report from the Temperance Committee detailed how the combat inflicted too huge an amount of suffering upon the people of Vietnam. It then detailed how U.S. support for South Vietnam siphoned money away from poverty programs in the United States and pitted citizen against citizen. This declaration therefore concluded that "if the Church, starting with the First Episcopal District, does not speak out against this unjust, obscene, genocidal war, it will place itself in the position of being accused of intemperance."[40]

AME Church officials and members added a Christian conviction to these otherwise secular opinions about the war. After cataloging a litany of deaths, including those of innocent women, men, and children, the Indiana Conference Committee on Special Resolutions explained that as a Christian community, abiding by the Methodist calling to evangelize and commitment to Christian morality,

> We must individually and collectively make a concerted effort to bring peace once more to this world. We can do this by intensifying our efforts to introduce men everywhere to the "Prince of Peace." We can do this by becoming more involved in the political process of our nation and support those candidates who stand and run on a platform of peace.

The Committee on Special Resolutions for the Chicago Conference echoed these exact sentiments because "we do claim to have the mind of Christ in terms of trying to live peaceably with all men." This report thus asserted that "while the church gives sanction to armed preparation and military training as a defense against attack and for the elimination of evil, it must proclaim that war is unchristian and peace is the goal of the church." Here again, the AME Church revealed a relatively moderate tone, not wanting to appear entirely pacifist. Rather, a close examination of this particular war, coupled with Christian convictions, led to these antiwar reports and resolutions from various districts. The denomination's mistrust of Richard Nixon had also contributed to this changed mindset about the Vietnam War. It urged AME members to campaign to end the war as a Christian duty.[41]

By 1972, these AME convictions against the war led many to endorse George McGovern's candidacy for president, another example of how Nixon's foreign and domestic policies lost the support of previously moderate to conservative Christians. The Western District AME Sunday School Convention's August 1972 gathering went directly to the point. They backed the McGovern ticket, stating that the Democrats "did adopt a platform which addresses itself to bringing a war in Vietnam to an end and bringing our servicemen home." While it is impossible to gauge the exact effect in terms of AME members who then voted a certain way, especially in light of Nixon's landslide election, such statements display the church in action, voicing an antiwar conviction and attempting to use moral suasion to alter the political process. The General Conference added to this movement by announcing a voter registration drive to get more black people to vote. The reasoning for this tactic included a list of factors, including opposition to the Vietnam War. Citing the extreme monetary cost and loss of human life, the General Conference sought to back a candidate who would better serve the American people with welfare programs and an end to war. B. J. Nolen lent his voice and the *Christian Recorder* to this cause as well. He asserted that "with the Presidential election fast approaching, the crescendo appears to be accelerating. Those who cannot countenance a continuation of hostilities in Indo-China feel that a pre-election cease-fire must be reached." With these election-year opinions, the AME distinguished itself from other denominations that often shied away from political endorsements for fear that they might alienate constituents. For going on two centuries, this church body thrived on a combination of evangelical outreach, Christian passion, and social action unlike most other church bodies, particularly within white Protestantism. With Nixon having alienated so many racial minorities with his domestic policies, his Vietnam agenda easily came under attack from a denomination that had turned against the war.[42]

Not surprisingly, the denomination addressed race within many of its antiwar convictions. Dr. Herman Branson, president of the AME-affiliated Wilberforce University in Ohio, led a caucus of fifteen presidents from black colleges who "confronted" Nixon about his record on civil rights, poverty, war, and specifically the shootings at Jackson State University. Outraged at the administration's record, they requested changes aimed at alleviating such suffering and neglect by the government. The conversation included the disproportionate number of black people who had fought the Vietnam War because of poverty and a lack of educational opportunities, which prompted African Americans to volunteer in disproportionate numbers for the service, a fact supported since then by historical documentation. After over two hours of conversation, Nixon promised to make changes and become more attentive, though the historical record offers little tangible proof that he followed through on this pledge. This lack of response contributed further to AME disdain for the war. Other reports that pertained to the Vietnam War included discussions of race, such as the approving story about the first black soldier buried in a white cemetery after losing his life in Southeast Asia and general comments about the black community's increasing opposition to the war. The fact that the war took money from poverty programs aimed in part at African Americans, forced black men to fight disproportionately, and came from an administration that had lost any respect from a majority of black leaders contributed to this denomination's antiwar platform.[43]

As with many of the churches and periodicals that had denounced the Vietnam War, B. J. Nolen combined a sense of thanksgiving with continued remorse when the United States withdrew military forces from Vietnam in January 1973. Rejoicing that the killing of Americans would stop, Nolen also cautioned that the war had not ended for the Vietnamese and persisted with criticism of the Nixon administration for policies related to the war. Calling the peace accord "a reason for rejoicing" and also a time for "prayerful reflection," the *Christian Recorder* editor stated that "the years of dying in a far off land in the strangest of wars in U.S. history seems at an end. The flower of the nation's manhood can now look forward to a life of living, instead of the next day, the next hour, the next moment that might well send an unseen, unheard bullet for an end that's instant." Nolen celebrated this end of war and the fact that "President Nixon again summons the nation to another new beginning. This evokes hope, a commodity this nation has wasted on Vietnam for a decade." Nonetheless, the nation's turmoil continued and Nixon sent other mixed messages that troubled Nolen. The question of amnesty for those who had evaded the draft offered one example for Nolen of Nixon's duplicity. On the one hand, he had settled matters with the North Vietnamese and even agreed to help in rebuilding that war-ravaged land; yet he refused to grant amnesty for those who had conscientiously disagreed with his wartime decisions. For Nolen, this smacked of hypocrisy and added fuel to the AME fire against the Nixon administration.[44]

Clearly a number of Christians shifted significantly in their understandings of the Vietnam War. While all of the periodicals and denominations discussed in this chapter altered their understanding to some extent, much of that change had to do with whether or not they supported Richard Nixon and/or their degree of belief in containment theory. However, some moderate and conservative Christians followed a less explicit trajectory. Those who had taken a moderate approach in the 1960s became more dogmatic in their antiwar pronouncements by the 1970s; moderate to conservative sentiment about the war gravitated toward a neutrality or mixed opinion about various aspects of diplomacy. For Catholics, this American journey in many ways mimicked that of the pope, Vatican, and global Catholicism during that same period. The church had diligently fostered a changed image, from Cold Warrior to neutral advocate for peace. That campaign worked its way into the American Catholic scene in a noticeable way. These Christians helped shape U.S. Christian opinions about the Vietnam War during the 1970s and demonstrate that many Christians had changed their mind about the war by the time of the U.S. withdrawal because of their theological convictions and mistrust of Richard M. Nixon.

Conclusion

The mixed Christian opinions about the Vietnam War from the 1960s still existed in the 1970s, though with less diversity and a larger population of those opposed to the war. *Christianity Today* and most within the Southern Baptist Convention persisted in their support for the war, arguing that it was essential for protecting the United States from Communist expansion and the rest of the world from atheism. For them, nothing had changed from the 1950s in terms of foreign policy outlooks, and so they supported Nixon's Southeast Asian policies. In addition to siding with Nixon regarding race, "law and order," and his courting of the evangelical vote, the Christian Right also began to wed itself to the Republican Party because of its conservative foreign policy. The same consistency in argument came from the *Christian Century, Commonweal, U.S. Catholic and Jubilee, Catholic World,* and the United Church of Christ. These institutions denounced the war as imperialistic and immoral as they became more and more vehement in their antiwar protesting. They especially criticized President Nixon, whom they felt lied to the American people regarding his promise to end the war. Containment theory had become an outmoded relic of the past that led to un-Christian fighting against the Vietnamese. Furthermore, they continued their antiwar campaigning until the United States had withdrawn its military forces, unlike many others within the antiwar movement who had tapered off their activism by the early 1970s. However, where the 1960s had included a group of periodicals and denominations that contributed a mixed opinion about the war, the 1970s witnessed that ambiguity dissipate as more groups denounced the war. The African Methodist Episcopal Church, *America,* and *Catholic Digest* had previously revealed disparate opinions about the Vietnam War but now came to oppose it.

Christians held opinions that ran the gamut from hostility toward the war to support for the president and his policies, all working to contribute their voice to the culture war over U.S. actions in Southeast Asia. Whether an institution's stance represented an alteration from what it argued in the 1960s or not, each entity clung to its theological and social roots when responding to the war, despite some occasional blurring of these distinctions. While studies have portrayed Americans as vastly changed by the war experience and unrest at home, this consistency within the way Christians arrived at their war opinions indicates that, when Christian America analyzed the Vietnam War, articulated contrasting opinions about it, and anguished over it, they—at the same time—remained true to traditions, theology, and methods of protest or social commentary. In other words, American Christians had not changed profoundly their *way* of formulating opinions despite engaging intimately in the conversation or altering their view of the Vietnam War itself. In political and religious commentary, Christian America contributes to 1970s examinations of the Vietnam War because it reflects the debate taking place throughout the nation. Grasping the role that U.S. Christians played in articulating Vietnam War perceptions contributes to our understandings of that era in that it reflects a large portion of American society and the way it understood the war. It also demonstrates the unique way in which religious faith helped shape the way Christians came to these conclusions about the war.

Conclusion

1975

By 1975, much of America had grown tired of foreign policy debates, a reality borne out in portions of the Christian community yet with significant exceptions. Many entities lost interest in global issues, as revealed in the fact that Christian sources that had previously contained numerous and lengthy articulations of foreign affairs viewpoints housed much less such discussion by 1975. Yet other Christians remained aware of both the Cold and Vietnam wars in their print media, assemblies, and churchwide discussions. From March 1975 to early July 1975, Christian America's reaction to events in Southeast Asia summarized where the 1960s and 1970s had taken their religious convictions about foreign policy, thus also summarizing their contribution to the culture war about foreign policy that had gone on for over a decade.

For Americans refusing to put their heads in the sand, the events in Vietnam that year demanded that they continue to monitor what was happening in Southeast Asia. After the United States agreed to a peace settlement with North Vietnam in January 1973, it removed its ground forces but never stopped providing economic and military aid to Nguyen Van Thieu's regime in South Vietnam. The Cold War mentality of resisting Communist expansion had not disappeared with the failure of U.S. actions during the Vietnam War. Neither had the oppression faced by the South Vietnamese from this dictatorial government, leading to a continued civil war between South Vietnam, the insurgent guerilla movements there, and infiltrations from the north. But the American public, led by Congress, had had enough; when President Ford requested renewed and increased funding to defend allies in Cambodia, Laos, and Vietnam, Congress refused. Without U.S. military fighting and with the withdrawal of funding for that region, the civil war came to a head in April 1975 when Communist forces and their allies spread throughout South Vietnam and ultimately took Saigon, renaming it Ho Chi Minh City and reuniting Vietnam as a Communist nation.[1]

Poignant coverage of what happened during the Communist advance throughout Southeast Asia made its way to the United States. Thousands of South Vietnamese citizens who had supported the Thieu regime and allied with the United States fled for their lives. As the Communists advanced and took over, they assassinated political and military enemies and placed neutral people in reeducation camps where they tortured them into supporting the Communist government. This included attacks against many in South Vietnam with whom the North had allied throughout the war. Those who made it out of Vietnam had risked their lives on makeshift boats, luckily boarded an airlift, or smuggled themselves in other ways. Dramatic footage of American helicopters landing at the U.S. embassy just before Saigon collapsed into chaos showed Vietnamese people climbing fences and fighting one another in a desperate effort to get out. The United States also publicized the airlift of hundreds of children from an orphanage who otherwise faced a bleak future; this accompanied pleas to adopt the children, many of whom were of mixed race because of relationships between Vietnamese women and American soldiers. Here the U.S. churches had a particularly important role to play in spring 1975; while the government did many things to assist these impoverished and now despondent people, churches also moved into action around the world and within the United States to provide food, shelter, clothing, and other assistance, including sponsoring the Vietnamese families who immigrated to the United States and orchestrating efforts to adopt orphaned children.[2]

The collapse of South Vietnam spurred *Christianity Today* to appeal for assistance for the refugees who swarmed out of that country. The influx of refugees united Christians of all stripes in a humanitarian outpouring of goodwill for these exiled people. Editor Edward Plowman explained that many missionaries who had fled for their lives from Vietnam turned their attention to resettling those in need, and at first providing basic necessities such as food and shelter in places such as Taiwan. He wrote that "hundreds of thousands of persons poured into coastal areas" and found scarce food and astronomical prices for life's staples. A July editorial concurred that all Christians should turn their attention toward this crisis by assisting those resettling in the United States: "These people are God's creation as much as native North Americans are, and He will do the rewarding. The Samaritan spirit calls for making room not only in our homes but in our hearts. Whatever one thinks about the Viet Nam war, the refugees should be extended a genuine welcome as fellow human beings."[3]

Though appeals for refugee assistance sought support from people no matter their opinion of the Vietnam War, editorials about the lessons Americans should learn from the U.S. defeat left little doubt as to the opinions of *Christianity Today* editors. A faith in the domino theory permeated comments to the effect that the North Vietnamese victory constituted proof positive of Communist expansionism: "Slowly but surely, Cambodia and South Viet Nam are coming under North Vietnamese domination." Editors lamented that the United States had become isolationist and would refuse future incursions into other nations if threatened by Communists. In classic evangelical allusions to Armageddon, they wrote that "the turmoil of today may well presage the end of Western and world culture as we have known them" because of this new attitude. A later editorial asserted that "the danger now is that politicians may be too cautious and fail to act even if national survival might be at stake." In other words, the periodical clung to the notion that only a show of military strength stopped Communist aggression. A later editorial asserted that Hanoi had triumphed in this regard because the Soviets and Chinese gave military aid to North Vietnam while the United States neglected its ally. Applying a biblical lesson to the situation, editors then abandoned previous support for Richard Nixon's foreign policy and proclaimed,

> The Bible demands morally consistent behavior, but the United States has been inconsistent. Richard Nixon and Henry Kissinger claimed to bring détente into being, and Washington cosied up to Peking and Moscow. Whatever "détente" means, it obviously did not mean that the Communists would stop sending supplies to Hanoi. If it is desirable to have détente with China and Russia, why not let the Communists take over South Viet Nam and perhaps all of Indochina and then seek détente with them? Nations reap as they have sown. The United States with its inconsistency in policies has sown the whirlwind, and it will reap the whirlwind.

This continued emphasis on a harsh anticommunism further paved the way for conservative Christians to back the Republican far Right and foreshadowed the triumph of Ronald Reagan's rise to power in 1980 on a platform of reigniting Cold War hostilities.[4]

The Southern Baptist Convention added to this conservative Christian perspective on the basis of the denomination's commitment to global outreach and mission work, especially pertaining to missionaries who had to flee South Vietnam when that country collapsed in April 1975. These missionaries reported on Communist cruelty as its forces advanced southward, to the point that some American missionaries almost lost their lives. No trauma better articulated this reality than that experienced by Robert C. Davis Jr. and Gene V. Tunnell. These two Southern Baptists assisted refugees in escaping from Danang as Communist forces moved into that region. On Easter weekend, the two escaped on an American freighter only hours before the city fell to Communist control. Though they had evacuated their families earlier, they had remained because of an obligation to the Vietnamese Christians and supporters of the United States, whom they knew would meet certain death if they stayed in the country. Yet the fact that many people had to remain there because Communist forces advanced too quickly devastated them. The periodical for the Foreign Mission Board, *Commission*, explained that "missionaries had to make decisions day by day, hour by hour, as events trampled on the heels of events."[5]

The peril described as missionaries fled led Southern Baptists to ponder with dread what would happen inside Vietnam now that the North had reunited the country. Baptist missionaries especially fretted about the fate of Christians and other Vietnamese who had remained faithful to the United States but were now trapped in Vietnam. The hostility of Communists toward them meant certain death for many, a fact that solidified the anti-Communist stance of the Southern Baptist Convention. The Communists lived up to this expectation of cruel action. They purged their enemies and even went after previous allies, all in a totalitarian quest for complete domination. Because of this reality, Southern Baptists who had served in Vietnam as missionaries stated that "the unknown events which will take place behind Communist lines haunt all missionaries. Dread and fear of what the Communists will do to those who have held public office are most intense." Missionaries only found solace in the fact that "earnest Christian people will continue to serve the Lord Jesus there and to cherish the faith planted deeply in their hearts" despite Communist persecution. In the end, Baptists were comforted by the promise that "we shall see many Vietnamese Christians in the presence of our Savior who will rejoice that they came to know him as the living Lord because missionaries sent by Southern Baptists so lovingly came." Unfortunately, many reports by Americans who fled Vietnam, including SBC missionaries, confirmed the worst fears of Communist atrocities. Such news did much to solidify SBC opinions toward a conservative foreign policy that continued to resist all things Communist.[6]

Once South Vietnam collapsed, the Southern Baptist Convention turned its attention to saving the refugees who had fled successfully. SBC President Jaroy Weber appealed to his denomination and even the president of the

United States to assist those desperate and often helpless people. He wrote to Gerald Ford that because of the "clear and present danger to the thousands of refugees who are now drifting around, we call on the U.S. government for a maximum effort to relieve the human suffering in South Vietnam and Cambodia. We ask that emergency flights to the U.S.A. of war orphans be continued." Even as he pleaded, the Southern Baptist Convention had gone into action to assist as many of the refugees as possible. R. Keith Parks, the Foreign Mission Board secretary for Southeast Asia, had developed a strategy to assist the refugees even before the final takeover of Saigon by the North Vietnamese. He marshaled all of the resources available to him in the region to get food, clothing, and shelter for refugees in Guam and other countries who had landed with literally nothing but the clothes they wore. Many of the SBC missionaries who had had to flee Vietnam turned their attention to "serving in exile" alongside the Vietnamese in these refugee camps. As William T. Roberson, one such missionary, explained, "They mill among the masses housed in tents and barracks to extend whatever ministry of compassion that may offer itself."[7]

Yet the Southern Baptist Convention had limited resources to apply to this endeavor and so appealed to its membership for more help. Daniel R. Grant explained pointedly in the *Arkansas Baptist* that "we have a choice between showing Christian compassion or showing that we have Christian love for them only as long as they stay 'over there.' I was glad that one of the signs carried in the audience that welcomed the Vietnamese refugees to Fort Chafee read 'Southern Baptists welcome you.'" He therefore asked Southern Baptists to contribute to any relief efforts when possible. The Foreign Mission Board echoed his concern, rushing to completely redo the June 1975 issue of *Commission* to appeal for aid from its readers. Editors especially asked for assistance to help Vietnamese Baptists who only had the church to turn to for assistance. Finally, messengers to the June national convention added their voice to the cause in a resolution: "the messengers of this session of the Southern Baptist Convention express their concern for their fellow human beings, pray for them, and that the churches and families be encouraged to pray for them, and to aid in their resettlement throughout our country." For a Christian body with a staunch anticommunist bent, the refugees' plight only intensified this hatred, thereby shaping this denomination's stance regarding foreign policy in 1975 toward an entrenched and traditionalist Cold War mentality.[8]

As expected, liberal Christians viewed the collapse of South Vietnam much differently. During the first weeks of April, as the South Vietnamese government barely clung to its power and inevitable defeat appeared on the horizon, *Christian Century* editors referred to U.S. policy in Southeast Asia as "our long-discredited attempt to shore up our 'ally'" in South Vietnam. Other reports stated to readers that the misery in South Vietnam had never ended, though too many Americans forgot about Vietnam after the U.S. withdrawal in January 1973. Importantly, this liberal Protestant periodical had persistently reminded readers since then about what had gone on in Vietnam, with U.S. financial and military support. It thus reported on unexploded bombs, military assassinations, and the continued oppression of the South Vietnamese by their own government. According to these editors and writers, the United States had not established "peace with honor" when it withdrew. If anything, the government clung to old thoughts about the region despite removing the actual troop presence. *Christian Century* editors and writers called this reality deceitful and immoral. This fact led editor James M. Wall to applaud the doves in Congress, who resisted the Ford administration's call for increased funding in order to "save" South Vietnam. Wall stated that "in doing so they headed off attempts to shunt their protests into legislative machinery that would have permitted continuing aid to Indochina under the sort of compromise that lets dovish legislators say, 'We did our best. But it wasn't enough.'" Wall appreciated that, this time, representatives who had promised a peace policy from Congress regarding Vietnam had achieved it.[9]

Yet the flood of refugees who fled South Vietnam in an effort to save their lives as Communists took over touched the liberal periodical just as much as its conservative counterpart, despite relief that the civil war had come to an end. In April, editors reported on the airlift of two thousand babies out of South Vietnam orphanages as a partial fulfillment of the United States' obligation to continue helping the people of that nation. But here *Christian Century* editors diverged from their evangelical colleagues, refusing to simply see this as a positive without noting the negative. In this case, that meant pointing out that the United States had an obligation to protect these children because many of them were of mixed American and Vietnamese heritage, born from Vietnamese mothers and American soldier fathers. Editors also feared that the United States publicized this evacuation to gain national and global favor, not simply because it was the right thing to do. Or, as another editorial wondered, "The influx of South Vietnamese refugees has aroused debate that is curiously, and perhaps inevitably, color-tinged. Would reactions be the same if they were South Germans? We took in 200,000 East Germans in the early 1950s and 40,000

Hungarians after the 1956 Hungarian revolt, with hardly a ripple." Editors grew frustrated that many Americans stopped giving support to the refugees as the issue continued throughout the year, and especially disliked the suggestion by some that the United States had no obligation toward the refugees. Racism plagued the matter, according to the *Christian Century*, despite the positive notion that the United States was saving the refugees. The liberal journal continued to educate about Vietnam even after the war had ended.[10]

The *Christian Century* also listed the lessons that the United States should learn from the collapse of South Vietnam. One lesson concerned the perception that Americans had of Vietnam after the Communists took over. Editors warned against blanket condemnations simply because a Communist government had won, hoping to avoid increased global tension or simplistic understandings of a complex nation. Editor James M. Wall acknowledged that the new regime would "have all the disadvantages of a dictatorship oriented to a Marxist philosophy." But he also concluded that it offered hope that the new government would be an improvement over the corrupt Thieu regime. Since the United States had lost and the Vietnamese civil war had ended with a Communist victory, Wall hoped for the best while admitting the possibility of the worst.[11]

Wall and others, however, directed most of their lessons to learn from the Vietnam War at the United States itself. Wall took the opportunity to call upon the government to tell the whole truth about Vietnam and to stop clouding the issue in Cold War rhetoric. He stated that "a whole generation of Americans has been cheated into believing they were fighting a necessary war. Unless they are told the truth by their leaders, their fury can also be anarchic and destructive." He also declared that the entire nation, including the antiwar movement, had to avoid placing blame for what happened on one side and instead come together to assess how to prevent such a catastrophe in the future. Wall feared that the nation, in order to avoid this continued tension, would want to "forget" what had happened without any reflection on the matter: "But it will not be healthy if we start forgetting before we forgive" each other and all of the participants involved. In other words, Wall called for reconciliation. A Lutheran pastor wrote an article for the *Christian Century* that concurred with its editor. Richard John Neuhaus asserted that "there could be no 'good ending' to this terrible war" and emphasized the horrific fighting that had finally brought it to an end. He, too, challenged the antiwar movement not to gloat, pointing out that the collapse of South Vietnam is part of our "success." We can hope and believe that the present agony is a lesser evil than the consequences of continuing warfare. Too many public figures are now scurrying for cover in an unseemly attempt to shed their share of responsibility both for the war and for the horror of its ending. As Christians, we must stand forth in the courage of our uncertainties, recognizing the moral ambiguity of all our positions, trusting the judgment of the future which is, finally, God's judgment.

This was the lesson that the periodical desperately tried to deliver to its readers so that they, too, would learn the appropriate meaning of the Vietnam War and thereby alter America's reliance on anticommunism. Though the periodical ultimately failed in this goal of changing the nation's outlook, it crusaded valiantly against the conservative impetus to engage in traditional Cold War tactics.[12]

The United Church of Christ joined the *Christian Century* in this liberal Christian campaign against U.S. foreign policy. In April 1975, just before Saigon collapsed and North Vietnam reunited the country, *A.D.* made several reports about Vietnam. A member of Clergy and Laity Concerned, an interdenominational body established to voice religious opposition to the Vietnam War, reminded readers that "peace did not come in South Vietnam" after the treaty that the United States and North Vietnam signed went into effect because "to our nation's dishonor, we have fueled the Thieu military forces and sustained his corrupt and repressive government." The UCC had long criticized the United States for backing corruption in South Vietnam simply because it opposed communism. With South Vietnam's government crumbling, UCC writers once again pointed out American blame for what had happened in order to teach readers the lesson they thought should be learned from what had occurred.[13]

A.D. also reported about a delegation that visited North Vietnam and that included its editor, James A. Gittings. His report underscored both his opposition to the containment and domino theories and his condemnation of the U.S. role in Vietnam. In explaining the fallacy of the idea that Vietnam was a danger to the United States, he asserted that *"China rather than the U.S. is seen as the major long-term threat to Vietnam's identity as a nation."* In other words, he told readers that China endangered Vietnam more than the United States, and any global tension would be between those two Communist countries. After that comment, he explained the reason North Vietnam had invited these church officials to visit: "Our delegation was received in the hope that we would return home to convey to Americans, over the heads of these much-discussed militarists, the desire of North Vietnamese for peace and time to rebuild." According to Gittings, North Vietnam did not represent part of a global Communist conspiracy. Rather, he stated that "it is clear that the present regime in South Vietnam is a corruption-ridden government that possesses no clear vision of democracy." Still in 1975, just before the fall of Saigon, UCC outlets reminded Americans that Vietnam suffered from instability wrought by American actions.[14]

The United Church of Christ's integration of concern for humanity with its foreign policy opinions especially manifested itself regarding the Vietnamese refugees. UCC President Robert V. Moss best articulated the UCC's position in statements and addresses that he made on behalf of the denomination. Moss and other UCC officials called in April 1975 for U.S. churches to support the World Council of Churches' appeal for one million dollars to assist Indochinese refugees because "this is the moment for the churches to define moral responsibility not in terms of secret diplomacy . . . but in terms of the value God places upon every one of his children." The statement specifically asked the United States to relocate and support Vietnamese people who had backed the Thieu regime on behalf of the United States. In other words, Moss and his associates pointed out the American responsibility that persisted despite the end to the Vietnamese civil war. He furthered his appeal to the General Synod, happy that the national church body had "assumed the responsibility on our behalf for re-settling five hundred families of Vietnamese refugees" but concerned that only 125 additional families got local congregational backing. He wanted his denomination to do more to assist those still suffering because of the war and U.S. actions and wrote to convince people to that end. The United Church of Christ continued the crusade against a blind American anti-Communist foreign policy and what this policy did to the world.[15]

Commonweal continued to condemn U.S. policy, thus continuing the Catholic lay periodical's move toward a new understanding of the Cold War, void of reactionary anticommunism. It dumbfounded the editors when President Ford and Secretary of State Kissinger requested the funding for South Vietnam from Congress. Though they acknowledged that the U.S. withdrawal of support would lead to ruin for previous allies, they asserted that "slaughter and devastation cannot be funded endlessly. There had to come a time when Congress had to say, 'Millions for humanitarian purposes, but not one cent more for killing.'" *Commonweal* placed blame for this situation squarely on the shoulders of Nixon's alleged peace with honor, stating that "the Paris Peace was designed to get the U.S. out as a direct participant in a war that had no popular backing among the American people; it was not real-istically designed to bring peace to the Vietnamese people." In other words, the liberal Catholic journal already knew what historians have subsequently confirmed: Nixon and his advisors knew that the peace would not last and only implemented it in order to avoid the ultimate collapse of South Vietnam from looking like an American, or more accurately Nixonian, failure. The first April editorial on what had happened in South Vietnam therefore con-cluded that the United States *did* still have an obligation to the Vietnamese who had supported it, but that this obligation was limited to humanitarian assistance.[16]

Subsequent editorial reflections in this Catholic journal confirmed this original understanding. Calling the collapse of both Cambodia and South Vietnam "an unmitigated disaster," editors lamented that

> hundreds of thousands have died needlessly or in vain, including 55,000 Americans. Tens of thousands stand in risk of reprisals for having come under the spell of the stranger from across the Pacific—who didn't belong there in the first place and who now retires, disgraced and a little humili-ated, but supported ever by the ideological *macho* that motivated the misadventure.

This statement encapsulated so much that *Commonweal* thought about U.S. foreign policy. On the one hand, it acknowledged the danger now faced by U.S. allies in South Vietnam, neither believing that the Communists would be benevolent nor ignoring the certain annihilation now faced by many peo-ple in that land. But it placed much of the blame on the United States, for a belligerent diplomacy that assumed it was always correct and could not even admit the failure of its Vietnam policy. However, editors hoped that a shift toward humanitarian aid to all of Vietnam could broker a peace in that region without escalating Cold War hostilities. Pointing out the success of détente with the Soviet Union and People's Republic of China, editors called for a similar negotiation with Vietnam that included "humanitarian aid to the poor Vietnamese people, regardless of what we think of the regime under which they live." This idea epitomized the way *Commonweal* wanted to shape its readership's opinion regarding American foreign policy.[17]

When the Vietnamese civil war ended, the Jesuit *America* took an antiwar perspective, a continuation of its reversal from prior support for U.S. policies. In early April, as thousands of South Vietnamese fled the country for their lives, editors stated that the broadcast images were "a painful reminder to the American public of a war they would like to forget." *America* thought the situation too important to allow this amnesia. The periodical also shunned militarism as a solution to that situation, and perhaps in general, when it denounced Ford's appeal for more funding and stated that "the point at issue is not U.S. responsibility to the people of Indochina but whether increased military assistance is the best way to exercise that responsibility at the present time." A week later, editors declared that U.S. foreign relations in Southeast Asia had resulted in "massive defeat" and supported the congressional decision to stop funding. By 1975 little of its reporting concerned foreign policy, despite the fact that in the previous decade *America* had usually mentioned it in reference to Vietnam. The failure of American action there had changed editorial minds.[18]

Though *America* turned against the Vietnam War later than had its Catholic peer magazines, by 1975 it, too, had changed its reliance on the domino theory. Conservatives in America, including Henry Kissinger, declared the "fall" of Cambodia and South Vietnam in 1975 to be proof positive of the domino theory. *America* had agreed during most of the Vietnam War but now came to see a different reality. Calling faith in containment theory and fear of the domino theory a "destructive delusion," editors in May 1975 wondered if government officials really believed that "a single adversary with a tightly knit strategy of conquest" existed or if they used this panic falsely to convince Americans to back the war. Either way, the Catholic periodical asserted that a truer reading of Vietnam revealed that the USSR and PRC vied against one another at times, and that within Vietnam the North Vietnamese and Vietcong leveraged for power. In other words, "the Communist movement was more complex in its internal relations than the image ever allowed it to be." For *America*, this was the painful lesson to learn from the Vietnam War.[19]

This changed approach brought *America* more in line with the humanist viewpoint regarding 1975 Vietnam that shaped other liberal reactions. The airlift of children from South Vietnam provided a case in point. Saving these innocent souls offered "small flashes of human decency and honor" in an otherwise complete tragedy. Yet editors worried about the fate of these young people once they got to the United States and hated the thought of their becoming a propaganda tool. They wanted the children given good homes and support, with no political agenda behind the generosity. Furthermore, *America* noted that saving these few children "should not distract us from the hard realities of our responsibilities for the vastly greater number of Vietnamese left behind." But *America* still concerned itself with Communist oppression of its citizens. Unlike its liberal colleagues, it combined the questioning of U.S. policy and apprehension for the South Vietnamese with a call for the world to criticize the treatment of people in all of Southeast Asia when Communists took over. Valuing human rights had to include a global outcry against the killing and maiming of innocent people despite the failure of U.S. policy in that region. Communism represented no less an evil to the Jesuit periodical than it had in previous years; what changed was their reaction to U.S. diplomacy, not their hatred of communism.[20]

This persistent anticommunism separated *America* sharply from periodicals such as *Commonweal* and the *Christian Century*. While *America* had moved toward a shared opinion with liberal counterparts about the Vietnam War, this hardly signaled a wholesale philosophical makeover. In articles and editorials, writers continued to denounce Communist regimes the world over and to worry about the fate of Christianity in those lands. This continued mistrust of Communists not only included the newly established governments in Southeast Asia but also those throughout Europe and Latin America. *America* felt that, despite lessons learned in Vietnam, the rest of the world still had a responsibility to champion protection of all people. The worst violators of human rights often came from Communist nations, a fact that the Jesuit periodical continued to point out to Catholic Americans.[21]

Unlike the Christian entities discussed above, which maintained an interest in foreign policy in 1975, reporting in smaller Catholic journals tapered off. *U.S. Catholic and Jubilee* said almost nothing. Only executive editor Robert E. Burns wrote about global issues when he continued the Claretian Fathers periodical's antiwar campaign: "With the South Vietnamese government now disintegrated, there is no moratorium on nonsensical statements about this dreadful war. Senator Barry Goldwater is quoted as saying that the war would have been over in a month if he had been elected President in 1964. As if a modern war can be 'won.' Will we ever learn?" Other than this antiwar statement, the magazine fell silent. But the Catholic periodical that had voiced an even stauncher antiwar platform by 1968 became even more quiet by not printing a single word about foreign affairs in 1975. *Catholic World* changed formats in 1972 to become *New Catholic World*. This shift altered much of the content and especially curtailed the inclusion of editorial opinions. In the early 1970s, many Christian publications suffered economically because of rising publishing and mailing costs; combined with U.S. society's penchant by 1975 for wanting to move away from foreign policy discussions, this transformation to *New Catholic World* eliminated one of the Catholic voices that had previously shaped diplomatic opinions. A similar lacuna manifested itself in the conservative *Catholic Digest*, which had always reported the least on foreign policy because its format did not include editorializing or as many original articles. A sporadic reference to communism and its nations appeared, but without the dogmatic disapproval. In other words, taken together, these three Catholic periodicals reflected an America grown weary of the conflict surrounding foreign affairs and by 1975 had moved to different topics.[22]

Of all the Christian entities discussed in this book, none offers a more confounding record for 1975 than does the African Methodist Episcopal Church. During the 1960s and earlier part of the 1970s, the AME had commented regularly on both the Cold and Vietnam wars. A number of sources from the church body weighed in on international affairs. The AME's racial identity contributed a particularly distinct voice in that leaders and lay people alike never shied away from social activism if called to it by events or circumstances. As we have seen, they lived out the heritage of a denomination created because of racial discrimination. Given this record, the nearly complete absence of a discussion on foreign policy in 1975 is stunning. Yet in the same sources that earlier contained a wealth of information, including the *Christian Recorder*, district conference records, and national statements, little to nothing remains to sketch out how the AME viewed the continuing Cold War or the collapse of South Vietnam.

This silence leaves historians to speculate about the AME Church during this pivotal year. Perhaps the AME Church simply reflects the rest of America, one scholars describe as weary of the Vietnam War and foreign relations and desperately wanting to "move on" and forget. That attitude of wanting to forget about foreign policy certainly pertained to Lutheran Americans in 1975. After a decade of vibrant debate about global issues, Lutherans spent much of 1975 trying to put the tension and angst of the Vietnam War era behind them. While this desire may explain AME silence in part, the denomination had not paralleled Lutheranism to this point. Additionally, though a longing to forget the recent turmoil may explain some reactions within the AME, it hardly squares with the denomination's legacy, which had never shied away from public debate about social issues. And ample evidence *does* exist to demonstrate the AME's continued vibrancy within the civil rights movement and broader conversation about race in America. Indeed, that fact lends some credence to the idea that at least some leaders and members merely wanted to move away from commenting on foreign policy.[23]

Another explanation may come from the lack of a formal AME archival system. While the Department of Research and Scholarship offers assistance to anyone who inquires and goes to great lengths to find materials, the fact remains that the denomination has no central archive that collects national, district, and local materials for historic preservation. This leaves historians only what accidentally remains from sporadic donations and the meticulous attempt by the head of that department to gather as much material as possible. Thus, the dearth of 1975 records may also or exclusively stem from the fact that what the denomination did say has been lost to time. Whether as a result of a combination of these factors or one in particular, the AME Church remains frustratingly silent compared to other Christian entities regarding 1975 and foreign relations.[24]

A thorny reality manifested itself in Christian reactions to foreign relations and global affairs in 1975. Throughout the 1960s and first half of the 1970s, periodicals and denominations took positions about the Cold and Vietnam wars that generally squared with their overall political leanings, either leftward or rightward, and that paralleled their theological convictions. Their historic background and context also influenced the way they understood these struggles. This reality did not disappear in 1975, but it did transform into something less definitive. While some Christians held fast to discussing foreign policy, others had begun to shy away from it. This circumstance plays into the notion of an America tired of war and debate, seeking to move beyond the divisions that had plagued the United States for over a decade. The culture war over diplomatic matters had abated, in larger America and within its Christian institutions. This very complexity within Christian reactions to Vietnam in 1975 becomes both an overview reflection of America in general and, at the same time, a way to understand how the Christian community shaped the way people responded to and acted within U.S. foreign relations.

Reflecting and Shaping Society

Christianity offers one lens through which to analyze American society's reactions to the Cold and Vietnam wars. Its institutions reflect foreign policy opinions from that era, presenting a spectrum of beliefs from far-right conservatives to far-left pacifists, with a majority of voices falling somewhere between these extremes. These are important voices to consider when studying the American culture war over foreign policy during these two decades.

Christian America also reflects the middle ground held by many people and institutions in the United States. These individuals trusted their government and began in 1964 with cautious support for the Vietnam War. By the

1970s, however, America's longest war took its toll on this faith. A government that had lied too often to its citizens combined with too many maimed and killed to sway more and more Christians to oppose the war. These moderate Christians help us to understand Americans who began the decade with a trust of the government and ended it with calls for a change in the United States' approach to Southeast Asia.

In addition to reflecting American society, Christian American entities wanted to shape foreign policy outlooks during this decade according to their religious convictions. Though this shaping is more difficult to assess because data does not exist to show exactly how and where Americans adopted their opinions on the basis of Christian periodical or denominational arguments, sources nonetheless imply how this took place. Christians often arrived at their stances about a myriad of issues, including diplomatic matters and war, on the basis of an institution's historical reaction to both religious and secular events. For example, *Christianity Today* and the Southern Baptist Convention framed their arguments in support of the Cold and Vietnam wars in the context of their missionary outreach. The Catholic press revealed the historic diversity of American Catholic opinions, with some clinging to the Vatican's traditional Cold War mantra while others followed the post–Vatican II Catholic move toward peace. The *Christian Century* and United Church of Christ took up liberal causes throughout the 1960s because of their humanist theology, including advocacy for civil rights and welfare programs, a legacy that bled into their disdain for America's participation in the arms race and Vietnam War. And the African Methodist Episcopal Church mixed a strain of conservatism regarding historical opposition to communism with a countervailing blast at U.S. race relations to shape its opinions about foreign affairs. Christians voiced strong convictions about the Cold and Vietnam wars through the traditional venues of writing, giving speeches, and assembling together. These public offerings had to have guided Americans in their thought processes. At the same time, this very diversity indicates that even when the church might have shaped society, it did so in a myriad of different ways that led to a spectrum of foreign policy opinions.

Christians especially wanted their theological convictions to sway American opinions. Regardless of our ability to gauge the actual influence that these Christians had, they strongly believed that they were influencing public opinion and, through it, government leaders. Evangelical piety meant that missionary work was necessary for saving souls and thus factored greatly into the way conservative Christians viewed the Cold and Vietnam wars. Humanist theologies worked for improvements in the condition of humanity the world over as a Christian obligation. When war destroyed people and their lands, liberal Christians therefore condemned it. When American Catholic bishops backed U.S. hostility to communism, so, too, did lay Catholics. But when other priests and eventually the pope condemned the Vietnam War, other Catholics followed suit. Many Americans have persistently articulated a Christian faith and throughout history have looked to their religion for answers to difficult secular issues. It stands to reason that the same thing happened during the 1960s and 1970s regarding the Cold and Vietnam wars. When Americans heard their church body or influential leaders warn about the danger of Communist expansionism, it had to play into their backing of U.S. policy. Protecting mission work or simply aiding fellow believers in other countries demanded this position. When liberal Christian leaders told their flock that the war was immoral, they hoped that people listened. When denominational resolutions or respected periodicals condemned the treatment of the Vietnamese or mass killings of soldiers and civilians on all sides, these Americans took it to heart, most likely joining the throngs of voters who more and more backed antiwar candidates or demanded action from Congress. And when historians examine that huge mass of middle Americans who began the Vietnam War in support of it but gradually turned against it, they can find reason for some of this evolution in the way Christian institutions called out to their constituencies for change and/or underwent that very change themselves.

Those seeking statistical data to prove how the church shaped society in this regard will be hard pressed to find it. In part, this difficulty stems from the many attitudes that existed, meaning that Christianity shaped opinions of every kind, without a clear-cut influence one way or another. Additionally, in the midst of this shaping, Christian lay leaders and clergy seldom stopped to calculate their actual influence. They were too busy doing the church's job of working with people and trying to affect those around them. Yet studying Christian America reveals that a combination of faith and institutional history helped some Americans formulate their understandings of the Cold and Vietnam wars. Christianity in some way shaped American opinions. We all must struggle to find out as much as we can about what this means.

Lessons Learned

Christian America both reflected and shaped opinions about the Cold and Vietnam wars during the 1960s and 1970s. Christianity therefore played a pivotal role in this national culture debate. It also represented the spectrum of American attitudes, from conservative backing of anything that the government argued for to liberal denunciations of the arms race and the Vietnam War, plus every imaginable middle ground between these opposites. We gain a better understanding of this era as we learn more and more about how religion played into what Americans believed about foreign policy, but more work must be done. What of the denominations not discussed in this book? Did Johnson or Nixon say anything publicly or behind the scenes that indicates how religion shaped their actions? What about other government leaders and their faith lives? Certainly more leaders than just Senator Mark O. Hatfield or a handful of politicians were guided by religious ideology. How do American religious convictions match popular opinion as a whole? And what other entities infused the debate over Vietnam with a religious conviction? These are just a few of the questions remaining to be answered.

The United States since World War II has established a legacy of military engagement around the world, and each time Christians have both condoned these excursions and denounced them. Knowing the churches' role in past situations better prepares us to comprehend the world around us today. Is the church reflecting or shaping attitudes about the wars in Iraq and Afghanistan and the War on Terrorism? How many people today look to their churches and religious leaders for guidance about how to understand foreign affairs? And does the government listen to the religious convictions of American people when formulating its foreign policy? If so, particularly given changes in the American religious landscape, including the decline of the traditional mainline churches and the rise of nondenominational churches, what branch of Christianity is dominant in the political realm and why? Without clear answers to these questions, the nation remains dangerously blind to the realities that shape our current, and past, understandings of war.

Notes

INTRODUCTION

1. David E. Settje, *Lutherans and the Longest War: Adrift on a Sea of Doubt about the Cold and Vietnam Wars, 1964–1975* (Lanham, MD: Lexington Books, 2007).

2. A note about my usage of "conservative," "liberal," and "moderate" is in order. Unless otherwise noted, by "conservative" I mean Christians who leaned rightward regarding both politics and religion. This meant a neoconservative outlook that sought limited government influence on society, laissez-faire economics, and yet a strong military and staunch anti-Communist Cold Warriorism. Religiously, conservatives tended toward biblical literalism, missionary outreach, and revivalism. Liberals, too, tended to apply a liberal philosophy to both their politics and their faith. Politically, they favored social justice movements, especially the civil rights movement and women's rights movement, and they questioned traditional Cold War outlooks as warlike and dangerous. They sought instead cooperation with Communist nations, disarmament, and reduced global tension. A theology of human improvement guided most liberals, in that they advocated programs and initiatives that bettered the human condition regardless of religious affiliation. Moderates fell somewhere between these polar opposites and will be described individually throughout the text, as each had unique circumstances and blendings of conservative and liberal politics and/or theologies.

3. Various manifestations of this section also appeared in the introduction to my first book, *Lutherans and the Longest War*.

4. Dimitry Pospielovsky, *The Russian Church under the Soviet Regime, 1917–1982* (Crestwood, NY: St. Vladimir's Seminary Press, 1984); Owen Chadwick, *The Christian Church in the Cold War* (New York: Penguin Books, 1992); Stephane Courtois, Nicolas Werth, Jean-Louis Panne, Andrzej Packowski, Karel Bartosek, and Jean-Louis Margolin, *The Black Book of Communism: Crimes, Terror, Repression* (Cambridge, MA: Harvard University Press, 1999); Dianne Kirby, ed., *Religion and the Cold War* (New York: Palgrave Macmillan, 2003); Elliott Abrams, *The Influence of Faith: Religious Groups and U.S. Foreign Policy* (Lanham, MD: Rowman and Littlefield, 2001).

5. Gordon H. Chang, *Friends and Enemies: The United States, China, and the Soviet Union, 1948–1972* (Stanford, CA: Stanford University Press, 1990).

6. Gary R. Hess, "The Unending Debate: Historians and the Vietnam War," in Michael J. Hogan, ed., *America in the World: The Historiography of American Foreign Relations since 1941* (Cambridge, MA: Cambridge University Press, 1995), 358–94; Robert Buzzanco, *Masters of War: Military Dissent and Politics in the Vietnam Era* (Cambridge: Cambridge

University Press, 1996); Allen J. Matusow, *The Unraveling of America: A History of Liberalism in the 1960s* (New York: Harper and Row, 1984); Robert S. McNamara, *In Retrospect: The Tragedy and Lessons of Vietnam* (New York: Random House Books, 1995).

7. Charles DeBenedetti and Charles Chatfield, *An American Ordeal: The Antiwar Movement of the Vietnam Era* (Syracuse, NY: Syracuse University Press, 1990); Mitchell K. Hall, *Because of Their Faith: CALCAV and Religious Opposition to the Vietnam War* (New York: Columbia University Press, 1990); Melvin Small, *Johnson, Nixon, and the Doves* (New Brunswick, NJ: Rutgers University Press, 1988); William J. Duiker, *Sacred War: Nationalism and Revolution in a Divided Vietnam* (New York: McGraw-Hill, 1995).

8. A brief note on my use of "communism" is necessary, particularly as used in reference to conservative Americans. While intellectuals, liberals to a greater and greater extent throughout the 1960s, and certainly contemporary scholars understand the nuances within "communism" and the profound differences between "communism" and "socialism," conservatives and many moderate Americans during the Cold War did not. They lumped Communists into one gigantic force to fear, and I therefore parallel their generic use of "communism" when referring to their discussions. Lisa McGirr, *Suburban Warriors: The Origins of the New American Right* (Princeton, NJ: Princeton University Press, 2001); Jonathan M. Schoenwald, *A Time for Choosing: The Rise of Modern American Conservatism* (New York: Oxford University Press, 2001); Mary C. Brennan, *Turning Right in the Sixties: The Conservative Capture of the GOP* (Chapel Hill: University of North Carolina Press, 1995); Dan T. Carter, *The Politics of Rage: George Wallace, the Origins of the New Conservatism, and the Transformation of American Politics* (Baton Rouge: Louisiana State University Press, 2000); John A. Andrew III, *The Other Side of the Sixties: Young Americans for Freedom and the Rise of Conservative Politics* (New Brunswick, NJ: Rutgers University Press, 1997); Donald T. Critchlow, *Phyllis Schlafly and Grassroots Conservatism: A Woman's Crusade* (Princeton, NJ: Princeton University Press, 2005); Patrick Allitt, *Religion in America since 1945: A History* (New York: Columbia University Press, 2003); Paul Boyer, *By the Bomb's Early Light: American Thought and Culture at the Dawn of the Atomic Age* (Chapel Hill: University of North Carolina Press, 1985).

9. Various portions of this section also appeared in the introduction to Settje, *Lutherans*.

10. This study employs a broad meaning for the terms "fundamentalism" and "evangelicalism." In the case of "fundamentalism," the term describes the theological understanding of people who interpreted the Bible as the inerrant word of God. Some evangelicals believed this as well, though not as universally. Fundamentalists traced their tradition back to the modernist controversy of the late nineteenth and early twentieth centuries. Evangelical history goes back farther in U.S. history to the First Great Awakening. Defining the words in their political context becomes more complex. Some fundamentalists clung to the theory that religion and politics should never intermingle and so claimed to stay out of secular discussions. However, by the early 1970s, evangelicals began efforts to influence political topics with conservative Christian thinking. But even these theorists insisted that they wanted a strict separation of church and state. Thus, although various evangelicals and fundamentalists differed in their actual practice of separating religion and politics, they all maintained that the two should not fraternize because religion represented God's will while secular topics were impure. The terms "evangelicalism" and "fundamentalism," then, indicate people who held to strict interpretations of the Bible; it must be emphasized

that all fundamentalists are evangelicals, but not all evangelicals are fundamentalists. It is also important to note that not everyone who adhered to these conservative religious principles also practiced conservative politics; it was possible to maintain liberal democratic ideals in conjunction with evangelical religious notions. The best discussion of early fundamentalism is George M. Marsden, *Fundamentalism and American Culture: The Shaping of Twentieth-Century Evangelicalism, 1870–1925* (New York: Oxford University Press, 1980). For a more extensive discussion of the terms "fundamentalism" and "evangelicalism," see Peter W. Williams, *America's Religions: Traditions and Cultures* (New York: Macmillan, 1990), 322, 351–54, and Martin E. Marty, *Pilgrims in Their Own Land: Five Hundred Years of Religion in America* (New York: Penguin Books, 1984), 470–71.

11. Patrick Allitt, *Religion in America since 1945: A History* (New York: Columbia University Press, 2003); Martin E. Marty, *Modern American Religion*, Volume 3, *Under God, Indivisible, 1941–1960* (Chicago: University of Chicago Press, 1996); T. Jeremy Gunn, *Spiritual Weapons: The Cold War and the Forging of an American National Religion* (Westport, CT: Praeger, 2009); James Hudnut-Beumler, *Looking for God in the Suburbs: The Religion of the American Dream and Its Critics, 1945–1965* (New Brunswick, NJ: Rutgers University Press, 1994); Mark David Hulsether, *Building a Protestant Left: Christianity and Crisis Magazine, 1941–1993* (Knoxville: University of Tennessee Press, 1999); William Inboden, *Religion and American Foreign Policy, 1945–1960: The Soul of Containment* (New York: Cambridge University Press, 2008); Seth Jacobs, "'Our System Demands the Supreme Being': The U.S. Religious Revival and the 'Diem Experiment,' 1954–55," *Diplomatic History* 25 (Fall 2001): 589–624; Angela M. Lahr, *Millennial Dreams and Apocalyptic Nightmares: The Cold War Origins of Political Evangelism* (New York: Oxford University Press, 2007); Gerald Sittser, *A Cautious Patriotism: The American Churches and the Second World War* (Chapel Hill: University of North Carolina Press, 1997); Stephen J. Whitfield, *The Culture of the Cold War* (Baltimore, MD: Johns Hopkins University Press, 1991).

12. Richard B. Miller, *Interpretations of Conflict: Ethics, Pacifism, and the Just-War Tradition* (Chicago: University of Chicago Press, 1991); Daniel C. Maguire, *The Horrors We Bless: Rethinking the Just-War Legacy* (Minneapolis: Fortress Press, 2007); Andrew LeRoy Pratt, "Religious Faith and Civil Religion: Evangelical Responses to the Vietnam War, 1964–1973" (Ph.D. diss., Southern Baptist Theological Seminary, 1988); Michael Walzer, *Just and Unjust War: A Moral Argument with Historical Illustrations* (New York: Basic Books, 1977); Jean Bethke Elshtain, ed., *Just War Theory* (New York: New York University Press, 1992).

13. A myriad of studies examine Christians who opposed the Vietnam War. The best overview of antiwar opinions is Charles DeBenedetti and Charles Chatfield, *An American Ordeal: The Antiwar Movement of the Vietnam Era* (Syracuse, NY: Syracuse University Press, 1990). Other examinations include Michael B. Friedland, *Lift Up Your Voice Like a Trumpet: White Clergy and the Civil Rights and Antiwar Movements, 1954–1973* (Chapel Hill: University of North Carolina Press, 1998); Hulsether, *Building a Protestant Left*; Mitchell K. Hall, *Because of Their Faith: CALCAV and Religious Opposition to the Vietnam War* (New York: Columbia University Press, 1990); Jill Kristine Gill, "'Peace Is Not the Absence of War but the Presence of Justice': The National Council of Churches' Reaction and Response to the Vietnam War, 1965–1972" (Ph.D. diss., University of Pennsylvania, 1996); Rick L. Nutt, *Toward Peacemaking: Presbyterians in the South and National Security, 1945–1983* (Tuscaloosa: University of Alabama Press, 1994).

14. For the best study of the NLF, see Robert K. Brigham's *Guerilla Diplomacy: The NLF's Foreign Relations and the Viet Nam War* (Ithaca, NY: Cornell University Press, 1999).

15. *Gallup Political Index: Gallup International* (Princeton, NJ: American Institute of Public Opinion, 1965–1969); *Gallup Opinion Index* (Princeton, NJ: American Institute of Public Opinion, 1970–1975); George H. Gallup, *The Gallup Poll: Public Opinion, 1935–1971*, vol. 3 (New York: Random House, 1972).

16. I did not include one of the historic peace churches, such as the Quakers, because they belong to the antiwar movement, which has already received a lot of historiographical coverage.

17. For a good review of *Christianity Today*'s history and efforts to influence the public, political, and diplomatic realm, see D. G. Hart, *That Old Time Religion in Modern America: Evangelical Protestantism in the Twentieth Century* (Chicago: Ivan R. Dee, 2002). Other studies, such as James Landers's *Weekly War: Newsmagazines and Vietnam* (Columbia: University of Missouri Press, 2004), have demonstrated the value of using news magazines to understand some of the cultural influences in the United States on the Vietnam War. Quentin J. Schultze's *Christianity and the Mass Media in America: Toward a Democratic Accommodation* (East Lansing: Michigan State University Press, 2003) also employed a comparison of *Christianity Today* and the *Christian Century* to gain a sense of religious effects on American society, in his case the interaction between the Christian press and mass media. By using *Christianity Today*, the *Christian Century*, and a variety of Catholic periodicals, this study mimics such successful glances into American attitudes by adding information about how the Christian press debated the Vietnam War. Marietta Chicorel, ed., *Ulrich's International Periodicals Directory*, Volume 2, *Arts, Humanities, Business, and Social Sciences*, 12th ed, (New York: Bowker, 1968): 1045.

18. My preliminary analysis of *Christianity Today*'s reaction to the Cold and Vietnam wars appeared in David E. Settje, "'Sinister' Communists and Vietnam Quarrels: The *Christian Century* and *Christianity Today* Respond to the Cold and Vietnam Wars," *Fides et Historia* 32 (Winter/Spring 2000): 81–97.

19. Hart, *That Old-Time Religion*, 151.

20. My preliminary analysis of the *Christian Century*'s reaction to the Cold and Vietnam wars appeared in Settje, "'Sinister' Communists," 81–97; Chicorel, *Ulrich's*, 779. Mark Hulsether's *Building a Protestant Left: Christianity and Crisis Magazine, 1941–1993* (Knoxville: University of Tennessee Press, 1999) provides an excellent model for using one periodical to represent liberal Protestantism, as this book does with the *Christian Century*. His argument regarding *Christianity and Crisis* and the Vietnam War in many way mirrors what this book will argue about the *Christian Century* (see Hulsether, pp. 125–34): the periodical began the 1960s in many ways supporting the United States and its Cold War militarism but drifted away from this stance the longer the Vietnam War persisted and the more U.S. actions in Southeast Asia came into question.

21. For the history of the *Christian Century*, see William R. Hutchinson, ed., *Between the Times: The Travail of the Protestant Establishment in America, 1900–1960* (Cambridge: Cambridge University Press, 1989).

22. *Statistical Abstract of the United States 90th Annual Edition* (Washington, D.C.: U.S. Department of Commerce, 1969): 42; the membership number cited here was for 1967. Further demonstrating the scholarly use of the press to study American Catholicism, Quentin J. Schultze's *Christianity and the Mass Media in America* employed three of

the periodicals to represent the Catholic press that this study examines: *Commonweal*, *America*, and *Catholic World*. Studying Catholic periodicals presents a myriad of options, none of which provides a perfect sampling unless one attempted to write about every possible Catholic publication; nonetheless, the sampling employed here includes a cross-section of theological and political attitudes within Catholic America, thus beginning the discussion of Catholic responses to the Vietnam War.

23. For the best histories of American Catholicism, see Jay P. Dolan, *The American Catholic Experience: A History from Colonial Times to the Present* (Notre Dame, IN: University of Notre Dame Press, 1992; for the quotation in this paragraph, see p. 426); Martin E. Marty, *A Short History of American Catholicism* (Allen, TX: Thomas More Publishing, 1995); Chester Gillis, *Roman Catholicism in America* (New York: Columbia University Press, 1999).

24. A preliminary comparison of *America* and *Commonweal* appeared in David E. Settje, "Dueling Catholic Periodicals: *America*'s and *Commonweal*'s Perceptions of the Cold and Vietnam Wars," *Catholic Social Science Review* 9 (2004): 249–64. Chicorel, *Ulrich's*, 897, 896, 1071.

25. Chicorel, *Ulrich's*, 1037, 1043.

26. Edward T. Brett, *The U.S. Catholic Press on Central America: From Cold War Anticommunism to Social Justice* (Notre Dame, IN: University of Notre Dame Press, 2003).

27. *Statistical*, 1969, 41; this membership number is from 1967.

28. Jesse C. Fletcher, *The Southern Baptist Convention: A Sesquicentennial History* (Nashville, TN: Broadman and Holman, 1994); Bill J. Leonard, *Baptists in America* (New York: Columbia University Press, 2005); David T. Morgan, *The New Crusades, the New Holy Land: Conflict in the Southern Baptist Convention, 1969–1991* (Tuscaloosa: University of Alabama Press, 1996).

29. *Statistical*, 1969, 42; for a reason not described in the *Statistical Abstract*, the reporting on denominational membership for the AME was for the year 1951 and was never updated throughout the years of this study, 1964–1975.

30. Howard D. Gregg, *History of the African Methodist Episcopal Church: The Black Church in Action* (Nashville, TN: AMEC Sunday School Union, 1980); C. Eric Lincoln and Lawrence H. Mamiya, *The Black Church in the African American Experience* (Durham, NC: Duke University Press, 1990); Anne H. Pinn and Anthony B. Pinn, *Fortress Introduction to Black Church History* (Minneapolis: Fortress Press, 2002).

31. *Statistical*, 1969, 42; these figures were for the year 1967.

32. DeBenedetti and Chatfield, *An American Ordeal*.

33. Louis H. Gunnemann, *The Shaping of the United Church of Christ: An Essay in the History of American Christianity* (Cleveland, OH: United Church Press, 1977) and *United and Uniting: The Meaning of an Ecclesial Journey* (Cleveland, OH: United Church Press, 1987).

34. Unfortunately, archival materials that assist this endeavor tend to be scarce, either because periodicals failed to preserve letters to the editor or because denominations lost or destroyed records due to space restrictions.

35. Michael S. Foley, *Dear Dr. Spock: Letters about the Vietnam War to America's Favorite Baby Doctor* (New York: New York University Press, 2005).

36. It must be noted, however, that many periodicals and institutions did not preserve all of their records. For example, it is very difficult to locate unpublished letters to the editor, which were often destroyed or lost over time.

1. "Omaha: Graham Worried," *Baptist Message* (hereafter *BM*) 80 (24 September 1964): 17; "Peace among Men," *United Church Herald* (hereafter *UCH*) 7 (15 December 1964): 18.

2. Patrick Allitt, *Religion in America since 1945: A History* (New York: Columbia University Press, 2003); Mark Hulsether, *Religion, Culture, and Politics in the Twentieth-Century United States* (New York: Columbia University Press, 2007); William Inboden, *Religion and American Foreign Policy, 1945–1960: The Soul of Containment* (New York: Cambridge University Press, 2008); Martin E. Marty, *Modern American Religion*, Vol. 3, *Under God, Indivisible, 1941–1960* (Chicago: University of Chicago Press, 1996); Warren L. Vinz, *Pulpit Politics: Faces of American Protestant Nationalism in the Twentieth Century* (Albany: State University of New York Press, 1997).

3. Les K. Adler, *The Red Image: American Attitudes toward Communism in the Cold War Era* (New York: Garland, 1991); H. W. Brands, *The Devil We Knew: Americans and the Cold War* (New York: Oxford University Press, 1993); David S. Foglesong, *The American Mission and the "Evil Empire": The Crusade for a "Free Russia" since 1881* (Cambridge: Cambridge University Press, 2007); Joel Kovel, *Red Hunting in the Promised Land: Anticommunism and the Making of America* (New York: Basic Books, 1994); Michael S. Sherry, *In the Shadow of War: The United States since the 1930s* (New Haven, CT: Yale University Press, 1995).

4. Charles DeBenedetti and Charles Chatfield, *An American Ordeal: The Antiwar Movement of the Vietnam Era* (Syracuse, NY: Syracuse University Press, 1990); Marty, *Under God*; Patrick Allitt, *Religion in America since 1945: A History* (New York: Columbia University Press, 2003).

5. David F. Schmitz, *Thank God They're on Our Side: The United States and Right-Wing Dictatorships, 1921–1965* (Chapel Hill: University of North Carolina Press, 1999) and *The United States and Right-Wing Dictatorships, 1965–1989* (Cambridge: Cambridge University Press, 2006).

6. John C. Bennett, "Shades of Red," *Christianity Today* (hereafter *CT*) 9 (20 November 1964): 23; "Red Is Red after All," *CT* 9 (4 December 1964): 31.

7. Robert Dallek, *Flawed Giant: Lyndon Johnson and His Times, 1961–1973* (New York: Oxford University Press, 1998); "All the King's Horses," *CT* 12 (16 February 1968): 28; Samuel H. Moffett, "Report from Korea: No Panic over 'Pueblo,'" *CT* 12 (16 February 1968): 37; Edward L. R. Elson, "Wrong Assumptions on Vietnam," *CT* 12 (16 February 1968): 33–34.

8. "The Czech Revolution," *CT* 12 (26 April 1968): 42; "The Czech Caterpillar Keeps Stirring," *CT* 12 (16 August 1968): 27–28; "Refining Czech Communism," *CT* 12 (13 September 1968): 33–35; "Will Rumania Be Next?" *CT* 12 (27 September 1968): 38.

9. L. Nelson Bell, "Recognize Your Enemy," *CT* 12 (19 July 1968): 21–22; Bela Udvarnoki, "Church and State behind the Iron Curtain," *CT* 8 (11 September 1964): 8–10.

10. Ellen Schrecker, *Many Are the Crimes: McCarthyism in America* (New York: Little, Brown, 1998); J. Edgar Hoover, "The Faith of Our Fathers," *CT* 8 (11 September 1964): 6–7.

11. The best Vatican histories of its Cold War policy are Eric O. Hanson, *The Catholic Church in World Politics* (Princeton, NJ: Princeton University Press, 1987) and Peter C. Kent and John F. Pollard, eds., *Papal Diplomacy in the Modern Age* (Westport, CT: Praeger Publishers, 1994).

12. "The Cold War," *America* 111 (3 October 1964): 372–73; "Moscow-Peking Unity," *America* 111 (21 November 1964): 651–52; "Storm Clouds Over Asia . . . ," *America* 111 (12 December 1964): 764–65.

13. "Kim Il Sung's Unfinished Revolution," *America* 118 (10 February 1968): 179–80; Benjamin Masse, "Threat of Communism Reconsidered," *America* 118 (17 February 1968): 211.

14. "Time Bomb in Czechoslovakia," *America* 118 (18 May 1968): 661–62; "Return to Harsh Reality," *America* 118 (31 August 1968): 115; "The Contagion of Freedom," *America* 118 (7 September 1968): 148; "Curtain Falls Slowly on Prague," *America* 119 (30 November 1968): 536–37.

15. Roy W. Gustafson to Fred. B. Rhodes Jr., 18 November 1968, Southern Baptist Historical Library and Archives (hereafter SBHLA), Fred Rhodes Papers, Box 2, "Graham, Billy—Evan. Assoc., Correspondence, 1967–1969."

16. Jack U. Harwell, "How Do Christians View Presidential Campaign?" *Christian Index* (hereafter *CI*) 147 (5 September 1968): 6; William A. Glenn, "The Iron and the Clay," *Alabama Baptist* (hereafter *AB*) 129 (13 August 1964): 9; "Omaha: Graham Worried," *BM* 80 (24 September 1964): 17; Al Morgan, "News from the Southern Baptist Convention," BPR, SBHLA, SBC Press Kits, Box 2, Folder 18.

17. Earl Ofari Hutchinson, *Black and Reds: Race and Class in Conflict, 1919–1990* (East Lansing: Michigan State University Press, 1995); Gerald Horne, *Black Liberation/Red Scare: Ben Davis and the Communist Party* (Newark, NJ: University of Delaware Press, 1994); Daniel Levine, *Bayard Rustin and the Civil Rights Movement* (New Brunswick, NJ: Rutgers University Press, 2000); Schrecker, *Many Are the Crimes*, 389–95. For the Lutheran debate, which in many respects paralleled the Southern Baptist Convention dialogue, see chapter 3 of David E. Settje, *Lutherans and the Longest War: Adrift on a Sea of Doubt about the Cold and Vietnam Wars, 1964–1975* (Lanham, MD: Lexington Books, 2007).

18. Richard N. Owen, "Observations by Owen," *Baptist and Reflector* (hereafter *BAR*) 134 (23 May 1968): 4–5; Leon Macon, "Communism and the Race Question," *AB* 129 (3 September 1964): 3. Several books have proven false the claims against King made by the FBI because of its resistance to the civil rights movement, a campaign led by J. Edgar Hoover, including David J. Garrow, *The FBI and Martin Luther King, Jr.: From "Solo" to Memphis* (New York: Norton, 1981) and Kenneth O'Reilly, *"Racial Matters": The FBI's Secret File on Black America, 1960–1972* (New York: Free Press, 1989).

19. James F. Cole, "Brothers or Keepers?" *BM* 84 (18 April 1968): 4–6; Richard N. Owen, *BAR* 130 (8 October 1964): 4.

20. Erwin L. McDonald, "The World Crisis," *Arkansas Baptist* (hereafter *AKB*) 63 (6 August 1964): 2–3.

21. "New Freedom Reported for Czech Baptists," Baptist Press Release (hereafter BPR), 30 July 1968, SBHLA, Baptist Press, Box 1968 June–December, "Baptist Press—Southern Baptist Convention, 1968; July"; Jack U. Harwell, "Czechoslovakia Shows True Face of Communism," *CI* 147 (12 September 1968): 6; "Czech Baptists Plead: 'Remain with Us Now!'" BPR, SBHLA, Baptist Press, 1 October 1968, Box 1968 June–December, "Baptist Press—Southern Baptist Convention, 1968: October"; "Czech Churches Confident," *Commission* 31 (November 1968): 33.

22. African Methodist Episcopal Church (hereafter AMEC), "Minutes of the Thirty-Seventh Session of the General Conference," May 1964, AME Department of Research and Scholarship (hereafter AMED), Nashville, TN, 85; AMEC, "Minutes of the Thirty-Seventh Session of the

General Conference," May 1964, AMED, Nashville, TN, 211–14. For good discussion of the international context of American race and foreign policy, see Thomas Borstelmann, *The Cold War and the Color Line: American Race Relations in the Global Arena* (Cambridge, MA: Harvard University Press, 2003); Azza Salama Layton, *International Politics and Civil Rights Policies in the United States, 1941–1960* (Cambridge: Cambridge University Press, 2000); Jonathan Rosenberg, *How Far the Promised Land? World Affairs and the American Civil Rights Movement from the First World War to Vietnam* (Princeton, NJ: Princeton University Press, 2006).

23. "Avoid Red Tactics in Campaign against Communism, Says Methodist Bishop," *Christian Recorder* (hereafter *CR*) 115 (8 December 1964): 14; "'I Love Thy Church, O God,'" *CR* 119 (16 April 1968): 3, 14; J. S. Johnson, "Excuses and Crimes," *CR* 119 (24 September 1968): 2, 14.

24. William E. Summers III, "Bishop Gibbs Hold Spirited West Kentucky Annual Conference," *CR* 119 (29 October 1968): 4; Sam M. Davis, "Straight to the Target," *CR* 119 (31 December 1968): 1, 13.

25. Taylor Branch, *At Canaan's Edge: America in the King Years, 1965–1968* (New York: Simon and Schuster, 2006); James H. Cone, *Martin and Malcolm and America: A Dream or a Nightmare?* (New York: Orbis Books, 1992).

26. AMEC, "Minutes of the Thirty-Seventh Session of the General Conference," May 1964, AMED, Nashville, TN; AMEC, "Minutes of the Thirty-Seventh Session of the General Conference," May 1964, AMED, Nashville, TN, 168–69; Indiana Annual Conference, AMEC, 130th Session of the Annual Conference Minutes, 20–25 August 1968, AMED, Nashville, TN.

27. Schmitz, *The United States*; Piero Gleijeses, "'Flee! The White Giants Are Coming!':The United States, Mercenaries, and the Congo, 1964–1965," in Peter L. Hahn and Mary Ann Heiss, eds., *Empire and Revolution: The United States and the Third World since 1945* (Columbus: Ohio State University Press, 2001): 71–93.

28. "Congo: The Rebel Arc," *CT* 9 (20 November 1964): 49; "Martyrdom in the Congo," *CT* 9 (18 December 1964): 24–25.

29. Edward T. Brett, *The U.S. Catholic Press on Central America: From Cold War Anticommunism to Social Justice* (Notre Dame, IN: University of Notre Dame Press, 2003).

30. Georgie Anne Geyer, "The Coming Revolution in Latin America," *U.S. Catholic* (hereafter *USC*) 34 (July 1968): 6–10; Robert E. Burns, "The Examined Life," *USC* 34 (December 1964): 2.

31. "The Church in Cuba," *America* 111 (12 December 1964): 769.

32. Ernest Timmons, "The Bone in Gomulka's Throat," *Catholic Digest* (hereafter *CD*) 29 (December 1964): 61–63.

33. "Moscow: Resigns Party," *BM* 80 (6 August 1964): 17; "Albania Says It's Atheist," *Commission* 31 (January 1968): 32; "'Atheist Ship' in Operation," *Commission* 31 (June 1968): 31.

34. For overviews of the Southern Baptist commitment to missionary work, see Bill J. Leonard, *Baptists in America* (New York: Columbia University Press, 2005) and Jesse C. Fletcher, *The Southern Baptist Convention: A Sesquicentennial History* (Nashville, TN: Broadman and Holman, 1994). Baker J. Cauthen, "They Stand the Test," *Commission* 27 (September 1964): 19; James D. Crane, "A New Day for Missions," *Commission* 31 (June 1968): 9–13 (emphasis in original).

35. Brian Crozier, *The Rise and Fall of the Soviet Empire* (Rockin, CA: Forum Press, 1999); Gainer E. Bryan Jr., "Since the Coup," *Commission* 31 (March 1968): 8–11.

36. DeBenedetti and Chatfield, *An American Ordeal*; Lawrence S. Wittner, *Rebels against War: The American Peace Movement, 1933–1983* (Philadelphia: Temple University Press, 1984).

37. "A Time for Cool Heads and Steady Hands," *Christian Century* (hereafter *CC*) 81 (28 October 1964): 1323–24; Hwa Yu, "China," *CC* 85 (27 November 1968): 1522.

38. "Religion under Communism," *CC* 85 (5 June 1968): 744; "The Crisis in Czechoslovakia," *CC* 85 (31 July 1968): 959–60; "Universal Moral Myopia," *CC* 85 (4 September 1968): 1095–96; Alan Geyer, "Czechoslovakia and the U.S.: Lament for Two Peoples," *CC* 85 (18 September 1968): 1160–61.

39. William A. Au, *The Cross, the Flag, and the Bomb: American Catholics Debate War and Peace, 1960–1983* (Westport, CT: Greenwood Press, 1985); Chester Gillis, *Roman Catholicism in America* (New York: Columbia University Press, 1999); DeBenedetti and Chatfield, *An American Ordeal*; John B. Sheerin, "Is Communism Caving In?" *Catholic World* (hereafter *CW*) 207 (May 1968): 50–51.

40. Erwin L. McDonald, "Anti-King Backlash," *AKB* 67 (23 May 1968): 3–4.

41. Rick Perlstein, *Before the Storm: Barry Goldwater and the Unmaking of the American Consensus* (New York: Hill and Wang, 2001); John M. Schoenwald, *A Time for Choosing: The Rise of Modern American Conservatism* (New York: Oxford University Press, 2001); Mary C. Brennan, *Turning Right in the Sixties: The Conservative Capture of the GOP* (Chapel Hill: University of North Carolina Press, 1995); Lisa McGirr, *Suburban Warriors: The Origins of the New American Right* (Princeton, NJ: Princeton University Press, 2001); "Johnson? Yes!" *CC* 81 (9 September 1964): 1099–1101; "The Atom: Slave or Master?" *CC* 81 (5 August 1964): 979–80.

42. "Repression Trend Accelerates," *CC* 85 (31 January 1968): 132–33; "Another Finger on the Button," *CC* 81 (14 October 1964): 1259–60; Donald E. MacInnis, "Maoism: The Religious Analogy," *CC* 85 (10 January 1968): 39–42. The periodical's stance on the PRC's admittance into the United Nations no doubt stemmed in part from the fact that the NCC's World Order Study Conference had advocated such a position since 1958, and the NCC made it an official policy in 1966. Furthermore, much of this reasoning can be found in *Christianity and Crisis*, which had established this Christian realism in its foreign policy outlook already in the 1950s. See Mark David Hulsether, *Building a Protestant Left*: Christianity and Crisis *Magazine, 1941–1993* (Knoxville: University of Tennessee Press, 1999).

43. "Persecutes Cuban Baptists," *CC* 81 (7 October 1964): 1230–31; "Order in the Streets," *CC* 81 (30 September 1964): 1195–96; Manuel Maldonado-Denis, "The Situation of Cuba's Intellectuals," *CC* 85 (17 January 1968): 78–80.

44. "Mutual Deterrence," *Commonweal* 81 (2 October 1964): 28–29; "Looking at China," *Commonweal* 81 (6 November 1964): 181–82; "Changes in Russia," *Commonweal* 81 (30 October 1964): 147–48; "The Great Society," *Commonweal* 81 (20 November 1964): 255–58.

45. "The New Men of Power," *Commonweal* 88 (12 April 1968): 93–94; William Pfaff, "Czechoslovakia Invaded," *Commonweal* 88 (6 September 1968): 581.

46. Louis H. Gunnemann, *The Shaping of the UCC: An Essay in the History of American Christianity* (Cleveland, OH: United Church Press, 1999): 60; Emily Brookes, "Christian Republicanism?" *UCH* 7 (1 September 1964): 5. Though a vast majority of United Church of Christ leaders and lay people took a more liberal stance regarding the Cold War, a minority existed within the church that argued for a harsher anti-Communist platform that agreed with conservative Christian counterparts. Though it is almost impossible to pinpoint the exact derivation of this unrest, it most likely came from the Evangelical and

German Reformed Church members who had disliked the activist stance of the newly created UCC since its founding in 1957. Yet they were such a minority voice that this study focuses on the much more prevalent liberal position of the denomination.

47. Reverend Ben M. Herbster, "Accents for the UCC in the 1967–69 Biennium," UCC, "Minutes Sixth General Synod, Cincinnati, Ohio, 22–29 June 1967.": pp. 149–58, reproduced from the General Synod Collection (hereafter GSC), United Church of Christ Archives (hereafter UCCA).

48. Eve and Paul Bock, "New Epoch for Czech Christians," *UCH* 11 (September 1968): 44–45; "Comment," *UCH* 11 (November 1968): 30.

49. Gunnemann, *Shaping*, 70; UCC, "Minutes Fifth General Synod, Chicago, Illinois, 1–7 July 1965," 65-GS-238, Report on the "Council for Christian SA, as finally adopted," pp. 82–91, 130–31, reproduced from the GSC, UCCA; UCC, "Minutes Fifth General Synod, Chicago, Illinois, 1–7 July 1965," 65-GS-256, Report on the "Council for Christian SA, as finally adopted," pp. 82–91, 136–40, reproduced from the GSC, UCCA; UCC, "Minutes Fifth General Synod, Chicago, Illinois, 1–7 July 1965," 65-GS-257, Report on the "Council for Christian SA, as finally adopted," pp. 82–91, 136–40, reproduced from the GSC, UCCA.

50. DeBenedetti and Chatfield, *An American*.

51. "The Pueblo Affair," *CC* 85 (7 February 1968): 155–56; John M. Swomley Jr., "Domestic Economic Bases of the Cold War," *CC* 85 (1 May 1968): 581–85.

52. Dennis Deletant, *Communist Terror in Romania: Gheorghiu-Dej and the Police State, 1948–1965* (New York: St. Martin's Press, 1999); Matthew M. Mestrovic, "Rumania Looks West," *Commonweal* 81 (25 September 1964): 10–12; Matthew M. Mestrovic, "Fall of a Communist Czar," *Commonweal* 87 (26 January 1968): 487–89.

53. David T. Morgan's *New Crusades, the New Holy Land: Conflict in the Southern Baptist Convention, 1969–1991* (Tuscaloosa: University of Alabama Press, 1996) provides a good study of the moderate versus conservative conflict within the SBC. Bill Dyal, "Missions and Peace" (1964?), SBHLA, Christian Life Commission (hereafter CLC), Box 24, "War and Peace—1960s, Folder 1."

54. Jonathan Rosenberg, *How Far the Promised Land? World Affairs and the American Civil Rights Movement from the First World War to Vietnam* (Princeton, NJ: Princeton University Press, 2006); B. J. Nolen, "Freedom and Civil Rights, the Acid Test of True Democracy," *CR* 119 (8 October 1968): 8; AMEC, "Minutes of the Thirty-Ninth Session of the General Conference," AMED, Nashville, Tennessee, 10–11.

55. Herman F. Reissig, "Is This United States Being Militarized?" *UCH* 7 (1 September 1964): 22–23; "New Facts and Trends," *Social Action* 31 (April 1965): 7; Charles M. Savage, "Dialogue in a Demanding World," *Keeping You Posted* 4 (June 1968): 6–7.

CHAPTER 2

1. Harold John Ockenga, "Report from Viet Nam," *Christianity Today* (hereafter *CT*) 12 (15 March 1968): 35; Martin E. Marty, "Please, Mr. Ho!" *Christian Century* (hereafter *CC*) 85 (24 January 1968): 127.

2. For the best sources on Christianity and Vietnam, especially in relation to antiwar activism, see Charles DeBenedetti and Charles Chatfield, *An American Ordeal: The Antiwar Movement of the Vietnam Era* (Syracuse, NY: Syracuse University Press, 1990); Jill

Kristine Gill, "'Peace Is Not the Absence of War but the Presence of Justice': The National Council of Churches' Reaction and Response to the Vietnam War, 1965–1972" (Ph.D. diss., University of Pennsylvania, 1996); Warren Goldstein, *William Sloane Coffin Jr.: A Holy Impatience* (New Haven, CT: Yale University Press, 2004); Mitchell K. Hall, *Because of Their Faith: CALCAV and Religious Opposition to the Vietnam War* (New York: Columbia University Press, 1990); Rick L. Nutt, *Toward Peacemaking: Presbyterians in the South and National Security, 1945–1983* (Tuscaloosa: University of Alabama Press, 1994); and Amanda Porterfield, *The Transformation of American Religion: The Story of a Late-Twentieth-Century Awakening* (New York: Oxford University Press, 2001); David E. Settje, *Lutherans and the Longest War: Adrift on a Sea of Doubt about the Cold and Vietnam Wars, 1964–1975* (Lanham, MD: Lexington Books, 2007).

3. "The Pope and World Peace," *CT* 8 (28 August 1964): 32; "Putting First Things Second," *CT* 12 (1 March 1968): 27.

4. "Viet Nam: The Spiritual War," *CT* 8 (25 September 1964): 53–54; "North Viet Nam Case Study," *CT* 13 (22 November 1968): 44–45.

5. "Force Meets Force," *America* 111 (15 August 1964): 146; "Sitting Ducks of Bien Hoa . . . ," *America* 111 (14 November 1964): 585; ". . . Government in Saigon," *America* 111 (14 November 1964): 585.

6. "The Question in Saigon," *America* 111 (19 September 1964): 286–87; "Fanaticism on the Rampage," *America* 118 (17 February 1968): 212; "Pope Paul's Easter Message," *America* 118 (27 April 1968): 555–56.

7. "Saigon's Hope for Tomorrow," *Catholic Digest* (hereafter *CD*) 32 (August 1968): 118–22; H. R. Kaplan, "The Quality of Mercy in Vietnam," *CD* 32 (September 1968): 121–25.

8. "Five Hundred Baptist Pastors Surveyed: Nixon, Wallace Favored by Most," Baptist Press Release (hereafter BPR), 5 August 1968, Southern Baptist Historical Library and Archives (hereafter SBHLA), Baptist Press, Box 1968 June–December, "Baptist Press— Southern Baptist Convention (hereafter SBC)—1968, August"; Ione Gray, "Vietnam Missionaries Assured of FMB Backing," *Baptist and Reflector* 134 (22 February 1968): 7.

9. Robert L. Dicken to H. Franklin Paschall, 29 May 1967, SBHLA, Franklin Paschall Papers, Box 14, "Viet Nam Conflict"; H. Franklin Paschall to Frank B. Best, 20 June 1967, SBHLA, Franklin Paschall Papers, Box 14, "Viet Nam Conflict"; H. Franklin Paschall to Mrs. Walton Brigman, 22 April 1968, SBHLA, Franklin Paschall Papers, Box 14, "Viet Nam Conflict."

10. C. R. Daley, "Should the United States Get Out of Vietnam?—No," *The Maryland Baptist* (hereafter *MD*) n.v. (5 September 1968): 3, 8; Hudson Baggett, "Peace at Any Price," *Alabama Baptist* 133 (16 May 1968): 2; T. B. Matson, "The Morality of Vietnam," *Baptist Message* (hereafter *BM*) 84 (21 March 1968): 3; "Chaplain Sees Dissent As Impeding War Effort," *BM* 84 (25 January 1968): 7.

11. Alfred H. Gilbert, "Bound to Win," *United Church Herald* (hereafter *UCH*) 11 (February 1968): 6; H. R. Mol, "Our Brother's Keeper," *UCH* 7 (March 1968): 11 (emphasis in original).

12. "Is President Swayed by Talk of War?" *CC* 81 (12 August 1964): 1006; "An Echo, Not a Choice," *CC* 81 (19 August 1964): 1028; "Getting Out of Vietnam," *CC* 81 (23 December 1964): 1582–83.

13. Howard Schomer, "Vietnam: The War Nobody Wants?" *CC* 85 (3 January 1968): 7–8. For secondary literature about the North Vietnamese relationship with the People's

Republic of China, see Qiang Zhai, *China and the Vietnam Wars, 1950–1975* (Chapel Hill: University of North Carolina Press, 2000) and Chen Jian, *Mao's China and the Cold War* (Chapel Hill: University of North Carolina Press, 2001).

14. J. Claude Evans, "Hawks Get a Feeding," *CC* 85 (31 January 1968): 134; Carl P. Zietlow, "Perspective on the Paris Peace Talks," *CC* 85 (19 June 1968): 810–11; Peter Berger, "Between Tyranny and Chaos," *CC* 85 (30 October 1968): 1365–70.

15. "Where Protest Counts," *CC* 85 (24 January 1968): 99–100 (emphasis in original); "We're Still at War," *CC* 85 (29 May 1968): 703–4; Prentiss Pemberton and Homer Page, "Translating Antiwar Protest into Political Power," *CC* 85 (3 January 1968): 11–14.

16. William M. Dyal Jr., "The 'Silent Shriek' of Baptists on Vietnam," 13 December 1966, SBHLA, Christian Life Commission (hereafter CLC), Box 24, "Vietnam—1965–1967— Folder 8" (emphasis in original).

17. Robert H. Hamill, "Madness and Sanity in Vietnam," 9 January 1966, SBHLA, CLC, Box 24, "War and Peace—1960s, Folder 1, Folder 19"; John R. Claypool, "The Moral Expense of War," 6 February 1966, SBHLA, CLC, Box 24, "War and Peace—1960s, Folder 2, Folder 20."

18. Robert Brigham, *Guerrilla Diplomacy: The NLF's Foreign Relations and the Viet Nam War* (Ithaca, NY: Cornell University Press, 1999); Richard A. Hunt, *Pacification: The American Struggle for Vietnam's Hearts and Minds* (Boulder, CO: Westview Press, 1995).

19. Henlee H. Barnette, "Should the United States Get Out of Vietnam?—Yes," *MD* n.v. (5 September 1968): 3, 8; "Michigan Baptists Adopt Resolutions on Race, War," BPR, 8 November 1968, SBHLA, Baptist Press, Box 1968 June–December, "Baptist Press— SBC—1968, November." For the history of Vietnam, see William J. Duiker, *Vietnam: Revolution in Transition*, 2nd ed. (Boulder, CO: Westview Press, 1995); Marilyn B. Young, *The Vietnam Wars, 1945–1990* (New York: HarperPerennial, 1991).

20. Erwin L. McDonald, "Bibles or Bombs," *Arkansas Baptist* (hereafter *AKB*) 67 (11 January 1968): 3; Erwin L. McDonald, "Attitude on War," *AKB* 67 (4 April 1968): 3.

21. "Students Plan Demonstration over SBC Silence on Issues," BPR, 23 May 1968, SBHLA, Baptist Press, Box 1968 January–May, "Baptist Press—SBC—1968, May"; Jim Newton, "Students Urge SBC to Face Issues: Pastors Say Don't Leave," BPR, 3 June 1968, SBHLA, Baptist Press, Box 1968 June–December, "Baptist Press—SBC—1968, June."

22. United Church of Christ (hereafter UCC), "Minutes Fifth General Synod," Chicago, Illinois, 1–7 July 1965, 65-GS-237 Report on the "Council for Christian SA, as finally adopted," pp. 82–91, 130–31, reproduced from the General Synod Collection (hereafter GSC), United Church of Christ Archives (hereafter UCCA); "Anguish over Vietnam: Readers Respond," *UCH* 11 (April 1968): 22–23.

23. UCC, "Minutes Sixth General Synod," Cincinnati, Ohio, 22–29 June 1967, 67-GS-220 Resolution of "Justice and Peace in Vietnam," pp. 132–34, reproduced from the GSC, UCCA; Reverend Ben M. Herbster, "Accents for the UCC in the 1967–69 Biennium," UCC, "Minutes Sixth General Synod," Cincinnati, Ohio, 22–29 June 1967, pp. 149–58, reproduced from the GSC, UCCA.

24. Alan Geyer, "Moral Dilemmas in Revolutionary Warfare," *Social Action* (hereafter *SA*) 33 (September 1966): 12–20; J. Stanley Stevens, "Power," *Keeping You Posted* (hereafter *KYP*) 4 (1 January 1968): 5 (emphasis in original); Arthur J. Secor, "The Military Establishment," *UCH* 11 (February 1968): 6.

25. Notebook, *UCH* 11 (April 1968): 37 (deletion in original); James L. Mengel, "Blood Baths and Brotherhood," *KYP* 4 (December 1968): 6.

26. "North Vietnam's Bloody Nose," *Commonweal* 80 (21 August 1964): 559–60; William Pfaff, "Vietnam: The Roots of Chaos," *Commonweal* 81 (6 November 1964): 183–90.

27. "Hope on the Horizon," *Commonweal* 89 (12 April 1968): 91–93; "Flawed Intentions," *Commonweal* 88 (3 May 1968): 195–96; "And Now Saigon," *Commonweal* 89 (15 November 1968): 235–36.

28. "Chances for Peace," *Commonweal* 87 (12 January 1968): 427–28; "McCarthy and Kennedy," *Commonweal* 88 (29 March 1968): 35–36; "The Politics of Peace," *Commonweal* 88 (21 June 1968): 396–97; "Vietnam: The Bleak Prospect," *Commonweal* 89 (6 December 1968): 331–32.

29. Robert E. Burns, "The Examined Life," *U.S. Catholic* (hereafter *USC*) 33 (March 1968): 2; Robert E. Burns, "The Examined Life," *USC* 33 (February 1968): 2.

30. Paul K. T. Sih, "Our China Policy: A Reappraisal," *Catholic World* (hereafter *CW*) 200 (November 1964): 84–90.

31. John B. Sheerin, C. S. P., "Is Communism Caving In?" *CW* 207 (May 1968): 50–51; Donald J. Wolf, "Vietnam Morality: Who Judges What, When, How?" *CW* 207 (June 1968): 107–10 (emphasis in original).

32. SBC, "Resolution Concerning Peace," SBC Resolutions, June 1966, www.SBC.net; SBC, "Resolution on Peace," SBC Resolutions, June 1967, www.SBC.net; SBC, "Resolution on Peace," SBC Resolutions, June 1968, www.SBC.net.

33. E. P. Wallace, "Letter to President Lyndon B. Johnson," *Christian Recorder* (hereafter *CR*) 118 (9 January 1968): 10; B. J. Nolen, "A.M.E. Unfinished Revolution," *CR* 118 (19 March 1968): 8.

34. African Methodist Episcopal Church (hereafter AMEC), "Minutes of the Thirty-Eighth Session of the General Conference," May 1968, AME Department of Research and Scholarship (hereafter AMED), Nashville, TN, 114–15; "Martin Luther King's Vietnam Stand Seen Harming Welfare of Millions of Negroes," *A.M.E. Church Review* 92 (January–March 1968): 23. Taylor Branch, *At Canaan's Edge: America in the King Years, 1965–68* (New York: Simon and Schuster, 2006); Michael Eric Dyson, *I May Not Get There With You: The True Martin Luther King Jr.* (New York: Simon and Schuster, 2000).

35. "Embry Chapel Asks: What Nation Always Wins in the End?" *CR* 118 (2 April 1968): 3, 13; "Dr. Blake: Pacifists Not Cowards or Disobedient to Christ's Word," *CR* 119 (30 July 1968): 4.

36. "Report on the State of the Country," *CR* 119 (5 November 1968): 2, 14; B. J. Nolen, "Christianity Is a Battlefield, Brother," *CR* 119 (12 November 1968): 8.

37. Karl A. Olsson, "Brave Men—Living and Dead," *CR* 118 (18 June 1968): 3, 11; Michigan Annual Conference, AMEC, 82nd Session of the Annual Conference Minutes, 3–8 September 1968, AMED, Nashville, TN.

38. "Stripped to the Foundations," *CT* 9 (4 December 1964): 3–12; "Advance in Adversity," *CT* 9 (18 December 1964): 44; David E. Kucharsky, "Viet Nam: The Vulnerable Ones," *CT* 12 (1 March 1968): 16–19.

39. John McLaughlin, "Saigon at War," *America* 119 (23 November 1968): 512–16.

40. "Plans Made Despite Danger," *Commission* 27 (September 1964): 31; Gainer E. Bryan Jr., "Baptist Missionaries Say Most Support Vietnam War," BPR, 24 January 1968, SBHLA, Baptist Press, Box 1968 January-May, "Baptist Press—SBC—1968, January"; Gainer E. Bryan Jr., "Herman Hayes Supports U.S. Vietnam Position," *BM* 84 (8 February 1968): 12; "Vietnam Report," *Commission* 31 (April 1968): 33.

41. "Revolt in Vietnam," *Commonweal* 92 (25 September 1964): 4; Harry Haas, "Catholics in North Vietnam," *Commonweal* 87 (9 February 1968): 558–61.

42. "Voice for the Voiceless," *CC* 85 (3 January 1968): 4–5; Tran Van Danh, "Six Hours That Changed the Vietnam Situation," *CC* 85 (6 March 1968): 289–91.

CHAPTER 3

1. Southern Baptist Convention (hereafter SBC), "Resolution on Extremism," SBC Resolutions, June 1970, www.SBC.net; United Church of Christ (hereafter UCC), "Minutes Eighth General Synod," Grand Rapids, Michigan, 25–29 June 1971, 71-GS-39/71-GS-40/71-GS-41/71-GS-42/71-GS-43/71-GS-44/71-GS-45/71-GS-46/71-GS-47 Response and Action "Peace and United States Power," pp. 41–45, reproduced from the General Synod Collection (hereafter GSC), UCC Archives (hereafter UCCA).

2. T. Jeremy Gunn, *Spiritual Weapons: The Cold War and the Forging of an American National Religion* (Westport, CT: Praeger, 2009).

3. Carl F. H. Henry, "The Evangel in Eastern Europe," *Christianity Today* (hereafter *CT*) 17 (2 February 1972): 34; B. P. Dotsenko, "From Communism to Christianity," *CT* 17 (5 January 1973): 4–12.

4. Edward E. Plowman, "Deep in the Heart of Eastern Europe," *CT* 17 (5 January 1973): 44–45; David E. Kucharsky, "Religious Oppression: Russian Revolution Yields Bitter Fruit," *CT* 14 (24 April 1970): 42.

5. "Russia and Rhodesia," *CT* 17 (27 October 1972): 28.

6. "China vs. Bangladesh," *CT* 16 (15 September 1972): 36; Thomas G. Paterson, J. Garry Clifford, and Kenneth J. Hagan, *American Foreign Relations: A History since 1895*, 4th ed. (Toronto: Heath, 1995).

7. Carl F. H. Henry, "China: The Lonely Remnant," *CT* 17 (13 October 1972): 44–46; Carl F. H. Henry, "China: The Lonely Remnant," *CT* 17 (10 November 1972): 34–35.

8. Dick Hillis, "Who Will Mourn Chairman Mao?" *CT* 17 (24 November 1972): 4–5.

9. "India's Reds Blow It Again," *America* 122 (4 April 1970): 362; "Oneupmanship in Asia," *America* 122 (6 June 1970): 600; "The View from Peking," *America* 127 (28 October 1972): 329.

10. "New Threat to Czech Churches," *America* 122 (18 April 1970): 402; "Hope for U.S.-Cuban Thaw," *America* 127 (2 December 1972): 463–64.

11. Herschel H. Hobbs, "Communism or Christian Sharing?" *Baptist and Reflector* 136 (7 May 1970): 2 (emphasis in original); "Peace Symbol? Are You Sure?" *Baptist Beacon* 18 (17 August 1970): 1.

12. "Swedish Baptist Papers Urge BWA Action against Repression," Baptist Press Release (hereafter BPR), 17 June 1970, Southern Baptist Historical Library and Archives (hereafter SBHLA), Baptist Press, Box 1970 June–December, "Baptist Press—SBC—1970, June 6–29"; BPR, "Baptist Leader Sees Communism Threat," *Baptist Message* 87 (31 August 1972): 4.

13. "Baptist Group Directs Resolutions to Russian and Israeli Governments," BPR, 20 October 1972, SBHLA, Baptist Press, Box 1972 July–December, "Baptist Press—SBC—1972, October"; "Diplomat from Russia Speaks at Baptist Dialogue Meeting," 13 February 1973, Baptist Press, SBHLA, SBC Press Kit.

14. Religious News Service, "Southern Baptist Leader Reports on White House China Briefing," 13 August 1971, SBHLA, Fred Rhodes Papers, Box 1, "Christian Fellowship

Work—Folder 10"; Baptist Press, "Thirty Religious Leaders Briefed by White House on China," 12 August 1971, SBHLA, Fred Rhodes Papers, Box 1, "Christian Fellowship Work—Folder 10."

15. Charles L. Culpepper Jr., "Taiwan: China's Phoenix?" *Commission* 33 (April 1970): 17–18; J. G. Goodwin Jr., "Republic of Korea: Freedom's Frontier," *Commission* 35 (December 1972): 21–22; "Biology Major Plans Career with Thailand Police Force," BPR, 27 April 1970, SBHLA, Baptist Press, Box 1970 January–May, "Baptist Press—SBC—1970, April"; Ronald C. Hill, "Thailand: Shangri-la in Search," *Commission* 35 (December 1972): 19–20.

16. "A Morality That Did Not Communicate," *Christian Century* (hereafter *CC*) 89 (15 November 1972): 1143–44; Cornish Rogers, "Winning without Honor," *CC* 89 (15 November 1972): 1146.

17. James Armstrong, "The Case for McGovern," *CC* 89 (1 November 1972): 1096–98.

18. William Jeffries, "Today's Cuba and U.S. Policy," *CC* 87 (6 May 1970): 560–63; "Castro's Uncashed Checks," *CC* 89 (29 November 1972): 1208.

19. Hwa Yu, "China," *CC* 89 (27 September 1972): 970; Hwa Yu, "China," *CC* 89 (25 October 1972): 1082.

20. Special Correspondent, "Toward 'Critical Cooperation': An East German Theological Stance," *CC* 89 (13 September 1972): 902–4.

21. Robert L. Bard and Lewis Kurlantzik, "An Unfair Tax That Should Be Paid," *CC* 90 (17 January 1973): 63; Michael Bourdeaux, "Russian Baptist Leader Imprisoned," *CC* 87 (1 July 1970): 830; Michael Bourdeaux, "Soviet Archbishop Released from Prison, Reinstated by Church," *CC* 87 (27 May 1970): 674–75.

22. UCC, "Minutes Eighth General Synod, Grand Rapids, Michigan, 25–29 June 1971," 71-GS-17 Adoption of "'The Faith Crisis': Goals and Objectives," pp. 22–24, reproduced from the GSC, UCCA; David M. Stowe, "The Global Village-Church," *A.D.* 1 (December 1972): 45.

23. Harry Emerson Fosdick, "The Unknown Soldier," *A.D.* 1 (November 1972): 31–34; Oliver G. Powell, "An Advent Calendar of Prayers," *A.D.* (December 1972): 8–14.

24. Milton H. Mater, "Christian Morality Demands the Deployment of the ABM," *United Church Herald* (hereafter *UCH*) 13 (May 1970): 7; "Salt and Savor," *UCH* 13 (May 1970): 21.

25. UCC, "Minutes Seventh General Synod, Boston, Massachusetts, 25 June–2 July 1969," 69-GS-135 Action on "The Report on the Council for Christian Social Action," pp. 127–28, reproduced from the GSC, UCCA; David Stowe, "China: The Church," *UCH* 13 (July 1968): 16; Huber F. Klemme to Arthur E. Higgins, 10 March 1972, UCCA, Council for Christian Social Action, UCC 90–9, Box 2, Folder 6; UCC, "Minutes Ninth General Synod, St. Louis, Missouri, 22–26 June 1973," 73-6EC-2 Resolution on Cuba, p. 74, reproduced from the GSC, UCCA.

26. "Cambodian Confusion," *Commonweal* 92 (17 April 1970): 107–8 (emphasis in original).

27. Ramsdell Gurney Jr., "Negotiating for Peace," *Commonweal* 97 (15 December 1972): 246–51; "Hijacking and Justice," *Commonweal* 97 (2 March 1973): 491–92.

28. Matthew Mestrovic, "Crisis in Yugoslavia," *Commonweal* 97 (24 November 1972): 173–74.

29. Robert E. Burns, "The Examined Life," *U.S. Catholic and Jubilee* 38 (January 1973): 2.

30. Wayne R. McKinney, M.D., "Lift Up Your Head, Tom Dooley," *Catholic Digest* 37 (December 1972): 33–37.

31. Nikita D. Roodkowsky, "Lenin (1887–1970)," *Catholic World* (hereafter *CW*) 211 (June 1970): 107–11; Carnegie S. Calian, "Rich Nations and Poor Nations Need Each Other," *CW* 216 (January/February 1973): 12–15.

32. James H. Foster, "Is God Dead?" *Christian Recorder* (hereafter *CR*) 121 (7 July 1970): 3; B. J. Nolen, "Religion's Relationship to Political Processes Factor as U.S. Primes for Elections," *CR* 123 (8 August 1972): 5; "Is Rock Music Demon Inspired?" *CR* 122 (28 May 1973): 2, 8; J. A. McQueen, "Or [*sic*] Times and the Church," *CR* 123 (23 June 1973): 8.

33. Indiana Annual Conference, African Methodist Episcopal Church (hereafter AMEC), 134th Session Conference Minutes, 29 August–1 September 1972, African Methodist Episcopal Department of Research and Scholarship (hereafter AMED), Nashville, TN; Michigan Annual Conference, AMEC, 87th Session of the Annual Conference Minutes, 28–31 August 1973, AMED, Nashville, TN.

34. "Hope—Now Horror in Nigeria," *CR* 121 (21 April 1970): 11; B. J. Nolen, "Foreign Mission Programs Undergo Dramatic Change," *CR* 123 (11 July 1972): 8, 16; "Churchman Asks Continued U.S. Presence in Korea," *CR* 123 (3 October 1972): 3–4.

35. "They Had a Dream: Paul Robeson," *CR* 121 (5 May 1970): 14.

36. AMEC, "Journal of the Eighty-Fourth Session of the Michigan Annual Conference," 4th Episcopal District, Inkster, MI, August 1970, AMED, Nashville, TN, 102–8; B. J. Nolen, "New Patriarch Faces Many Challenges," *CR* 123 (15 August 1972): 5; H. A. Belin Jr., "A Man Worth Examining," *CR* 122 (2 July 1973): 4.

37. "Soviet Youth Pick-Up," *CR* 121 (21 April 1970): 5; B. J. Nolen, "Good Signs in America," *CR* 123 (26 September 1972): 5.

38. Chicago Annual Conference, AMEC, 88th Session of the Annual Conference Minutes, 8–13 September 1970, AMED, Nashville, TN; Philadelphia Annual Conference of the First Episcopal District, AMEC, 156th Session of the Annual Conference Minutes, 23–28 May 1972, AMED, Nashville, TN; B. J. Nolen, "Spiritual Vitality, Religion, and Politics Highlight the First Six Months of 1972," *CR* 123 (1 August 1972): 5, 8.

CHAPTER 4

1. George C. Herring, *America's Longest War: The United States and Vietnam, 1950–1975*, 4th ed. (New York: McGraw Hill, 2001); Jeffrey Kimball, *Nixon's Vietnam War* (Lawrence: University of Kansas Press, 1998); Marilyn B. Young, *The Vietnam Wars, 1945–1990* (New York: HarperPerennial, 1991).

2. Herring, *America's*; Kimball, *Nixon's*; Young, *The Vietnam*; William A. Gordon, *The Fourth of May: Killings and Coverups at Kent State* (Buffalo. NY: Prometheus Books, 1990); James A. Michener, *Kent State: What Happened and Why* (New York: Random House, 1971).

3. Herring, *America's*; Kimball, *Nixon's*; Young, *The Vietnam*; William J. Duiker, *Vietnam: Revolution in Transition*, 2nd ed. (Boulder, CO: Westview Press, 1995).

4. David E. Settje, *Lutherans and the Longest War: Adrift on a Sea of Doubt about the Cold and Vietnam Wars, 1964–1975* (Lanham, MD: Lexington Books, 2007); Patrick Allitt, *Religion in America since 1945: A History* (New York: Columbia University Press, 2003); Michael B. Friedland, *Lift Up Your Voice Like a Trumpet* (Chapel Hill: University of North Carolina Press, 1998); Mitchell K. Hall, *Because of Their Faith: CALCAV and Religious Opposition to the Vietnam War* (New York: Columbia University Press, 1990); Jay P. Dolan, *The American Catholic Experience: A History from Colonial Times to the Present* (Notre

Dame, IN: University of Notre Dame Press, 1992): 428; Chester Gillis, *Roman Catholicism in America* (New York: Columbia University Press, 1999).

5. "Cambodia and Israel," *Christianity Today* (hereafter *CT*) 14 (22 May 1970): 21–22; "On Leaving It to Hanoi," *CT* 17 (13 October 1972): 36.

6. Billy Graham, *Just As I Am: The Autobiography of Billy Graham* (San Francisco: Harper-Collins, 1997); Richard V. Pierard, "Billy Graham and Vietnam: From Cold Warrior to Peacemaker," *Christian Scholar's Review* 10 (1980): 37–51; William Martin, *A Prophet with Honor: The Billy Graham Story* (New York: William Morrow, 1991); Paul Boyer, *By the Bomb's Early Light: American Thought and Culture at the Dawn of the Atomic Age* (Chapel Hill: University of North Carolina Press, 1994); Billy Graham, "A Clarification," *CT* 17 (19 January 1973): 36.

7. Carl F. H. Henry, "Evangelical Renewal," *CT* 17 (5 January 1973): 42–43.

8. Hudson Baggett, "Where Is Our Gratitude?" *Alabama Baptist* (hereafter *AB*) 135 (21 May 1970): 2; Hudson Baggett, "Beyond the Election," *AB* 137 (9 November 1972): 2.

9. James A. Lester, "Campus Violence," *Baptist and Reflector* (hereafter *BAR*) 136 (14 May 1970): 4; David A. Risinger, "POW Scores Treason: Tells Faith's Values," *Ohio Baptist and Messenger* n.v. (26 July 1973): 8.

10. "Convention Press Conferences: Carl Bates," *Baptist Message* (hereafter *BM)* 86 (11 June 1970): 13, 16; Baptist Press, "Thirty Religious Leaders Briefed by White House on Red China," 12 August 1971, Southern Baptist Historical Library and Archives (hereafter SBHLA), Fred Rhodes Papers, Box 1, "Christian Fellowship Work—Folder 10."

11. James F. Cole, "One War Is Over, Another Rages On," *BM* 88 (1 February 1973): 2; Jack U. Harwell, "Vietnam War Is Over: What Happens Now?" *Christian Index* 152 (1 February 1973): 2; James A. Lester, "Thanksgiving for Cease-Fire," *BAR* 139 (1 February 1973): 4; J. Troy Prince, "Under the North Star: Missionary Diary," *Alaska Baptist Messenger* 28 (February 1973): 4.

12. Southern Baptist Convention (hereafter SBC), "Resolution on Peace," SBC Resolutions, June 1970, www.SBC.net; SBC, "Resolution on Achieving World Peace," SBC Resolutions, June 1972, www.SBC.net; "Resolutions as Adopted by the Convention," *BM* 87 (23 November 1972): 4; SBC, "Resolution on Southeast Asia," SBC Resolutions, June 1973, www.SBC.net.

13. "Who Cries for These?" *CT* 14 (3 July 1970): 22–23; Edward E. Plowman, "The Peace of God in South Viet Nam," *CT* 17 (22 December 1972): 32–33.

14. "Vietnam Servicemen Build Faster Than Destroy, SBC Leader Says," Baptist Press Release (hereafter BPR), 31 July 1970, SBHLA, Baptist Press, Box 1970 June–December, "Baptist Press—SBC—1970, June 6–29"; Walter R. Delamarter, "A Strategy for Vietnam," *Commission* 33 (April 1970): 22–29; Mrs. Ronald D. Merrell, "South Vietnam Lotus Country," *Commission* 36 (February 1973): 21–22; Baker J. Cauthen, "Facing a New Year," *Commission* 36 (January 1973): 29; "Vietnam Peace Affords Opportunity, Uncertainty," BPR, 26 January 1973, SBHLA, Baptist Press, Box 1973 January–June 1973, "Baptist Press—SBC—1973, January."

15. Cornish Rogers, "Toward a 'Pax Americana,'" *Christian Century* (hereafter *CC*) 89 (29 November 1972): 1209–10.

16. James Armstrong, "The Case for McGovern," *CC* 89 (1 November 1972): 1096–98.

17. "Laos and the Burden of History," *CC* 87 (8 April 1970): 411; "Sanctuaries and Temples: Misery in Cambodia," *CC* 87 (24 June 1970): 780.

18. Jill Drum Floerke, "Vietnam Cease-Fire Will Not Bring Reconciliation: Don Luce," *CC* 90 (28 February 1973): 263–64; "'Honorable' Peace: Final Self-Deception," *CC* 90 (7 February 1973): 139.

19. "Cold-Blooded Aggression," *Commonweal* 92 (15 May 1970): 211–13; "Kent and Cambodia," *Commonweal* 92 (22 May 1970): 235–36.

20. "When the Shooting Stops," *Commonweal* 97 (10 November 1972): 123–24 (emphasis in original); "Peace Now," *Commonweal* 97 (5 January 1973): 291–92; "After the Cease-Fire," *Commonweal* 97 (9 February 1972): 411–12.

21. "CCSA International Relations Head Speaks on Cambodia," *Keeping You Posted* 6 (June 1970): 3; James E. Wagner, "Nixon's Dance of Death," *United Church Herald* (hereafter *UCH*) 13 (July 1970): 6; Harry Applewhite, "Another Father, Two Sons, and a Daughter for Peace," *A.D.* 1 (October 1972): 56–59; United Church of Christ (hereafter UCC), "Minutes Ninth General Synod, St. Louis, Missouri, 22–26 June 1973," 73-GS-15 Resolution on "Cambodia Bombing," p. 17, reproduced from the General Synod Collection (hereafter GSC), UCC Archives (hereafter UCCA).

22. Roger L. Shinn, "Our Cause Is Not Just," *CC* 89 (1 November 1972): 1099–1103 (emphasis in original).

23. "The Possibility of Peace," *CC* 89 (8 November 1972): 1121; "Evacuating the Children," *CC* 90 (3 January 1973): 3.

24. Martin E. Marty, "A Peace Movement Requiem," *CC* 90 (14 February 1973): 215. For studies of the peace movement's positive impact, see Charles DeBenedetti and Charles Chatfield, *An American Ordeal: The Antiwar Movement of the Vietnam Era* (Syracuse, NY: Syracuse University Press, 1990); Melvin Small, *Johnson, Nixon, and the Doves* (New Brunswick, NJ: Rutgers University Press, 1988).

25. Robert E. Burns, "The Extremist Life," *U.S. Catholic and Jubilee* (hereafter *USC*) 35 (July 1970): 2.

26. W. Evan Golder, "War Resister's Sanctuary," *USC* 37 (November 1972): 34–36.

27. John B. Sheerin, "Psychological Causes and Effects of Atrocities," *Catholic World* (hereafter *CW*) 211 (April 1970): 2–3; James B. Kelly, "The Ravaged Soil of Vietnam," *CW* 211 (May 1970): 71–73; Thomas J. Gumbleton, "War Never Again!" *New CW* 215 (September/October 1972): 203–5.

28. Foy Valentine to Bishop James Armstrong, 8 November 1971, SBHLA, Christian Life Commission (hereafter CLC), Box 18, "Peace 1970–1975—Folder 9"; "Baptist Leaders Rejoice at Peace, Mourn Johnson," BPR, 25 January 1973, SBHLA, Baptist Press, Box 1973 January–June, "Baptist Press—SBC—1973, January"; Frank Stagg, "Christian Conscience and War," 20 April 1969, SBHLA, CLC, Box 24, "War—Stagg: Christian Conscience and War—1969—Folder 21."

29. UCC, "Minutes Seventh General Synod, Boston, Massachusetts, 25 June–2 July 1969," 69-GS-142 Statement on "Vietnam by the Report Committees on CCSA and BHM," pp. 133–34, reproduced from the GSC, UCCA.

30. UCC, "Minutes Eighth General Synod, Grand Rapids, Michigan, 25–29 June 1971," 71-GS-64 Action on "Peace and United States Power," pp. 64–66, reproduced from the GSC, UCCA; UCC, "Minutes Eighth General Synod, Grand Rapids, Michigan, 25–29 June 1971," 71-GS-48 Resolution on "The Pentagon Papers and the Indochina War," pp. 45, 140–41, reproduced from the GSC, UCCA; UCC, "Minutes Eighth General Synod, Grand Rapids, Michigan, 25–29 June 1971," 71-GS-81 Resolution on "Courage and Witness of Philip and Daniel Berrigan," p. 76, reproduced from the GSC, UCCA.

31. Reverend Robert V. Moss, "An Address to the Eighth General Synod," UCC, "Minutes Eighth General Synod, Grand Rapids, Michigan, 22–29 June 1971," pp. 143–49, reproduced from the GSC, UCCA; Reverend Robert V. Moss, "An Address to the Closing Session," UCC, "Minutes Eighth General Synod, Grand Rapids, Michigan, 22–29 June 1971," pp. 216–17, reproduced from the GSC, UCCA.

32. "Comment," *UCH* 13 (June 1970): 28 (emphasis in original); "U.S. Accused of Crimes against Peace," *A.D.* 1 (December 1972): 56.

33. "At Stake in Cambodia," *America* 122 (11 April 1970): 384; "From Cease-fire to Peace?" *America* 127 (11 November 1972): 379.

34. "Rhetoric: Valid and Invalid," *America* 127 (9 September 1972): 135; "Cease-fire at Last," *America* 128 (3 February 1973): 79; "Investment in Peace," *America* 128 (24 February 1973): 159.

35. Mary McGrory, "'Illicit' Bombs Away," *America* 127 (7 October 1972): 249; "Any Hope for Peace Talks?" *America* 127 (30 December 1972): 559–60; "Peace! Peace! And There Is No Peace," *America* 128 (13 January 1973): 9.

36. Kevin A. Devine, "People Are Like That," *Catholic Digest* 37 (March 1973): 97.

37. Dean J. Kotlowski, *Nixon's Civil Rights: Politics, Principle, and Policy* (Cambridge, MA: Harvard University Press, 2001).

38. Alfred Lee Henderson, "Shooting at Kent State Attacked by Minister," *Christian Recorder* (hereafter *CR*) 121 (7 July 1970): 15; "Bishop Says Protests of Students Compels Church to Face Issues," *CR* 121 (23 June 1970): 5; "Resolution Committee Report," *CR* 121 (28 July 1970): 12 (emphasis in original).

39. B. J. Nolen, "Spiritual Vitality, Religion, and Politics Highlight the First Six Months of 1972," *CR* 123 (1 August 1972): 5, 8; B. J. Nolen, "Ongoing World Conflicts Raise Anew Religion's Role in Quest for Peace," *CR* 123 (19 September 1972): 8.

40. African Methodist Episcopal Church (hereafter AMEC), "Journal of the Eighty-Fourth Session of the Michigan Annual Conference," 4th Episcopal District, Inkster, MI, August 1970, AME Department of Research and Scholarship (hereafter AMED), Nashville, TN, 102–8; AMEC, "Journal of the One Hundred Thirty-Second Session of the Indiana Annual Conference," 4th Episcopal District, Fort Wayne, IN, September 1970, AMED, Nashville, TN, 230; New York Annual Conference, AMEC, 151st Session of the Annual Conference Minutes, 15–18 May 1973, AMED, Nashville, TN.

41. Indiana Annual Conference, AMEC, 132nd Session of the Annual Conference Minutes, 1–6 September 1970, AMED, Nashville, TN; Chicago Annual Conference, AMEC, 88th Session of the Annual Conference Minutes, 8–13 September 1970, AMED, Nashville, TN.

42. W. F. McIntosh Jr., "Black Methodists Endorse McGovern," *CR* 123 (29 August 1972): 1, 3; "A.M.E. Church in U.S. Voter Registration Drive," *CR* 123 (26 September 1972): 1, 4; B. J. Nolen, "Religious Activists Step Up Pressure to End Hostilities in Southeast Asia," *CR* 123 (7 November 1972): 4–5.

43. "Black Educators Tell President of 'Anger, Outrage, Frustration,'" *CR* 121 (23 June 1970): 4, 12; "Black GI, Killed in Vietnam, 'Integrates' a Cemetery," *CR* 121 (30 June 1970): 4; Christian G. Appy, *Working-Class War: American Combat Soldiers and Vietnam* (Chapel Hill: University of North Carolina Press, 1993); Herman Graham III, *The Brothers' Vietnam War: Black Power, Manhood, and the Military Experience* (Gainesville: University Press of Florida, 2003); James E. Westheider, *Fighting on Two Fronts: African Americans and the Vietnam War* (New York: New York University Press, 1997).

44. B. J. Nolen, "Rejoicing and Prayerful Reflection: Ceasefire in Vietnam!" *CR* 123 (22 January 1973): 1; B. J. Nolen, "Amnesty . . . No Forgiving?" *CR* 123 (12 February 1973): 4, 7.

CONCLUSION

1. George C. Herring, *America's Longest War: The United States and Vietnam, 1950–1975* (New York: McGraw Hill, 1979); Marilyn B. Young, *The Vietnam Wars, 1945–1990* (New York: HarperPerennial, 1991); Lewis Sorley, *A Better War: The Unexamined Victories and Final Tragedy of America's Last Years in Vietnam* (New York: Harvest Books, 1999); James H. Willbanks, *Abandoning Vietnam: How America Left and South Vietnam Lost Its War* (Lawrence: University Press of Kansas, 2004); J. Edward Lee and Toby Haynsworth, *White Christmas in April: The Collapse of South Vietnam, April 1975* (New York: Peter Lang, 1999).

2. William J. Duiker, *The Communist Road to Power in Vietnam*, 2nd ed. (Boulder, CO: Westview Press, 1996); Charles E. Neu, ed., *After Vietnam: Legacies of a Lost War* (Baltimore, MD: Johns Hopkins University Press, 2000); Herring, *America's*; Young, *Vietnam*; Sorley, *Better*; Willbanks, *Abandoning*; Lee and Haynsworth, *White*.

3. Edward E. Plowman, "Suffering in South Viet Nam," *Christianity Today* (hereafter *CT*) 19 (11 April 1975): 31–33; "Making Room for the Refugees," *CT* 19 (4 July 1975): 47–48.

4. "Storms and More Storms," *CT* 19 (11 April 1975): 27–28; "What to Remember about Viet Nam," *CT* 19 (23 May 1975): 45–46; "The Indochina Fiasco," *CT* 19 (25 April 1975): 27.

5. Leland Webb, "Farewell to Vietnam," *Commission* 38 (June 1975): 1–5; William T. Roberson, "Baptist Missionaries Escape as Communists Take Danang," 11 April 1975, Baptist Press Release, Southern Baptist Historical Library and Archives (hereafter SBHLA), SBC Press Kit.

6. William T. Roberson, "Anguish Plagues Baptist Missionaries to Vietnam," 6 May 1975, Baptist Press Release, SBHLA, SBC Press Kit; "All Missionaries Out of Laos," *Christian Index* 154 (5 June 1975): 3; Baker J. Cauthen, "Vietnam," *Commission* 38 (June 1975): 45.

7. "Weber Urges President Ford to More Action in S.E. Asia," 8 April 1975, Baptist Press Release, SBHLA, SBC Press Kit; William T. Roberson, "Vietnam Missionary Relates Uncertainty Facing Refugees," 21 May 1975, Baptist Press Release, SBHLA, SBC Press Kit.

8. Daniel R. Grant, "Christian Compassion and Vietnamese Refugees," *Arkansas Baptist* 74 (29 May 1975): 4; "Crisis Coverage," *Commission* 38 (June 1975): 0; Southern Baptist Convention, "Resolution on Vietnamese Refugees," SBC Resolutions, June 1975, www.SBC.net.

9. "Politics in Foreign Policy," *Christian Century* (hereafter *CC*) 92 (9 April 1975): 347; Doug Hostetter, "Quang Tri Province: Sown with Seeds of Death," *CC* 92 (2 April 1975): 324–25; James M. Wall, "When Liberals Become Conservative," *CC* 92 (2 April 1975): 323.

10. Rescuing Vietnam Orphans: Mixed Motives," *CC* 92 (16 April 1975): 374–75; "Underlines," *CC* 92 (4 June 1975): 566–67 (emphasis in original).

11. James M. Wall, "Receiving the Refugees," *CC* 92 (21 May 1975): 515–16.

12. James M. Wall, "American Hearts and Minds Deceived," *CC* 92 (16 April 1975): 371–72; Richard John Neuhaus, "Vietnam: No Good Ending," *CC* 92 (9 April 1975): 349.

13. Mitchell K. Hall, *Because of Their Faith: CALCAV and Religious Opposition to the Vietnam War* (New York: Columbia University Press, 1990); George W. Webber, "Frankly Shocked," *A.D.* 4 (April 1975): 8–9.

14. James A. Gittings, "What We Learned in North Vietnam," *A.D.* 4 (April 1975): 32–34 (emphasis in original); James A. Gittings, "Time to Think about Morals," *A.D.* 4 (April 1975): 34–35.

15. "Moss Urges End to Indochina Suffering," *A.D.* 4 (June 1975): 55; Reverend Robert V. Moss, "Jesus Frees and Unites: The Context of Our Meeting; An Address to the Tenth General Synod," United Church of Christ, "Minutes Tenth General Synod, Minneapolis, Minnesota, 27 June 1975," pp. 124–27, reproduced from the General Synod Collection, United Church of Christ Archives.

16. "Kissinger Fails," *Commonweal* 102 (11 April 1975): 36.

17. "Involvement's Last Hours," *Commonweal* 102 (25 April 1975): 67–68; "After Vietnam," *Commonweal* 102 (23 May 1975): 131–32.

18. "The Politics of Tragedy," *America* 132 (5 April 1975): 250; "Final Curtain in Indochina?" *America* 132 (12 April 1975): 271–72.

19. "The Question of Dominoes," *America* 132 (10 May 1975): 350.

20. "Decisions and Distraction . . . ," *America* 132 (19 April 1975): 290; "Our Other Asian Allies," *America* 132 (17 May 1975): 370.

21. "Perceptions of Peace," *America* 132 (24 May 1975): 390; "Silence in Cambodia," *America* 132 (3 May 1975): 330.

22. Robert E. Burns, "The Examined Life," *U.S. Catholic and Jubilee* 40 (June 1975): 2; Dan Finlay, "Some Pilgrims Still Walk," *Catholic Digest* 39 (April 1975): 90–96.

23. Howard D. Gregg, *History of the African Methodist Episcopal Church: The Black Church in Action* (Nashville, TN: AMEC Sunday School Union, 1980); C. Eric Lincoln and Lawrence H. Mamiya, *The Black Church in the African American Experience* (Durham, NC: Duke University Press, 1990); Anne H. Pinn and Anthony B. Pinn, *Fortress Introduction to Black Church History* (Minneapolis: Fortress Press, 2002).

24. David E. Settje, *Lutherans and the Longest War: Adrift on a Sea of Doubt about the Cold and Vietnam Wars, 1964–1975* (Lanham, MD: Lexington Books, 2007).

Bibliography

PERIODICALS AND NEWSPAPERS

A.D. (United Church of Christ/Presbyterian Church of America)
Advance (Lutheran Church–Missouri Synod; hereafter LCMS)
Alabama Baptist (Alabama Baptist Convention)
Alaska Baptist Messenger (Alaska Baptist Convention)
A.M.E. Church Review (African Methodist Episcopal Church)
America (Catholic, Jesuit)
Arkansas Baptist (Arkansas Baptist Convention)
Baptist and Reflector (Tennessee Baptist Convention)
Baptist Message (Louisiana Baptist Convention)
Catholic Digest (Catholic Publishing Center of the College of St. Thomas)
Catholic World (Catholic, Paulist Fathers)
Christian Century (Independent Protestant)
Christian Index (Georgia Baptist Convention)
Christian Recorder (African Methodist Episcopal Church)
Christianity Today (Independent Protestant)
Commentator (American Lutheran Church; hereafter ALC)
Commission (Southern Baptist Convention Foreign Mission Board)
Commonweal (Lay Catholic)
Engage (United Church of Christ)
Engage/Social Action (United Church of Christ)
Florida Baptist Witness (Florida Baptist Convention)
Focus (Lutheran Council USA; hereafter LCUSA; began in 1967)
Illinois Baptist (Illinois Baptist Convention)
In Step (LCUSA; began in 1970, formerly *A Mighty Fortress*)
Interchange (LCUSA; began in 1967)
Jubilee (Independent Catholic)
Keeping You Posted (United Church of Christ)
Lutheran (Lutheran Church of America; hereafter LCA)
Lutheran Social Concern (LCUSA; began in 1972, previously *Lutheran Social Welfare*;
    stopped publication in 1974)
Lutheran Social Welfare (LCUSA; began in 1968, previously *Lutheran Social Welfare
    Quarterly*; became *Lutheran Social Concern* in 1972)
Lutheran Social Welfare Quarterly (LCA; became *Lutheran Social Welfare* in 1968)

Lutheran Standard (ALC)
Lutheran Witness (LCMS)
Lutheran Witness Reporter (LCMS; began in May 1965)
Lutheran Woman's Quarterly (LCMS)
Lutheran Women (LCA)
A Mighty Fortress (National Lutheran Council/LCUSA; became *In Step* in 1970)
Minister's Information Service (LCA)
New Catholic World (Catholic, Paulist Fathers)
News Bureau (LCUSA; began in 1967)
Scope (ALC)
Social Action (United Church of Christ)
This Day (LCMS; ceased publication in 1971)
United Church Herald (United Church of Christ)
U.S. Catholic (Catholic, Claretian Fathers at St. Jude Seminary)
World Encounter (LCA)

ARCHIVES

African Methodist Episcopal Church, Nashville, TN. Department of Research and
    Scholarship.
Billy Graham Center, Wheaton College, Wheaton, IL. Evangelical Archives and
    Repository.
Concordia Lutheran Seminary, St. Louis, MO. Library.
Concordia University Chicago, River Forest, IL. Library.
DePaul University, Chicago, IL. Richardson Library.
Dominican University, River Forest, IL. Library.
Evangelical Lutheran Church in America Headquarters, Chicago, IL. Department of
    Denominational Archives.
Lutheran Church–Missouri Synod, Concordia Historical Institute, St. Louis, MO. Depart-
    ment of Archives.
North Central College, Naperville, IL. Oesterle Library.
Presbyterian Historical Society, Philadelphia, PA. Presbyterian Church (USA).
Southern Baptist Headquarters, Nashville, TN. Historical Library and Archives.
Trinity Lutheran Seminary, Columbus, OH. Library.
United Church of Christ Headquarters, Cleveland, OH. Archives.
University of Chicago, Chicago, IL. Regenstein Library.
Wheaton College, Wheaton, IL. Library.

ARTICLES, BOOKS, AND DISSERTATIONS

Abrams, Elliott, ed. *The Influence of Faith: Religious Groups and U.S. Foreign Policy.*
    Lanham, MD: Rowman and Littlefield, 2001.
Adams, David L., and Ken Schurb, eds. *The Anonymous God: The Church Confronts Civil
    Religion and American Society.* Saint Louis, MO: Concordia Publishing House, 2004.
Adler, Les K. *The Red Image: American Attitudes toward Communism in the Cold War Era.*
    New York: Garland, 1991.

Ahlstrom, Sydney E. *A Religious History of the American People*. New Haven, CT: Yale University Press, 1972.

Aijazuddin, F. S., ed. *The White House and Pakistan: Secret Declassified Documents, 1969–1974*. New York: Oxford University Press, 2002.

Aitken, Jonathan. *Nixon: A Life*. Washington, DC: Regnery, 1993.

Allin, Dana H. *Cold War Illusions: America, Europe, and Soviet Power, 1969–1989*. New York: St. Martin's Press, 1994.

Allitt, Patrick. *Religion in America since 1945: A History*. New York: Columbia University Press, 2003.

Alonso, Harriet Hyman. *Peace as a Women's Issue: A History of the U.S. Movement for World Peace and Women's Rights*. Syracuse, NY: Syracuse University Press, 1993.

Alperovitz, Gar. *Atomic Diplomacy: Hiroshima and Potsdam*. Boulder, CO: Pluto Press, 1994.

Ambrose, Stephen E. *Nixon*. Volume 1, *The Education of a Politician, 1913–1962*. New York: Touchstone Books, 1987.

———. *Nixon*. Volume 3, *Ruin and Recovery, 1973–1990*. New York: Touchstone Books, 1991.

Anderson, David L. *Trapped by Success: The Eisenhower Administration and Vietnam, 1953–1961*. New York: Columbia University Press, 1991.

Anderson, Terry H. *The Movement and the Sixties: Protest in America from Greensboro to Wounded Knee*. New York: Oxford University Press, 1995.

———. *The Sixties*. 3rd ed. New York: Pearson Longman, 2007.

Andrew, John A. III. *The Other Side of the Sixties: Young Americans for Freedom and the Rise of Conservative Politics*. New Brunswick, NJ: Rutgers University Press, 1997.

Appleby, Joyce, Lynn Hunt, and Margaret Jacob. *Telling the Truth about History*. New York: Norton, 1994.

Appy, Christian G. *Working-Class War: American Combat Soldiers and Vietnam*. Chapel Hill: University of North Carolina Press, 1993.

———, ed. *Cold War Constructions: The Political Culture of United States Imperialism, 1945–1966*. Amherst: University of Massachusetts Press, 2000.

Asselin, Pierre. *A Bitter Peace: Washington, Hanoi, and the Making of the Paris Peace Agreement*. Chapel Hill: University of North Carolina Press, 2002.

Au, William A. *The Cross, the Flag, and the Bomb: American Catholics Debate War and Peace, 1960–1983*. Westport, CT: Greenwood Press, 1985.

Augustine, Saint. *Concerning the City of God against the Pagans*. Trans. by John O'Meara. New York: Penguin Books, 1984.

Austin, Randall Dean. "Caution Christian Soldiers: The Mainline Protestant Churches and the Cold War." Ph.D. diss., University of Arkansas, 1997.

Avery, William O. *Empowered Laity: The Story of the Lutheran Laity Movement*. Minneapolis: Augsburg Fortress Press, 1997.

Avorn, Jerry L. *Up against the Ivy Wall: A History of the Columbia Crisis*. New York: Atheneum, 1970.

Bachman, John W. *Together in Hope: Fifty Years of Lutheran World Relief*. Minneapolis: Kirk House Publishers, 1995.

Bachmann, E. Theodore. *The United Lutheran Church in America, 1918–1962*. Minneapolis: Fortress Press, 1997.

Baer, H. David. *The Struggle of Hungarian Lutherans under Communism*. College Station: Texas A&M University Press, 2006.

Bailey, Beth. *Sex in the Heartland*. Cambridge, MA: Harvard University Press, 1999.

Bailey, Beth, and David Farber, eds. *America in the Seventies*. Lawrence: University Press of Kansas, 2004.

Baritz, Loren. *Backfire: A History of How American Culture Led Us into Vietnam and Made Us Fight the Way We Did*. New York: William Morrow, 1985.

Becker, Jasper. *Hungry Ghosts: Mao's Secret Famine*. New York: Free Press, 1996.

Bennett, David H. *The Party of Fear: The American Far Right from Nativism to the Militia Movement*. New York: Vintage Books, 1988.

Bentley, Eric, ed. *Thirty Years of Treason: Excerpts from Hearings before the House Committee on Un-American Activities, 1938–1968*. New York: Thunder's Mouth Press, 2002.

Berkowitz, Edward D. *Something Happened: A Political and Cultural Overview of the Seventies*. New York: Columbia University Press, 2006.

Berman, Larry. *Perfect Spy: The Incredible Double Life of Pham Xuan An, Time Magazine Reporter and Vietnamese Communist Agent*. New York: Smithsonian Books, 2007.

Bernstein, Carl, and Bob Woodward. *All the President's Men*. New York: Warner Books, 1974.

Beschloss, Michael R. *Taking Charge: The Johnson White House Tapes, 1963–1964*. New York: Simon and Schuster, 1997.

———, ed. *Reaching for Glory: Lyndon Johnson's Secret White House Tapes, 1964–1965*. New York: Simon and Schuster, 2001.

Bill, James A. *George Ball: Behind the Scenes in U.S. Foreign Policy*. New Haven, CT: Yale University Press, 1997.

Billingsley, Kenneth Lloyd. *Hollywood Party: How Communism Seduced the American Film Industry in the 1930s and 1940s*. Rocklin, CA: Forum Publishing, 1998.

Billingsley, William J. *Communists on Campus: Race, Politics, and the Public University in Sixties North Carolina*. Athens: University of Georgia Press, 1999.

Blumhofer, Edith L., ed. *Religion, Politics, and the American Experience: Reflections on Religion and American Public Life*. Tuscaloosa: University of Alabama Press, 2002.

Bodroghkozy, Aniko. *Groove Tube: Sixties Television and the Youth Rebellion*. Durham, NC: Duke University Press, 2001.

Borstelmann, Thomas. *Apartheid's Reluctant Uncle: The United States and Southern Africa in the Early Cold War*. New York: Oxford University Press, 1993.

———. *The Cold War and the Color Line: American Race Relations in the Global Arena*. Cambridge, MA: Harvard University Press, 2001.

Boudarel, Georges, and Nguyen Van Ky. *Hanoi: City of the Rising Dragon*. Lanham, MD: Rowman and Littlefield, 2002.

Bowman, John S., ed. *The World Almanac of the Vietnam War*. New York: World Almanac, 1985.

Boyer, Paul. *By the Bomb's Early Light: American Thought and Culture at the Dawn of the Atomic Age*. Chapel Hill: University of North Carolina Press, 1985.

———. *Fallout: A Historian Reflects on America's Half-Century Encounter with Nuclear Weapons*. Columbus: Ohio State University Press, 1998.

———. *When Time Shall Be No More: Prophecy Belief in Modern American Culture*. Cambridge, MA: Harvard University Press, 1992.

Bradley, Mark Philip. *Imagining Vietnam and America: The Making of Postcolonial Vietnam, 1919–1950*. Chapel Hill: University of North Carolina Press, 2000.

Branch, Taylor. *At Canaan's Edge: America in the King Years, 1965–68*. New York: Simon and Schuster, 2006.

———. *Parting the Waters: America in the King Years, 1954–1963*. New York: Simon and Schuster, 1988.

———. *Pillar of Fire: America in the King Years, 1963–1965*. New York: Simon and Schuster, 1998.

Brands, H. W. *The Devil We Knew: Americans and the Cold War*. New York: Oxford University Press, 1993.

Braun, Mark E. *A Tale of Two Synods: Events That Led to the Split between Wisconsin and Missouri*. Milwaukee, MN: Northwestern Publishing House, 2003.

Brennan, Mary C. *Turning Right in the Sixties: The Conservative Capture of the GOP*. Chapel Hill: University of North Carolina Press, 1995.

———. *Wives, Mothers, and the Red Menace: Conservative Women and the Crusade against Communism*. Boulder: University of Colorado Press, 2008.

Brett, Edward T. *The U.S. Catholic Press on Central America: From Cold War Anticommunism to Social Justice*. Notre Dame, IN: University of Notre Dame Press, 2003.

Brigham, Robert K. *Guerilla Diplomacy: The NLF's Foreign Relations and the Viet Nam War*. Ithaca, NY: Cornell University Press, 1999.

Broadwater, Jeff. *Eisenhower and the Anti-Communist Crusade*. Chapel Hill: University of North Carolina Press, 1992.

Brown, Judith M., and Rosemary Foot, eds. *Hong Kong's Transitions, 1842–1997*. New York: St. Martin's Press, 1997.

Buckingham, Peter H. *America Sees Red: Anticommunism in America, 1870s to 1980s*. Claremont, CA: Regina Books, 1988.

Bundy, William. *A Tangled Web: The Making of Foreign Policy in the Nixon Presidency*. New York: Hill and Wang, 1998.

Burgess, John P. *The East German Church and the End of Communism*. New York: Oxford University Press, 1997.

Burns, Stewart. *Social Movements of the 1960s: Searching for Democracy*. New York: Twayne, 1990.

Busch, Andrew E. *Reagan's Victory: The Presidential Election of 1980 and the Rise of the Right*. Lawrence: University Press of Kansas, 2005.

Buzzanco, Robert. *Masters of War: Military Dissent and Politics in the Vietnam Era*. Cambridge: Cambridge University Press, 1996.

———. *Vietnam and the Transformation of American Life*. Malden, MA: Blackwell Publishers, 1999.

Cahill, Lisa Sowle. *Love Your Enemies: Discipleship, Pacifism, and Just War Theory*. Minneapolis, MN: Fortress Press, 1994.

Campbell, James T. *Songs of Zion: The African Methodist Episcopal Church in the United States and South Africa*. Chapel Hill: University of North Carolina Press, 1998.

Caplow, Theodore, Howard M. Bahr, John Modell, and Bruce A. Chadwick. *Recent Social Trends in the United States, 1960–1990*. Montreal: McGill-Queen's University Press, 1991.

Capps, Walter H. *The Unfinished War: Vietnam and the American Conscience*. Boston: Beacon Press, 1982.

Caro, Robert A. *The Years of Lyndon Johnson: The Path to Power*. New York: Knopf, 1982.

Carpenter, Joel A. *Revive Us Again: The Reawakening of American Fundamentalism.* New York: Oxford University Press, 1997.

Carroll, Peter N. *It Seemed Like Nothing Happened: America in the 1970s.* New Brunswick, NJ: Rutgers University Press, 1982.

Carter, Dan T. *The Politics of Rage: George Wallace, the Origins of the New Conservativism, and the Transformation of American Politics.* Baton Rouge: Louisiana State University Press, 1995.

Castile, George Pierre. *To Show Heart: Native American Self-Determination and Federal Indian Policy, 1960–1975.* Tucson: University of Arizona Press, 1998.

Chadwick, Owen. *The Christian Church in the Cold War.* New York: Penguin Books, 1992.

Chalmers, David. *And the Crooked Places Made Straight: The Struggle for Social Change in the 1960s.* Baltimore, MD: Johns Hopkins University Press, 1991.

Chambers, Whittaker. *Witness.* Washington, DC: Regenery Publishing, 1952.

Chang, George H. *Friends and Enemies: The United States, China, and the Soviet Union, 1948–1972.* Palo Alto, CA: Stanford University Press, 1990.

Chong, Denise. *The Girl in the Picture: The Story of Kim Phuc, the Photograph, and the Vietnam War.* New York: Viking Press, 1999.

Cimino, Richard, ed. *Lutherans Today: American Lutheran Identity in the Twenty-first Century.* Grand Rapids, MI: Eerdmans, 2003.

Cobb, William W. Jr. *The American Foundation Myth in Vietnam: Reigning Paradigms and Raining Bombs.* Lanham, MD: University Press of America, 1998.

Cone, James H. *Martin and Malcolm and America: A Dream or a Nightmare?* Maryknoll, NY: Orbis Books, 1991.

Corber, Robert J. *Homosexuality in Cold War America: Resistance and the Crisis of Masculinity.* Durham, NC: Duke University Press, 1997.

———. *In the Name of National Security: Hitchcock, Homophobia, and the Political Construction of Gender in Postwar America.* Durham, NC: Duke University Press, 1993.

Courtois, Stephane, Andrzej Paczkowski, and Karel Bartosek. *The Black Book of Communism: Crimes, Terror, Repression.* Cambridge, MA: Harvard University Press, 1999.

Critchlow, Donald T. *Phyllis Schlafly and Grassroots Conservatism: A Woman's Crusade.* Princeton, NJ: Princeton University Press, 2005.

Crowley, Monica. *Nixon in Winter: His Final Revelations about Diplomacy, Watergate, and Life out of the Arena.* New York: Random House, 1998.

Crozier, Brian. *The Rise and Fall of the Soviet Empire.* Rocklin, CA: Forum Publishing, 1999.

Curtin, Michael. *Redeeming the Wasteland: Television Documentary and Cold War Politics.* New Brunswick, NJ: Rutgers University Press, 1995.

Dallek, Robert. *Flawed Giant: Lyndon Johnson and His Times, 1961–1973.* New York: Oxford University Press, 1998.

———. *Lone Star Rising: Lyndon Johnson and His Times, 1908–1960.* New York: Oxford University Press, 1991.

———. *Nixon and Kissinger: Partners in Power.* New York: HarperCollins, 2007.

Davidson, Phillip B. *Vietnam at War: The History, 1946–1975.* New York: Oxford University Press, 1988.

Davis, Nathaniel. *A Long Walk to Church: A Contemporary History of Russian Orthodoxy.* Boulder, CO: Westview Press, 1995.

Dean, John W. III. *Blind Ambition: The White House Years*. New York: Simon and Schuster, 1976.

Dean, Robert. *Imperial Brotherhood: Gender and the Making of Cold War Foreign Policy*. Amherst: University of Massachusetts Press, 2001.

DeBenedetti, Charles, and Charles Chatfield. *An American Ordeal: The Antiwar Movement of the Vietnam Era*. Syracuse: Syracuse University Press, 1990.

Deletant, Dennis. *Communist Terror in Romania: Gheorghiu-Dej and the Police State, 1948–1965*. New York: St. Martin's Press, 1999.

D'Emilio, John. *Lost Prophet: The Life and Times of Bayard Rustin*. Chicago: University of Chicago Press, 2003.

———. *Sexual Politics, Sexual Communities: The Making of a Homosexual Minority in the United States, 1940–1970*. Chicago: University of Chicago Press, 1998.

Di Leo, David L. *George Ball, Vietnam, and the Rethinking of Containment*. Chapel Hill: University of North Carolina Press, 1991.

Disno, Richard W. "American Lutheran Historiography: A Regional Approach." In The Lutheran Historical Conference, vol. 13 (1988), *American Lutheranism: Crisis in Historical Consciousness?* Minneapolis: Augsburg Publishing House, 1990.

Divine, Robert A. *The Sputnik Challenge: Eisenhower's Response to the Soviet Satellite*. New York: Oxford University Press, 1993.

Dolan, Jay P. *The American Catholic Experience: A History from Colonial Times to the Present*. Notre Dame, IN: University of Notre Dame Press, 1992.

Dower, John W. *War without Mercy: Race and Power in the Pacific War*. New York: Pantheon Books, 1986.

Drinnon, Richard. *Facing West: The Metaphysics of Indian-Hating and Empire-Building*. Norman: University of Oklahoma Press, 1997.

Dudziak, Mary L. *Cold War Civil Rights: Race and the Image of American Democracy*. Princeton, NJ: Princeton University Press, 2000.

Duiker, William J. *Ho Chi Minh: A Life*. New York: Hyperion, 2000.

———. *Sacred War: Nationalism and Revolution in a Divided Vietnam*. New York: McGraw Hill, 1995.

———. *The Communist Road to Power in Vietnam*. 2nd ed. Boulder, CO: Westview Press, 1996.

———. *Vietnam: Revolution in Transition*. 2nd ed.. Boulder, CO: Westview Press, 1995.

Dyson, Michael Eric. *I May Not Get There With You: The True Martin Luther King, Jr.* New York: Simon and Schuster, 2000.

Ehrhart, W. D. *Passing Time: Memoir of a Vietnam Veteran against the War*. Jefferson, NC: McFarland, 1986.

Ehrlichman, John. *Witness to Power: The Nixon Years*. New York: Simon and Schuster, 1982.

Elbaum, Max. *Revolution in the Air: Sixties Radicals Turn to Lenin, Mao, and Che*. New York: Verso Books, 2006.

Ellwood, Robert S. *The Sixties Spiritual Awakening: American Religion Moving from Modern to Postmodern*. New Brunswick, NJ: Rutgers University Press, 1994.

Elshtain, Jean Bethke, ed. *Just War Theory*. New York: New York University Press, 1992.

Emerson, Gloria. *Winners and Losers: Battles, Retreats, Gains, Losses, and Ruins from the Vietnam War*. New York: Harcourt Brace Jovanovich, 1976.

Emery, Fred. *Watergate: The Corruption of American Politics and the Fall of Richard Nixon.* New York: Times Books, 1994.

Engelhardt, Tom. *The End of Victory Culture: Cold War America and the Disillusioning of a Generation.* New York: Basic Books, 1995.

Enloe, Cynthia. *Bananas, Beaches, and Bases: Making Feminist Sense of International Politics.* Berkeley: University of California Press, 1990.

Esherick, Joseph W., Paul G. Pickowicz, and Andrew G. Walder, eds. *The Chinese Cultural Revolution as History.* Palo Alto, CA: Stanford University Press, 2006.

Fackre, Gabriel. *Believing, Caring, and Doing in the United Church of Christ: An Interpretation.* Cleveland, OH: United Church Press, 2005.

Fadiman, Anne. *The Spirit Catches You and You Fall Down: A Hmong Child, Her American Doctors, and the Collision of Two Cultures.* New York: Farrar, Straus, and Giroux, 1997.

Fairbank, John K., and Edwin O. Reischauer. *China: Tradition and Transformation.* Boston: Houghton Mifflin, 1989.

Fariello, Griffin. *Red Scare: Memories of the American Inquisition.* New York: Avon Books, 1995.

Fernlund, Kevin J., ed. *The Cold War American West, 1945–1989.* Albuquerque: University of New Mexico Press, 1998.

Field, Hermann, and Kate Field. *Trapped in the Cold War: The Ordeal of an American Family.* Palo Alto, CA: Stanford University Press, 1999.

Findlay, James F. Jr. *Church People in the Struggle: The National Council of Churches and the Black Freedom Movement, 1950–1970.* New York: Oxford University Press, 1993.

Finke, Roger, and Rodney Starks. *The Churching of America, 1776–1990: Winners and Losers in Our Religious Economy.* New Brunswick, NJ: Rutgers University Press, 1992.

FitzGerald, Frances. *Fire in the Lake: The Vietnamese and the Americans in Vietnam.* New York: Vintage Books, 1972.

Flamm, Michael W. *Law and Order: Street Crime, Civil Unrest, and the Crisis of Liberalism in the 1960s.* New York: Columbia University Press, 2005.

Fletcher, Jesse C. *The Southern Baptist Convention: A Sesquicentennial History.* Nashville, TN: Broadman and Holman, 1994.

Flynn, George Q. *The Draft, 1940–1973.* Lawrence: University Press of Kansas, 1993.

Flynt, Wayne. *Alabama Baptists: Southern Baptists in the Heart of Dixie.* Tuscaloosa: University of Alabama Press, 1998.

Fogelsong, David S. *America's Secret War against Bolshevism: U.S. Intervention in the Russian Civil War, 1917–1920.* Chapel Hill: University of North Carolina Press, 1995.

———. *The American Mission and the "Evil Empire": The Crusade for a "Free Russia" since 1881.* New York: Cambridge University Press, 2007.

Foley, Michael S. *Confronting the War Machine: Draft Resistance during the Vietnam War.* Chapel Hill: University of North Carolina Press, 2003.

———, ed. *Dear Dr. Spock: Letters about the Vietnam War to America's Favorite Baby Doctor.* New York: New York University Press, 2005.

Fousek, John. *To Lead the Free World: American Nationalism and the Cultural Roots of the Cold War.* Chapel Hill: University of North Carolina Press, 2000.

Fowler, Robert Booth. *A New Engagement: Evangelical Political Thought, 1966–1976.* Grand Rapids, MI: Eerdmans, 1982.

Fox, Richard W. *Jesus in America: Personal Savior, Cultural Hero, National Obsession*. San Francisco: HarperCollins, 2005.

Franklin, H. Bruce. *M.I.A.; or, Mythmaking in America: How and Why Belief in Live POWs Has Possessed a Nation*. Brooklyn, NY: Lawrence Hill Books, 1992.

Freedman, Lawrence. *Kennedy's Wars: Berlin, Cuba, Laos, and Vietnam*. New York: Oxford University Press, 2000.

Fried, Richard M. *The Russians Are Coming! The Russians Are Coming! Pageantry and Patriotism in Cold-War America*. New York: Oxford University Press, 1998.

Friedland, Michael Brooks. *Lift Up Your Voice like a Trumpet: White Clergy and the Civil Rights and Antiwar Movements, 1954–1973*. Chapel Hill: University of North Carolina Press, 1998.

Fry, Joseph A. *Debating Vietnam: Fulbright, Stennis, and Their Senate Hearings*. Lanham, MD: Rowman and Littlefield, 2006.

Fursenko, Aleksandr, and Timothy Naftali. *"One Hell of a Gamble": Krushchev, Castro, Kennedy, and the Cuban Missile Crisis, 1958–1964*. London: Pimlico, 1999.

Gaddis, John Lewis. *Strategies of Containment: A Critical Appraisal of Postwar American National Security Policy*. New York: Oxford University Press, 1982.

———. "The Emerging Post-Revisionist Synthesis on the Origins of the Cold War." *Diplomatic History* 7 (Summer 1983): 171–204.

Gaiduk, Ilya A. *The Soviet Union and the Vietnam War*. Chicago: Ivan R. Dee, 1996.

Galchutt, Kathryn M. *The Career of Andrew Schulze, 1924–1968: Lutherans and Race in the Civil Rights Era*. Macon, GA: Mercer University Press, 2005.

Gallup, George H. *The Gallup Poll: Public Opinion, 1935–1971*. Vol. 3. New York: Random House, 1972.

Garber, Majorie, and Rebecca L. Walkowitz, eds. *Secret Agents: The Rosenberg Case, McCarthyism, and Fifties America*. New York: Routledge, 1995.

Gardner, Lloyd C. *Pay Any Price: Lyndon Johnson and the Wars for Vietnam*. Chicago: Ivan R. Dee, 1995.

Garfinkle, Adam. *Telltale Hearts: The Origins and Impact of the Vietnam Antiwar Movement*. New York: St. Martin's Press, 1995.

Garrow, David J. *The FBI and Martin Luther King, Jr.: From Solo to Memphis*. New York: Norton, 1981.

Garver, John W. *Protracted Contest: Sino-Indian Rivalry in the Twentieth Century*. Seattle: University of Washington Press, 2001.

Gibbs, Nancy, and Michael Duffy. *The Preacher and the Presidents: Billy Graham in the White House*. New York: Center Street, 2007.

Gibson, James William. *The Perfect War: The War We Couldn't Lose and How We Did*. New York: Vintage Books, 1986.

———. *Warrior Dreams: Violence and Manhood in Post-Vietnam America*. New York: Hill and Wang, 1994.

Gilbert, James. *Another Chance: Postwar America, 1945–1985*. Belmont, CA: Wadsworth, 1981.

———. *Redeeming Culture: American Religion in an Age of Science*. Chicago: University of Chicago Press, 1997.

Gilbert, W. Kent. *Commitment to Unity: A History of the Lutheran Church in America*. Philadelphia: Fortress Press, 1988.

Gill, Jill Kristine. "'Peace Is Not the Absence of War but the Presence of Justice': The National Council of Churches' Reaction and Response to the Vietnam War, 1965–1972." Ph.D. diss., University of Pennsylvania, 1996.

Gillis, Chester. *Roman Catholicism in America*. New York: Columbia University Press, 1999.

Gitlin, Todd. *The Sixties: Years of Hope, Days of Rage*. New York: Bantam Books, 1987.

Glendon, Mary Ann. *A World Made New: Eleanor Roosevelt and the Universal Declaration of Human Rights*. New York: Random House, 2001.

Goldstein, Warren. *William Sloane Coffin Jr.: A Holy Impatience*. New Haven, CT: Yale University Press, 2004.

Gordon, William A. *The Fourth of May: Killings and Coverups at Kent State*. Buffalo: Prometheus, 1990.

Gottlieb, Annie. *Do You Believe in Magic: The Second Coming of the Sixties Generation*. New York: Time Books, 1987.

Graebner, Alan. *Uncertain Saints: The Laity in the Lutheran Church–Missouri Synod, 1900–1970*. Westport, CT: Greenwood Press, 1975.

Graham, Billy. *Just As I Am: The Autobiography of Billy Graham*. San Francisco: Harper-SanFrancisco, 1997.

Graham, Herman III. *The Brothers' Vietnam War: Black Power, Manhood, and the Military Experience*. Gainesville: University Press of Florida, 2003.

Greenberg, David. *Nixon's Shadow: The History of an Image*. New York: Norton, 2003.

Greene, Graham. *The Quiet American*. New York: Penguin Books, 1973.

Gregg, Howard D. *History of the African Methodist Episcopal Church: The Black Church in Action*. Nashville, TN: AMEC Sunday School Union, 1980.

Griffith, Robert. *The Politics of Fear: Joseph R. McCarthy and the Senate*. Amherst: University of Massachusetts Press, 1970.

Gritsch, Eric W. *Fortress Introduction to Lutheranism*. Minneapolis: Fortress Press, 1994.

Gritsch, Eric W., and Robert W. Jenson. *Lutheranism: The Theological Movement and Its Confessional Writings*. Philadelphia: Fortress Press, 1976.

Gunn, T. Jeremy. *Spiritual Weapons: The Cold War and the Forging of an American National Religion*. Westport, CT: Praeger, 2009.

Gunnemann, Louis H. *The Shaping of the United Church of Christ: An Essay in the History of American Christianity*. Cleveland, OH: United Church Press, 1999.

———. *United and Uniting: The Meaning of an Ecclesial Journey*. New York: United Church Press, 1987.

Guth, James L., John C. Green, Corwin E. Smidt, Lyman A. Kellstedt, and Margaret M. Poloma. *The Bully Pulpit: The Politics of Protestant Clergy*. Lawrence: University Press of Kansas, 1997.

Gutierrez, David G. *The Columbia History of Latinos in the United States since 1960*. New York: Columbia University Press, 2004.

Hagan, John. *Northern Passage: American Vietnam War Resisters in Canada*. Cambridge, MA: Harvard University Press, 2001.

Hahn, Peter L., and Mary Ann Heiss, eds. *Empire and Revolution: The United States and the Third World since 1945*. Columbus: Ohio State University Press, 2001.

Halberstam, David. *Ho*. New York: Vintage Books, 1971.

Haldeman, H. R. *The Haldeman Diaries: Inside the Nixon White House*. New York: Putnam, 1994.

Hall, Mitchell K. *Because of Their Faith: CALCAV and Religious Opposition to the Vietnam War*. New York: Columbia University Press, 1990.

———. *Crossroads: American Popular Culture and the Vietnam Generation*. Lanham, MD: Rowman and Littlefield, 2005.

Hallin, Daniel C. *The "Uncensored War": The Media and Vietnam*. Berkeley: University of California Press, 1986.

Hamilton, Michael P. *The Vietnam War: Christian Perspectives*. Grand Rapids, MI: Eerdmans, 1967.

Hammond, William M. *Public Affairs: The Military and the Media*. Washington, DC: Center of Military History, United States Army, 1988.

———. *Reporting Vietnam: Media and Military at War*. Lawrence: University of Kansas Press, 1998.

Hankins, Barry. *Uneasy in Babylon: Southern Baptist Conservatives and American Culture*. Tuscaloosa: University of Alabama Press, 2002.

Hanson, Eric O. *The Catholic Church in World Politics*. Princeton, NJ: Princeton University Press, 1987.

Harlow, Luke E., and Mark A. Noll, eds. *Religion and American Politics: From the Colonial Period to the Present*. 2nd ed. New York: Oxford University Press, 2007.

Harper, Keith, ed. *American Denominational History: Perspectives on the Past, Prospects for the Future*. Tuscaloosa: University of Alabama Press, 2008.

Hart, D. G. *That Old-Time Religion in Modern America: Evangelical Protestantism in the Twentieth Century*. Chicago: Ivan R. Dee, 2002.

Hartmann, Susan M. *From Margin to Mainstream: American Women and Politics since 1960*. New York: McGraw Hill, 1996.

Harvey, Paul, and Philip Goff, eds. *The Columbia Documentary History of Religion in America since 1945*. New York: Columbia University Press, 2005.

Heale, M. J. *American Anticommunism: Combating the Enemy Within, 1830–1970*. Baltimore, MD: Johns Hopkins University Press, 1990.

Heineman, Kenneth J. *Campus Wars: The Peace Movement at American State Universities in the Vietnam Era*. New York: New York University Press, 1993.

———. *God Is a Conservative: Religion, Politics, and Morality in Contemporary America*. New York: New York University Press, 1998.

Heiss, Mary Ann. *Empire and Nationhood: The United States, Great Britain, and Iranian Oil, 1950–1954*. New York: Columbia University Press, 1997.

Henriksen, Margot A. *Dr. Strangelove's America: Society and Culture in the Atomic Age*. Berkeley: University of California Press, 1997.

Herman, Arthur. *Joseph McCarthy: Reexamining the Life and Legacy of America's Most Hated Senator*. New York: Free Press, 2000.

Herr, Michael. *Dispatches*. New York: Vintage Books, 1968.

Herring, George C. *America's Longest War: The United States and Vietnam, 1950–1975*. New York: McGraw-Hill, 1979.

Hess, Gary R. "The Unending Debate: Historians and the Vietnam War." In Michael J. Hogan, ed., *America in the World: The Historiography of American Foreign Relations since 1941*. Cambridge: Cambridge University Press, 1995.

Hixson, Walter L. *Parting the Curtain: Propaganda, Culture, and the Cold War, 1945–1961*. New York: St. Martin's Press, 1998.

————. *The Myth of American Diplomacy: National Identity and U.S. Foreign Policy*. New Haven, CT: Yale University Press, 2008.

Hoffman, Oswald C. J., and Ronald J. Schlegel. *What More Is There to Say but Amen: The Autobiography of Dr. Oswald C. J. Hoffmann*. St. Louis: Concordia Publishing House, 1996.

Holm, Tom. *Strong Hearts, Wounded Souls: Native American Veterans of the Vietnam War*. Austin: University of Texas Press, 1996.

Horne, Gerald. *Black Liberation/Red Scare: Ben Davis and the Communist Party*. Newark: University of Delaware Press, 1994.

————. *Class Struggle in Hollywood, 1930–1950: Moguls, Mobsters, Stars, Reds, and Trade Unionists*. Austin: University of Texas Press, 2001.

————. *Fire This Time: The Watts Uprising and the 1960s*. Charlottesville: University Press of Virginia, 1995.

Howard, Gerald, ed. *The Sixties: The Art, Attitudes, Politics, and Media of Our Most Explosive Decade*. New York: Marlowe, 1995.

Huchthausen, Peter. *K-19: The Widowmaker; The Secret Story of the Soviet Nuclear Submarine*. Washington, DC: National Geographic Society, 2002.

Hudnut-Beumler, James. *Looking for God in the Suburbs: The Religion of the American Dream and Its Critics, 1945–1965*. New Brunswick, NJ: Rutgers University Press, 1994.

Hulsether, Mark David. *Building a Protestant Left*: Christianity and Crisis *Magazine, 1941–1993*. Knoxville: University of Tennessee Press, 1999.

————. *Religion, Culture, and Politics in the Twentieth-Century United States*. New York: Columbia University Press, 2007.

Hunt, Andrew E. *The Turning: A History of Vietnam Veterans against the War*. New York: New York University Press, 1999.

Hunt, Michael H. *Crises in U.S. Foreign Policy: An International History Reader*. New Haven, CT: Yale University Press, 1996.

————. *Ideology and U.S. Foreign Policy*. New Haven, CT: Yale University Press, 1987.

————. *Lyndon Johnson's War: America's Cold War Crusade in Vietnam, 1945–1968*. New York: Hill and Wang, 1996.

Hunt, Richard A. *Pacification: The American Struggle for Vietnam's Hearts and Minds*. Boulder, CO: Westview Press, 1995.

Hunter, James Davison. *American Evangelicalism: Conservative Religion and the Quandary of Modernity*. New Brunswick, NJ: Rutgers University Press, 1983.

Hunter, Jane. *The Gospel of Gentility: American Women Missionaries in Turn-of-the-Century China*. New Haven, CT: Yale University Press, 1984.

Hutchinson, Earl Ofari. *Blacks and Reds: Race and Class in Conflict, 1919–1990*. East Lansing: Michigan State University Press, 1995.

Hutchison, William R. *Errand to the World: American Protestant Thought and Foreign Missions*. Chicago: University of Chicago Press, 1987.

————, ed. *Between the Times: The Travail of the Protestant Establishment in America, 1900–1960*. Cambridge: Cambridge University Press, 1989.

Inboden, William. *Religion and American Foreign Policy, 1945–1960: The Soul of Containment*. New York: Cambridge University Press, 2008.

Inglis, Fred. *The Cruel Peace: Everyday Life and the Cold War*. New York: Basic Books, 1991.

Iriye, Akira. "Western Perceptions and Asian Realities." *The Harmon Memorial Lectures in Military History*. United States Air Force Academy, 1981: 1–15.

Isaacs, Arnold R. *Vietnam Shadows: The War, Its Ghosts, and Its Legacy.* Baltimore, MD: Johns Hopkins University Press, 1997.

Jacobs, Seth. *America's Miracle Man in Vietnam: Ngo Dinh Diem, Religion, Race, and U.S. Intervention in Southeast Asia, 1950–1957.* Durham, NC: Duke University Press, 2004.

———. "'Our System Demands the Supreme Being': The U.S. Religious Revival and the 'Diem Experiment,' 1954–55." *Diplomatic History* 25 (Fall 2001): 589–624.

Jeffords, Susan. *The Remasculinization of America: Gender and the Vietnam War.* Bloomington: Indiana University Press, 1989.

Jeffreys-Jones, Rhodri. *Changing Differences: Women and the Shaping of American Foreign Policy, 1917–1994.* New Brunswick, NJ: Rutgers University Press, 1995.

———. *Peace Now! American Society and the Ending of the Vietnam War.* New Haven, CT: Yale University Press, 1999.

Jenkins, Philip. *Cold War at Home: The Red Scare in Pennsylvania, 1945–1960.* Chapel Hill: University of North Carolina Press, 1999.

———. *Decade of Nightmares: The End of the Sixties and the Making of Eighties America.* New York: Oxford University Press, 2006.

Jespersen, T. Christopher. *American Images of China, 1931–1949.* Palo Alto, CA: Stanford University Press, 1996.

Jian, Chen. *Mao's China and the Cold War.* Chapel Hill: University of North Carolina Press, 2001.

Johnson, James Turner. *The Holy War Idea in Western and Islamic Traditions.* University Park: Pennsylvania State University Press, 1997.

Johnson, Jeff G. *Black Christians: The Untold Lutheran Story.* St. Louis: Concordia Publishing House, 1991.

Jones, Howard. *Death of a Generation: How the Assassinations of Diem and JFK Prolonged the Vietnam War.* New York: Oxford University Press, 2003.

Jones, Howard, and Randall B. Woods. "The Origins of the Cold War: A Symposium." *Diplomatic History* 17 (Spring 1993): 251–310.

Joseph, Peniel E. *Waiting 'Til the Midnight Hour: A Narrative History of Black Power in America.* New York: Henry Holt, 2006.

Kaplan, Amy, and Donald E. Pease, eds. *Cultures of United States Imperialism.* Durham, NC: Duke University Press, 1993.

Kauffman, Christopher J. "Politics, Programs, and Protests: Catholic Relief Services in Vietnam, 1954–1975." *Catholic Historical Review* 91 (April 2005): 223–50.

Kent, Peter C., and John F. Pollard, eds. *Papal Diplomacy in the Modern Age.* Westport, CT: Praeger, 1994.

Kent, Stephen A. *From Slogans to Mantras: Social Protest and Religious Conversion in the Late Vietnam War Era.* Syracuse, NY: Syracuse University Press, 2001.

Kersten, Lawrence L. *The Lutheran Ethic: The Impact of Religion on Laymen and Clergy.* Detroit, MI: Wayne State University Press, 1970.

Kessler, Lawrence D. *The Jiangyin Mission Station: An American Missionary Community in China, 1895–1951.* Chapel Hill: University of North Carolina Press, 1996.

Kimball, Jeffrey. *Nixon's Vietnam War.* Lawrence: University Press of Kansas, 1998.

———. *The Vietnam War Files: Uncovering the Secret History of Nixon-Era Strategy.* Lawrence: University Press of Kansas, 2004.

Kirby Dianne, ed. *Religion and the Cold War.* New York: Palgrave Macmillan. 2003.

Kissinger, Henry. *White House Years*. Boston: Little, Brown, 1979.

———. *Years of Upheaval*. Boston: Little, Brown, 1982.

Klehr, Harvey, and John Earl Haynes. *Venona: Decoding Soviet Espionage in America*. New Haven, CT: Yale University Press, 1999.

Klehr, Harvey, John Earl Haynes, and Kyrill M. Anderson. *The Soviet World of American Communism*. New Haven, CT: Yale University Press, 1998.

Klehr, Harvey, John Earl Haynes, and Fridrikh Igorevich Firsov. *The Secret World of American Communism*. New Haven, CT: Yale University Press, 1995.

Klein, Christa R. *Politics and Policy: The Genesis and Theology of Social Statements in the Lutheran Church in America*. Minneapolis: Fortress Press, 1989.

Kotlowski, Dean J. *Nixon's Civil Rights: Politics, Principle, and Policy*. Cambridge, MA: Harvard University Press, 2001.

Kovel, Joel. *Red Hunting in the Promised Land: Anticommunism and the Making of America*. New York: Basic Books, 1994.

Krenn, Michael L. *Black Diplomacy: African Americans and the State Department, 1945–1969*. London: M. E. Sharpe, 1999.

Kruse, Kevin M. *White Flight: Atlanta and the Making of Modern Conservatism*. Princeton, NJ: Princeton University Press, 2005.

Kuisel, Richard F. *Seducing the French: The Dilemma of Americanization*. Berkeley: University of California Press, 1993.

Kusch, Frank. *All-American Boys: Draft Dodgers in Canada from the Vietnam War*. Westport, CT: Praeger, 2001.

Kutler, Stanley I. *The Wars of Watergate: The Last Crisis of Richard Nixon*. New York: Knopf, 1990.

———, ed. *Abuse of Power: The New Nixon Tapes*. New York: Touchstone Books, 1997.

Kuznick, Peter J., and James Gilbert, eds. *Rethinking Cold War Culture*. Washington, DC: Smithsonian Institution Press, 2001.

LaFeber, Walter. *America, Russia, and the Cold War, 1945–1966*. New York: John Wiley, 1967.

Lagerquist, L. DeAne. *From Our Mothers' Arms: A History of Women in the American Lutheran Church*. Minneapolis: Augsburg Publishing House, 1987.

———. *The Lutherans*. Westport, CT: Praeger, 1999.

Lahr, Angela M. *Millennial Dreams and Apocalyptic Nightmares: The Cold War Origins of Political Evangelicalism*. New York: Oxford University Press, 2007.

Landers, James. *The Weekly War: Newsmagazines and Vietnam*. Columbia: University of Missouri Press, 2004.

Larson, Deborah Welch. *Anatomy of Mistrust: U.S.-Soviet Relations during the Cold War*. Ithaca, NY: Cornell University Press, 1997.

Lasch, Christopher. *The Culture of Narcissism: American Life in an Age of Diminishing Expectations*. New York: Norton, 1979.

Lassiter, Matthew D. *The Silent Majority: Suburban Politics in the Sunbelt South*. Princeton, NJ: Princeton University Press, 2006.

Layne, Christopher. *The Peace of Illusions: American Grand Strategy from 1940 to the Present*. Ithaca, NY: Cornell University Press, 2006.

Layton, Azza Salama. *International Politics and Civil Rights Policies in the United States, 1941–1960*. Cambridge: Cambridge University Press, 2000.

Leab, Daniel J. *I Was a Communist for the FBI: The Unhappy Life and Times of Matt Cvetic*. University Park: Pennsylvania State University Press, 2000.

Lederer, William J., and Eugene Burdick. *The Ugly American*. New York: Norton, 1965.

Lee, J. Edward, and Toby Haynsworth, eds. *White Christmas in April: The Collapse of South Vietnam, 1975*. New York: Peter Lang, 1999.

Leffler, Melvyn P. *A Preponderance of Power: National Security, the Truman Administration, and the Cold War*. Palo Alto, CA: Stanford University Press, 1992.

———. "The Cold War: What Do 'We Now Know'?" *American Historical Review* 104 (April 1999): 501–24.

Leonard, Bill J. *Baptists in America*. New York: Columbia University Press, 2005.

———. *God's Last and Only Hope: The Fragmentation of the Southern Baptist Convention*. Grand Rapids, MI: Eerdmans, 1990.

Levine, Daniel. *Bayard Rustin and the Civil Rights Movement*. New Brunswick, NJ: Rutgers University Press, 2000.

Levy, David W. *The Debate over Vietnam*. Baltimore, MD: Johns Hopkins University Press, 1991.

Lewis, Lionel S. *Cold War on Campus: A Study of the Politics of Organizational Control*. New Brunswick, NJ: Transaction, 1988.

Lieberman, Robbie. *The Strangest Dream: Communism, Anticommunism, and the U.S. Peace Movement, 1945–1963*. Syracuse, NY: Syracuse University Press, 2000.

Lienesch, Michael. *Redeeming America: Piety and Politics in the New Christian Right*. Chapel Hill: University of North Carolina Press, 1993.

Lincoln, C. Eric, and Lawrence H. Mamiya. *The Black Church in the African American Experience*. Durham, NC: Duke University Press, 1990.

Lockhart, Greg. *Nation in Arms: The Origins of the People's Army of Vietnam*. Wellington, New Zealand: Allen and Unwin, 1989.

Lodwick, Kathleen L. *Crusaders against Opium: Protestant Missionaries in China, 1874–1917*. Lexington: University Press of Kentucky, 1996.

Logevall, Fredrik. *Choosing War: The Lost Chance for Peace and the Escalation of War in Vietnam*. Berkeley: University of California Press, 1999.

Logevall, Fredrik, and Andrew Preston, eds. *Nixon in the World: American Foreign Relations, 1969–1977*. New York: Oxford University Press, 2008.

Lorence, James J. *The Suppression of* Salt of the Earth: *How Hollywood, Big Labor, and Politicians Blacklisted a Movie in Cold War America*. Albuquerque: University of New Mexico Press, 1999.

Lowe, Peter, ed. *The Vietnam War*. New York: St. Martin's Press, 1998.

Lucas, Scott. *Freedom's War: The American Crusade against the Soviet Union*. New York: New York University Press, 1999.

Lutz, Catherine A., and Jane L. Collins. *Reading National Geographic*. Chicago: University of Chicago Press, 1993.

Lutz, Charles P. *Loving Neighbors Far and Near: U.S. Lutherans Respond to a Hungry World*. Minneapolis: Augsburg Fortress Press, 1994.

———, ed. *Church Roots: Stories of Nine Immigrant Groups That Became the American Lutheran Church*. Minneapolis: Augsburg Publishing House, 1985.

MacFarquhar, Roderick, and Michael Schoenhals. *Mao's Last Revolution*. Cambridge, MA: Harvard University Press, 2006.

MacMillan, Margaret. *Nixon and Mao: The Week That Changed the World*. New York: Random House, 2007.

MacPherson, Myra. *Long Time Passing: Vietnam and the Haunted Generation*. New York: Anchor Books, 1984.

Maguire, Daniel C. *The Horrors We Bless: Rethinking the Just-War Legacy*. Minneapolis: Fortress Press, 2007.

Mahony, Phillip, ed. *From Both Sides Now: The Poetry of the Vietnam War and Its Aftermath*. New York: Scribner Poetry, 1998.

Mann, Robert. *A Grand Delusion: America's Descent into Vietnam*. New York: Basic Books, 2001.

Maraniss, David. *They Marched into Sunlight: War and Peace, Vietnam and America, October 1967*. New York: Simon and Schuster, 2003.

Marr, David G. *Vietnam 1945: The Quest for Power*. Berkeley: University of California Press, 1995.

Marsden, George M. *Fundamentalism and American Culture: The Shaping of Twentieth-Century Evangelism, 1870–1925*. New York: Oxford University Press, 1980.

———. *Religion and American Culture*. New York: Harcourt Brace College Publishers, 1990.

Marty, Martin E. *Modern American Religion*. Vol. 3, *Under God, Indivisible, 1941–1960*. Chicago: University of Chicago Press, 1996.

———. *Pilgrims in Their Own Land: Five Hundred Years of Religion in America*. New York: Penguin Books, 1984.

———. *A Short History of American Catholicism*. Allen, TX: Thomas More Publishing, 1995.

Mason, Katrina R. *Children of Los Alamos: An Oral History of the Town Where the Atomic Age Began*. New York: Twayne, 1995.

Mason, Robert. *Richard Nixon and the Quest for a New Majority*. Chapel Hill: University of North Carolina Press, 2004.

Mastny, Vojtech. *The Cold War and Soviet Insecurity: The Stalin Years*. New York: Oxford University Press, 1996.

Matusow, Allen J. *Nixon's Economy: Booms, Busts, Dollars, and Votes*. Lawrence: University Press of Kansas, 1998.

———. *The Unraveling of America: A History of Liberalism in the 1960s*. New York: Harper-Collins, 1984.

May, Elaine Tyler. *Homeward Bound: American Families in the Cold War Era*. New York: Basic Books, 1988.

McBeth, H. Leon. *The Baptist Heritage: Four Centuries of Baptist Witness*. Nashville, TN: Broadman Press, 1987.

McCormick, Thomas J. *America's Half-Century: United States Foreign Policy in the Cold War*. Baltimore, MD: Johns Hopkins University Press, 1989.

McEnaney, Laura. *Civil Defense Begins at Home: Militarization Meets Everyday Life in the Fifties*. Princeton, NJ: Princeton University Press, 2000.

McGirr, Lisa. *Suburban Warriors: The Origins of the New American Right*. Princeton, NJ: Princeton University Press, 2001.

McKnight, Gerald D. *The Last Crusade: Martin Luther King, Jr., the FBI, and the Poor People's Campaign*. Boulder, CO: Westview Press, 1998.

McLeod, Hugh. *The Religious Crisis of the 1960s*. New York: Oxford University Press, 2007.

McMahon, Robert J. *The Limits of Empire: The United States and Southeast Asia since World War II*. New York: Columbia University Press, 1999.

McManners, John, ed. *The Oxford History of Christianity*. New York: Oxford University Press, 1993.

McMaster, H. R. *Dereliction of Duty: Lyndon Johnson, Robert McNamara, the Joint Chiefs of Staff, and the Lies That Led to Vietnam*. New York: HarperPerennial, 1997.

McNamara, Robert S. *In Retrospect: The Tragedy and Lessons of Vietnam*. New York: Random House Books, 1995.

McNamara, Robert S., James G. Blight, and Robert K. Brigham. *Arugment without End: In Search of Answers to the Vietnam Tragedy*. New York: PublicAffairs, 1999.

McNeal, Patricia. *Harder Than War: Catholic Peacemaking in Twentieth-Century America*. New Brunswick, NJ: Rutgers University Press, 1992.

Mead, Frank S., revised by Samuel S. Hill. "Lutheran." *Handbook of Denominations in the United States*. Nashville, TN: Abingdon Press, 1995.

Melton, J. Gordon. *A Will to Choose: The Origins of African American Methodism*. Lanham, MD: Rowman and Littlefield, 2007.

Meyerowitz, Joanne, ed. *Not June Cleaver: Women and Gender in Postwar America, 1945–1960*. Philadelphia: Temple University Press, 1994.

Michener, James A. *Kent State: What Happened and Why*. New York: Random House, 1971.

Mieczkowski, Yanek. *Gerald Ford and the Challenges of the 1970s*. Lexington: University Press of Kentucky, 2005.

Miller, Douglas T. *On Our Own: Americans in the Sixties*. Lexington, MA: Heath, 1996.

Miller, Richard B. *Interpretations of Conflict: Ethics, Pacifism, and the Just-War Tradition*. Chicago: University of Chicago Press, 1991.

Miller, Timothy. *The Sixties Commune: Hippies and Beyond*. Syracuse, NY: Syracuse University Press, 1999.

Mishler, Paul C. *Raising Reds: The Young Pioneers, Radical Summer Camps, and Communist Political Culture in the United States*. New York: Columbia University Press, 1999.

Mitchell, Greg. *Tricky Dick and the Pink Lady: Richard Nixon vs. Helen Gahagan Douglas— Sexual Politics and the Red Scare, 1950*. New York: Random House, 1998.

Moise, Edwin E. *Tonkin Gulf and the Escalation of the Vietnam War*. Chapel Hill: University of North Carolina Press, 1996.

Mooney, James W., and Thomas R. West, eds. *Vietnam: A History and Anthology*. St. James, NY: Brandywine Press, 1994.

Moore, Barrington Jr. *Moral Purity and Persecution in History*. Princeton, NJ: Princeton University Press, 2000.

Morgan, David T. *The New Crusades, the New Holy Land: Conflict in the Southern Baptist Convention, 1969–1991*. Tuscaloosa: University of Alabama Press, 1996.

Morgan, Joseph G. *The Vietnam Lobby: The American Friends of Vietnam, 1955–1975*. Chapel Hill: University of North Carolina Press, 1997.

Moser, Richard. *The New Winter Soldiers: GI and Veteran Dissent during the Vietnam Era*. New Brunswick, NJ: Rutgers University Press, 1996.

Nadel, Alan. *Containment Culture: American Narratives, Postmodernism, and the Atomic Age*. Durham, NC: Duke University Press, 1995.

Nash, Philip. *The Other Missiles of October: Eisenhower, Kennedy, and the Jupiters, 1975–1963*. Chapel Hill: University of North Carolina Press, 1997.

Nelson, E. Clifford, ed. *The Lutherans in North America*. Philadelphia: Fortress Press, 1980.

Nelson, Keith L. *The Making of Détente: Soviet-American Relations in the Shadow of Vietnam*. Baltimore, MD: Johns Hopkins University Press, 1995.

Neu, Carles E., ed. *After Vietnam: Legacies of a Lost War*. Baltimore, MD: Johns Hopkins University Press, 2000.

Newman, Mark. *Getting Right with God: Southern Baptists and Desegregation, 1945–1995*. Tuscaloosa: University of Alabama Press, 2001.

Nhu Tang, Truong. *A Viet Cong Memoir*. New York: Vintage Books, 1985.

Nicosia, Gerald. *Home to War: A History of the Vietnam Veterans' Movement*. New York: Crown, 2001.

Ninkovich, Frank. *Modernity and Power: A History of the Domino Theory in the Twentieth Century*. Chicago: University of Chicago Press, 1994.

Noll, Mark A. *A History of Christianity in the United States and Canada*. Grand Rapids, MI: Eerdmans, 1992.

Nutt, Rick L. *Toward Peacemaking: Presbyterians in the South and National Security, 1945–1983*. Tuscaloosa: University Press of Alabama, 1994.

Oakes, Guy. *The Imaginary War: Civil Defense and American Cold War Culture*. New York: Oxford University Press, 1994.

Olson, Gregory A. *Mansfield and Vietnam: A Study of Rhetorical Adaptation*. East Lansing: Michigan State University Press, 1995.

O'Neill, Dan. *The Firecracker Boys*. New York: St. Martin's Press, 1994.

O'Neill, William L. *Coming Apart: An Informal History of America in the 1960s*. New York: Random House, 1971.

Oppenheimer, Mark. *Knocking on Heaven's Door: American Religion in the Age of the Counterculture*. New Haven, CT: Yale University Press, 2003.

O'Reilly, Kenneth. *"Racial Matters": The FBI's Secret File on Black America, 1960–1972*. New York: Free Press, 1989.

Oshinsky, David M. *A Conspiracy So Immense: The World of Joe McCarthy*. New York: Free Press, 1983.

Oudes, Bruce, ed. *From The President: Richard Nixon's Secret Files*. New York: Harper and Row, 1989.

Pahl, Jon. *Empire of Sacrifice: The Religious Origins of American Violence*. New York: New York University Press, 2010.

———. *Hopes and Dreams of All: The International Walther League and Lutheran Youth in American Culture, 1893–1993*. Chicago: Wheat Ridge Ministries, 1993.

———. *Youth Ministry in Modern America: 1930 to the Present*. Peabody, MA: Hendrickson, 2000.

Park, Chung-Shin. *Protestantism and Politics in Korea*. Seattle: University of Washington Press, 2003.

Partner, Peter. *God of Battles: Holy Wars of Christianity and Islam*. Princeton, NJ: Princeton University Press, 1997.

Paterson, Thomas G. *Meeting the Communist Threat: Truman to Reagan*. New York: Oxford University Press, 1988.

Paterson, Thomas G., J. Garry Clifford, and Kenneth J. Hagan. *American Foreign Relations: A History since 1895*. Lexington, MA: Heath, 1995.

Peck, James. *Washington's China: The National Security World, the Cold War, and the Origins of Globalism*. Amherst: University of Massachusetts Press, 2006.

Pells, Richard H. *The Liberal Mind in a Conservative Age: American Intellectuals in the 1940s and 1950s*. New York: Harper and Row, 1985.

Perlstein, Rick. *Before the Storm: Barry Goldwater and the Unmaking of the American Consensus*. New York: Hill and Wang, 2001.

———. *Nixonland: The Rise of a President and the Fracturing of America*. New York: Scribner, 2008.

Pierard, Richard. "Billy Graham and Vietnam: From Cold Warrior to Peacemaker." *Christian Scholars Review* 10 (1980): 37–51.

Pinn, Anne H., and Anthony B. Pinn. *Fortress Introduction to Black Church History*. Minneapolis: Fortress Press, 2002.

Plummer, Brenda Gayle. *Rising Wind: Black Americans and U.S. Foreign Affairs, 1935–1960*. Chapel Hill: University of North Carolina Press, 1996.

Porterfield, Amanda. *The Transformation of American Christianity: The Story of a Late-Twentieth-Century Awakening*. New York: Oxford University Press, 2001.

Pospielovsky, Dimitry. *The Russian Church under the Soviet Regime, 1917–1982*. 2 vols. Crestwood, NY: St. Vladimir's Seminary Press, 1984.

Powers, Richard Gid. *Not without Honor: The History of American Anticommunism*. New York: Free Press, 1995.

Poyo, Gerald E. *Cuban Catholics in the United States, 1960–1980: Exile and Integration*. Notre Dame, IN: University of Notre Dame Press, 2007.

Prados, John. *Vietnam: The History of an Unwinnable War, 1945–1975*. Lawrence: University Press of Kansas, 2009.

Pratt, Andrew LaRoy. "Religious Faith and Civil Religion: Evangelical Responses to the Vietnam War, 1964–1973." Ph.D. diss., Southern Baptist Theological Seminary, 1988.

Preston, William Jr. *Aliens and Dissenters: Federal Suppression of Radicals, 1903–1933*. Urbana: University of Illinois Press, 1963.

Quinn-Judge, Sophie. *Ho Chi Minh: The Missing Years, 1919–1941*. Berkeley: University of California Press, 2002.

Rabe, Stephen G. *The Most Dangerous Area of the World: John F. Kennedy Confronts Communist Revolution in Latin America*. Chapel Hill: University of North Carolina Press, 1999.

Raboteau, Albert J. *Canaan Land: A Religious History of African Americans*. New York: Oxford University Press, 1999.

Ramirez, Juan. *A Patriot After All: The Story of a Chicano Vietnam Vet*. Albuquerque: University of New Mexico Press, 1999.

Reeves, Richard. *President Kennedy: Profile of Power*. New York: Simon and Schuster, 1993.

———. *President Nixon: Alone in the White House*. New York: Simon and Schuster, 2001.

Reinitz, Richard. *Irony and Consciousness: American Historiography and Reinhold Niebuhr's Vision*. Lewisburg, PA: Bucknell University Press, 1980.

Rhodes, Richard. *Dark Sun: The Making of the Hydrogen Bomb*. New York: Simon and Schuster, 1995.

———. *The Making of the Atomic Bomb*. New York: Touchstone Books, 1986.

Robert, Dana L. "From Missions to Mission to Beyond Missions: The Historiography of American Protestant Foreign Missions since World War II." In Harry S. Stout and D. G. Hart, eds., *New Directions in American Religious History*. New York: Oxford University Press, 1997.

Robin, Ron. *The Making of the Cold War Enemy: Culture and Politics in the Military-Intellectual Complex*. Princeton, NJ: Princeton University Press, 2001.

Rochester, Stuart I., and Frederick Kiley. *Honor Bound: American Prisoners of War in Southeast Asia, 1961–1973*. Annapolis, MD: Naval Institute Press, 1999.

Roof, Wade Clark, and William McKinney. *American Mainline Religion: Its Changing Shape and Future*. New Brunswick, NJ: Rutgers University Press, 1987.

Rorabaugh, W. J. *Berkeley at War: The 1960s*. New York: Oxford University Press, 1989.

Rose, Kenneth D. *One Nation Underground: The Fallout Shelter in American Culture*. New York: New York University Press, 2001.

Rose, Lisle A. *The Cold War Comes to Main Street: America in 1950*. Lawrence: University Press of Kansas, 1999.

Rosenberg, Jonathan. *How Far the Promised Land? World Affairs and the American Civil Rights Movement from the First World War to Vietnam*. Princeton, NJ: Princeton University Press, 2006.

Rotter, Andrew J. "Christians, Muslims, and Hindus: Religion and U.S.-South Asian Relations, 1947–1954." *Diplomatic History* 24 (Fall 2000): 593–640 (with commentary by Robert Dean, Robert Buzzanco, and Patricia R. Hill).

———. *Comrades at Odds: The United States and India, 1947–1964*. Ithaca, NY: Cornell University Press, 2000.

———. *The Path to Vietnam: Origins of the American Commitment to Southeast Asia*. Ithaca, NY: Cornell University Press, 1987.

Rowe, John Carlos, and Rick Berg, eds. *The Vietnam War and American Culture*. New York: Columbia University Press, 1991.

Said, Edward W. *Culture and Imperialism*. New York: Vintage Books, 1994.

———. *Orientalism*. New York: Vintage Books, 1978.

Sands, Kathleen M., ed. *God Forbid: Religion and Sex in American Public Life*. New York: Oxford University Press, 2000.

Sarotte, M. E. *Dealing with the Devil: East Germany, Détente, and Ostpolitik, 1969–1973*. Chapel Hill: University of North Carolina Press, 2001.

Schmidt, Jean Miller. *Souls or the Social Order: The Two-Party System in American Protestantism*. Brooklyn, NY: Carlson Publishing, 1991.

Schmitz, David F. *Thank God They're on Our Side: The United States and Right-Wing Dictatorships, 1921–1965*. Chapel Hill: University of North Carolina, 1999.

———. *The United States and Right-Wing Dictatorships, 1965–1989*. Cambridge: Cambridge University Press, 2006.

Schoenwald, Jonathan M. *A Time for Choosing: The Rise of Modern American Conservatism*. New York: Oxford University Press, 2001.

Scholastic Magazines Editors. *What You Should Know about Communism and Why*. New York: Scholastic Book Services, 1962.

Schrecker, Ellen. *Many Are the Crimes: McCarthyism in America*. Boston: Little, Brown, 1998.

Schroeder, Steven. *A Community and a Perspective: Lutheran Peace Fellowship and the Edge of the Church, 1941–1991.* Lanham, MD: University Press of America, 1993.

Schroth, Raymond A., S.J. *The American Jesuits: A History.* New York: New York University Press, 2007.

Schulman, Bruce J. *Lyndon B. Johnson and American Liberalism: A Brief Biography with Documents.* New York: St. Martin's Press, 1995.

———. *The Seventies: The Great Shift in American Culture, Society, and Politics.* New York: Da Capo Press, 2001.

Schulman, Bruce J., and Julian E. Zelizer, eds. *Rightward Bound: Making America Conservative in the 1970s.* Cambridge, MA: Harvard University Press, 2008.

Schultz, Richard H. Jr. *The Secret War against Hanoi: Kennedy's and Johnson's Use of Spies, Saboteurs, and Covert Warriors in North Vietnam.* New York: HarperCollins, 1999.

Schultze, Quentin J. *Christianity and the Mass Media in America: Toward a Democratic Accommodation.* East Lansing: Michigan State University Press, 2003.

Schulzinger, Robert D. *A Time for War: The United States and Vietnam, 1941–1975.* New York: Oxford University Press, 1997.

Scott, Joan Wallach. *Gender and the Politics of History.* New York: Columbia University Press, 1988.

Settje, David E. "Dueling Catholic Periodicals: *America*'s and *Commonweal*'s Perceptions of the Cold and Vietnam Wars, 1964–1975." *Catholic Social Science Review* 9 (2004): 249–64.

———. "A Historian's View of Current Ethics: Vietnam and Iraq Compared." *Journal of Lutheran Ethics* 4 (August 2004): http://www.elca.org/scriptlib/dcs/jle/article. asp?aid=338.

———. "Justifiable War or an Offense to the Conscience? Lutheran Responses to the Vietnam War, 1964–1975." *Lutherans in America: A Twentieth-Century Retrospective; Lutheran Historical Conference Essays and Reports* 19 (2000): 20–47.

———. "Lutheran Women Warriors: Gender and the Cold and Vietnam Wars, 1964–1975." *Reexamining Conflict and Cooperation: Implications for Current Understandings of American Lutheranism; Lutheran Historical Conference Essays and Reports* 20 (2002): 132–58.

———. *Lutherans and the Longest War: Adrift on a Sea of Doubt about the Cold and Vietnam Wars, 1964–1975.* Lanham, MD: Lexington Books, 2007.

———. "'Sinister' Communists and Vietnam Quarrels: *The Christian Century* and *Christianity Today* Respond to the Cold and Vietnam Wars." *Fides et Historia* 32 (Winter/Spring 2000): 81–97.

Sherry, Michael S. *Gay Artists in Modern American Culture: An Imagined Conspiracy.* Chapel Hill: University of North Carolina Press, 2007.

———. *In the Shadow of War: The United States since the 1930s.* New Haven, CT: Yale University Press, 1995.

Sherwin, Martin J. *A World Destroyed: Hiroshima and the Origins of the Arms Race.* New York: Vintage Books, 1973.

Sirgiovanni, George. *An Undercurrent of Suspicion: Anti-Communism in America during World War II.* New Brunswick, NJ: Transaction Publishers, 1990.

Sittser, Gerald L. *A Cautious Patriotism: The American Churches and the Second World War.* Chapel Hill: University of North Carolina Press, 1997.

Slotkin, Richard. *Gunfighter Nation: The Myth of the Frontier in Twentieth-Century America*. New York: Atheneum Books, 1992.

Small, Melvin. *Antiwarriors: The Vietnam War and the Battle for America's Hearts and Minds*. Lanham, MD: Scholarly Resources, 2003.

———. *At the Water's Edge: American Politics and the Vietnam War*. Chicago: Ivan R. Dee, 2005.

———. *Covering Dissent: The Media and the Anti-Vietnam War Movement*. New Brunswick, NJ: Rutgers University Press, 1994.

———. *Democracy and Diplomacy: The Impact of Domestic Politics on U.S. Foreign Policy, 1789–1994*. Baltimore, MD: Johns Hopkins University Press, 1996.

———. *Johnson, Nixon, and the Doves*. New Brunswick, NJ: Rutgers University Press, 1988.

———. *The Presidency of Richard Nixon*. Lawrence: University Press of Kansas, 1999.

Smith, Oran P. *The Rise of Baptist Republicanism*. New York: New York University Press, 1997.

Solberg, Richard W. *Lutheran Higher Education in North America*. Minneapolis: Augsburg Publishing House, 1985.

———. *Open Doors: The Story of Lutherans Resettling Refugees*. St. Louis, MO: Concordia Publishing House, 1992.

Sorley, Lewis. *A Better War: The Unexamined Victories and Final Tragedy of America's Last Years in Vietnam*. New York: Harvest Books, 1999.

Staub, Michael E., ed. *The Jewish 1960s: An American Sourcebook*. Waltham, MA: Brandeis University Press, 2004.

Steigerwald, David. *The Sixties and the End of Modern America*. New York: St. Martin's Press, 1995.

Stephanson, Anders. *Kennan and the Art of Foreign Policy*. Cambridge, MA: Harvard University Press, 1989.

Stern, Mark. *Calculating Visions: Kennedy, Johnson, and Civil Rights*. New Brunswick, NJ: Rutgers University Press, 1992.

Stevens, Richard L. *Mission on the Ho Chi Minh Trail: Nature, Myth, and War in Viet Nam*. Norman: University of Oklahoma Press, 1995.

Stormer, John A. *None Dare Call It Treason*. New York: Buccaneer Books, 1964.

Sueflow, August R. *Heritage in Motion: Readings in the History of the Lutheran Church–Missouri Synod, 1962–1995*. St. Louis, MO: Concordia Publishing House, 1998.

Sugrue, Thomas J. *The Origins of the Urban Crisis: Race and Inequality in Postwar Detroit*. Princeton, NJ: Princeton University Press, 1996.

Summers, Anthony. *The Arrogance of Power: The Secret World of Richard Nixon*. New York: Penguin Books, 2000.

Swerdlow, Amy. *Women Strike for Peace: Traditional Motherhood and Radical Politics in the 1960s*. Chicago: University of Chicago Press, 1993.

Taylor, Sandra C. *Vietnamese Women at War: Fighting for Ho Chi Minh and the Revolution*. Lawrence: University Press of Kansas, 1999.

Tentler, Leslie Woodcock, ed. *The Church Confronts Modernity: Catholicism since 1950 in the United States, Ireland, and Quebec*. Washington, DC: Catholic University Press of America, 2007.

Tipton, Steven M. *Getting Saved from the Sixties: Moral Meaning in Conversion and Cultural Change*. Berkeley: University of California Press, 1982.

Todd, Mary. *Authority Vested: A Story of Identity and Change in the Lutheran Church–Missouri Synod*. Grand Rapids, MI: Eerdmans, 2000.

Tollefson, James W. *The Strength Not to Fight: Conscientious Objectors of the Vietnam War in Their Own Words*. Washington, DC: Brassey's, 2000.

Tomes, Robert R. *Apocalypse Then: American Intellectuals and the Vietnam War, 1954–1975*. New York: New York University Press, 1998.

Tucker, Nancy Bernkopf. "Taiwan Expendable? Nixon and Kissinger Go to China." *Journal of American History* 92 (June 2005): 109–35.

Ung, Loung. *First They Killed My Father: A Daughter of Cambodia Remembers*. New York: HarperCollins, 2000.

Unger, Irwin, and Debi Unger. *America in the 1960s*. St. James, NY: Brandywine Press, 1988.

Unruh, Elisabeth Annice. "Equality Denied: Lutheran Responses to the Equal Rights Amendment." *Journal of the Lutheran Historical Conference*. Forthcoming.

Van DeMark, Brian. *Into the Quagmire: Lyndon Johnson and the Escalation of the Vietnam War*. New York: Oxford University Press, 1995.

Van Devanter, Lynda. *Home before Morning: The Story of an Army Nurse in Vietnam*. Amherst: University of Massachusetts Press, 1983.

von der Mehden, Fred. R. *Religion and Modernization in Southeast Asia*. Syracuse, NY: Syracuse University Press, 1986.

Vinz, Warren L. *Pulpit Politics: Faces of American Protestant Nationalism in the Twentieth Century*. Albany: State University of New York, 1997.

Von Rohr, John. *The Shaping of American Congregationalism, 1620–1957*. Cleveland, OH: Pilgrim Press, 1992.

Wagnleitner, Reinhold. *Coca-Colonization and the Cold War: The Cultural Mission of the United States in Austria after the Second World War*. Chapel Hill: University of North Carolina Press, 1994.

Walker, J. Samuel. "Historians and Cold War Origins: The New Consensus." In Gerald K. Haines and J. Samuel Walker, eds., *American Foreign Relations: A Historiographical Review*. Westport, CT: Greenwood Press, 1981.

Walter, Ingrid. "One Year after Arrival: The Adjustment of Indochinese Women in the United States." *International Migration* 19 (1981): 129–52.

Walter, Ingrid, and Cordelia Cox. "Resettlement in the United States of Unattached and Unaccompanied Indochinese Refugee Minors by Lutheran Immigration and Refugee Services." *International Migration* 17 (1979): 139–61.

Walzer, Michael. *Just and Unjust Wars: A Moral Argument with Historical Illustrations*. 2nd ed. New York: Basic Books, 1992.

Washington, James Melvin. *Frustrated Fellowship: The Black Baptist Quest for Social Power*. Macon, GA: Mercer University Press, 2004.

Wehrle, Edmund F. *Between a River and a Mountain: The AFL-CIO and the Vietnam War*. Ann Arbor: University of Michigan Press, 2005.

Weigand, Kate. *Red Feminism: American Communism and the Making of Women's Liberation*. Baltimore, MD: Johns Hopkins University Press, 2001.

Weigel, George. *The Final Revolution: The Resistance Church and the Collapse of Communism*. New York: Oxford University Press, 1992.

Weisbrot, Robert. *Freedom Bound: A History of America's Civil Rights Movement*. New York: Plume Books, 1990.

Wells, Ronald A. *The Wars of America: Christian Views*. Macon, GA: Mercer University Press, 1991.

Wells, Tom. *The War Within: America's Battle over Vietnam*. New York: Henry Holt, 1994.

———. *Wild Man: The Life and Times of Daniel Ellsberg*. New York: Palgrave, 2001.

Weseley-Smith, Peter. *Unequal Treaty, 1897–1997: China, Great Britain, and Hong Kong's New Territories*. New York: Oxford University Press, 1983.

Westad, Odd Arne, ed. *Brothers in Arms: The Rise and Fall of the Sino-Soviet Alliance, 1945–1963*. Stanford, CA: Stanford University Press, 1998.

Westheider, James E. *Fighting on Two Fronts: African Americans and the Vietnam War*. New York: New York University Press, 1997.

Whitfield, Stephen J. *The Culture of the Cold War*. Baltimore, MD: Johns Hopkins University Press, 1991.

Wiederaenders, Robert C., ed. *Historical Guide to Lutheran Church Bodies of North America*. St Louis, MO: Lutheran Historical Conference, 1998.

Willbanks, James H. *Abandoning Vietnam: How America Left and South Vietnam Lost Its War*. Lawrence: University Press of Kansas, 2004.

Williams, Peter W. *America's Religions: Traditions and Cultures*. New York: Macmillan, 1990.

Williams, William Appleman. *The Tragedy of American Diplomacy*. New York: Norton, 1959; reprint 1988.

Wilmore, Gayraud S. *Black Religion and Black Radicalism: An Interpretation of the Religious History of African Americans*. 3rd ed. Maryknoll, NY: Orbis Books, 1998.

Wittner, Lawrence S. "Peace Movements and Foreign Policy: The Challenge to Diplomatic Historians." *Diplomatic History* 11 (Fall 1987): 355–70.

———. *Rebels against War: The American Peace Movement, 1933–1983*. Philadelphia: Temple University Press, 1984.

Woods, Jeff. *Black Struggle, Red Scare: Segregation and Anti-Communism in the South, 1948–1968*. Baton Rouge: Louisiana State University Press, 2004.

Woods, Randall Bennett. *Fulbright: A Biography*. Cambridge: Cambridge University Press, 1995.

———. *J. William Fulbright, Vietnam, and the Search for a Cold War Foreign Policy*. Cambridge: Cambridge University Press, 1998.

Wuthnow, Robert. *The Restructuring of American Religion: Society and Faith since World War II*. Princeton, NJ: Princeton University Press, 1988.

Wyatt, Clarence R. *Paper Soldiers: The American Press and the Vietnam War*. Chicago: University of Chicago Press, 1993.

Yergin, Daniel. *Shattered Peace: The Origins of the Cold War*. New York: Penguin Books, 1977.

Young, Marilyn B. *The Vietnam Wars, 1945–1990*. New York: HarperPerennial, 1991.

Zamoyski, Adam. *Holy Madness: Romantics, Patriots, and Revolutionaries, 1776–1871*. New York: Viking Press, 1999.

Zaroulis, Nancy, and Gerald Sullivan. *Who Spoke Up? American Protest against the War in Vietnam, 1963–1975*. Garden City, NY: Doubleday, 1984.

Zhai, Qiang. *China and the Vietnam Wars, 1950–1975*. Chapel Hill: University of North Carolina Press, 2000.

Zhufeng, Luo, ed. *Religion under Socialism in China*. Armonk, NY: M. E. Sharpe, 1991.

Index

Svec, Stanislav, 37
Swomley, John M., 55

Taiwan, 26, 107, 162
Ten Commandments, 34
Tennessee Baptist Convention, 35–36, 133
Tet Offensive, 64, 66–67, 90
Thailand, 107
Thieu, Nguyen Van, 128, 161–62, 167–68
Tito, Josip Broz, 64, 118
Truman, Harry S., 24
Tunnell, Gene V., 164

Udvarnoki, Bela, 31
United Church Herald, 18, 23, 57, 114; and
  pleas for peace, 52–54; and Vietnam
  War, 70, 78–79, 81, 150
United Church of Christ (UCC), 2, 23,
  187–88n46; and collapse of South
  Vietnam, 168–69; and monograph's
  methodology, 10, 18–20; and Nixon's
  Cold War policies, 95–96, 112–16, 126;
  and Nixon's Vietnam policies, 142–43,
  147–50; and questioning of monolithic
  communism, 52–55; and views of U.S.
  policy, 57–59; and views of Vietnam
  War, 70–71, 78–81
United Nations, 26, 86; and China, 50–52,
  54, 101, 187n42; and the Congo, 41
Union of Soviet Socialist Republics, 3–4,
  6–7; and invasion of Czechoslovakia,
  25–26, 30, 33, 37, 39, 47–48, 52–53, 88; and
  monolithic communism, 27–45, 50–51,
  73, 163; and relationship with United
  States, 25, 40, 51–52, 97–98, 170; and
  religious persecution, 96, 100, 105–6, 112,
  122–23; and Sino-Soviet relationship, 4,
  26, 41, 46–47, 56, 63–64, 103
Union Theological Seminary, 28, 143
United Methodist Church, 109, 139
United States Arms Control and Disarma-
  ment Agency, 54
United States Information Agency, 87
Urban League, 40
U.S. Catholic, 14, 42–43; and views of
  Vietnam War, 84–85

U.S. Catholic and Jubilee, 118–19, 144–45,
  172
U.S. Catholic Press on Central America
  (Brett), 15
U.S.S. Maddox, 63
USSR. *See* Union of Soviet Socialist
  Republics

Valentine, Foy, 16, 75–76, 146–47
Vatican, 14, 43
Vatican II. *See* Second Vatican Council
Vietnam War: and antiwar Christians,
  71–82; and Christian support for, 65–71;
  and Christian views of during Johnson
  administration, 45–46, 61–94; and
  Christian views during Nixon adminis-
  tration, 127–60; and civil war in, 9–10;
  and lessons learned from, 13, 161–77
Vietnamese orphans, 162, 166
Vietnamese Overseas Buddhist Associa-
  tion, 93; and lessons learned from by
  U.S., 162–77
Vietnamization, 127, 130, 142, 149
Voice of America, 124
Voting Rights Act of 1965, 17

Wagner, James E., 142
Wall, James M., 166–67
Wankiwucz, Melchoir, 29
War on Terrorism, 21–22, 177
Watergate crisis, 130, 150
Weber, Jaroy, 164–65
West Pakistan, 101, 109
Western Recorder, 70
Whole Earth-Whole People, 112–13
Wittner, Lawrence, 46
Wolf, Donald J., 85–86
Women's rights movement, 13, 18
World Council of Churches, 88, 169
World War II, 3, 6

Young, Whitney, 40
Yu, Hwa, 110–11
Yugoslavia, 64, 118

Zietlow, Carl P., 73–74

About the Author

DAVID E. SETTJE is an associate professor of history at Concordia University Chicago and author of *Lutherans and the Longest War: Adrift on a Sea of Doubt about the Cold and Vietnam Wars.*